BUDAPEST

INSIGHT *City* GUIDES

Produced & Directed by Hans Höfer
Edited by Hans-Horst Skupy
Photography by Helene Hartl, Hans-Horst Skupy,
János Stekovics and others
Translated by Susan James

APA
PUBLICATIONS

ABOUT THIS BOOK

Budapest tops the list of the most strategically situated European capital cities. Experts have agreed on its pre-eminence for a long time, and it is no accident that the Hungarian capital has in recent years managed to capture its place in the sun among the European capitals on the tourist belt. The mass flight of East Germans has been responsible for putting Budapest back into the headlines of the international press.

On the threshold of the 1990s, Hungary is a country in the process of far-reaching changes, the scene of a fascinating social and political experiment. A country of the Eastern bloc is opening up to the West without any great reservations, and no longer viewing the West as a cradle of the "counter-revolution" but as a guarantor of the flourishing development of the country. Those bound by dogma and those who juggle with the facts of history are retreating, a new kind of "socialism with a human face" is taking shape, the countdown for the future is running, and nowhere can these forward-looking tendencies be felt as significantly as in this very capital city, which gathers all the creative forces of the country to itself.

The newly-achieved self-confidence has literally coloured the appearance of the city. It is as if the collected dust and rubble of decades is being confronted with a huge scrubbing brush. Painting and cleaning is going on everywhere, facades are being restored, the old houses renovated, new hotels are being built. The department responsible for historic buildings and monuments is busy round the clock. A more beautiful Budapest, one ever more open to the influences of the times, is being created.

Cityguide: Budapest, another APA Publications' volume in its red-cover series of guides on the world's most beautiful and important cities is dedicated to feeling the pulse of Budapest, a city of traditions on the threshold of a new life. *Cityguides* take a detailed and emphatic look at the cultural and economic capitals of the world, following the example of the famous *Insight Guides*, which to date have covered more than a hundred travel destinations.

Words at Work

The task of devising the concept for *Cityguide: Budapest* and choosing the authors for the great variety of text contributions fell to **Hans-Horst Skupy**, a multi-talented author and photographer. He was born in Bratislava and has lived in southern Germany for many years. Skupy has published several travel guides, put together a book of aphorisms, and has a number of contributions – on topics which range from sundials to Gorbachev – to his credit. He is drawn to Budapest and to Hungary at every possible opportunity, and it comes as no surprise that his archive of photographs of Hungary now contains more than 10,000 pictures.

The sights of Budapest and its surroundings are brought to the reader by **Dr Wolfgang Libal**, one of the most well-informed experts on Hungary, who lives in Vienna. Born in Prague, he was for many years an editor and correspondent with the German news agency

H.- H. Skupy   *W. Libal*   *M. Radkai*

Deutsche Presseagentur, covering south-eastern Europe. Among his more important published works is a volume on Hungary, much praised in expert circles.

The so-called "good life" in Budapest, which can now be led by a growing number of its present-day citizens, is described by **Eugen-Géza von Pogány**, one of those Central Europeans at home in the Danube valley, regardless of national boundaries. Born in Hungary, he is a gourmet and *bon vivant*, a publisher of cookery books and similar easily digested material, and also a political journalist.

Marton Radkai, who earlier worked on *Insight Guide: Hungary*, for which he was project editor, contributed the short chapters on Raoul Wallenberg, the cemeteries of Budapest and the traffic problems.

György Sebestyén, a Hungarian who has made a name for himself as a novelist in Austria, where he is chairman of the national PEN club, wrote on the introductory "Capital of Nostalgia".

Several younger authors have contributed their analytical essays to round off the picture of Budapest provided by this *Cityguide*.

Peter Martos, who was born in Budapest and now lives in Vienna, claims that Europe is his real homeland. The editor-in-chief of the Viennese daily paper *Die Presse* has a background in international politics and within his office – who else would they choose? – he is the last word on all matters Hungarian. For this book, Martos describes "the other Budapest".

Karl Stipsicz, born in Vienna to an old Hungarian family, was educated in Budapest.

A qualified economist and the author for a book on Hungary, he is an expert on the country and works in the Eastern Europe department of Austrian television. Stipsicz wrote the chapters "Chiselled and Cast" and "The Metropolis".

Krisztina Koenen was born in Budapest and lives in Vienna. The contribution by this dedicated journalist about the Hungarian National Bank and its fluctuating history was first published in the magazine section of the German newspaper *Frankfurter Allgemeine Zeitung*. A correspondent for southeast Europe for the German magazine *Der Spiegel*, she followed up the traces left by the world-famous Budapest psychoanalysts, while **Robert Sterk**, the editor of the contemporary magazine *Wiener*, examined Budapest's role as a European tourist attraction.

Frames in Focus

Apart from the pictures contributed by Hans-Horst Skupy and his travelling companion **Helene Hartl**, a number of other photographers are represented in *Cityguide: Budapest*.

They include **Rainer Fichel** from Hamburg, whose pictures have also appeared in *Geo* and *Merian*, as well as **Pierro Guerrini**, also a well-travelled Italian, whose work has appeared in a number of well-known publications. Lastly, the young Hungarian photographer **János Stekovics**, who lives in West Germany and who made his mark with an exhibition of portraits of rural Hungarians, also contributed some original pictures of Budapest.

CONTENTS

TRAVEL TIPS

CITY OF CONTRADICTIONS

What a city! On the threshold of the 1990s, parliament and the media of this nominally socialist country are passionately debating the long overdue reforms of the political and social systems, and especially the economy. Otto von Habsburg, nephew of the Emperor and penultimate King of Hungary Franz Joseph (not exactly popular among the Magyars), held a speech (in Hungarian!) at the Karl Marx University in the spring of 1989. His subject: European unity. About 1,500 gave him a standing ovation and sang the national anthem "God bless the Hungarians".

There is an air of melancholy about Budapest, also known as the "Paris of the East" on account of its many cafes, theatres, museums and nightclubs. The weight of history which oppresses the city seems too great. Huns, Mongols, Turks and Habsburgs, Romanians, the Gestapo, the Wehrmacht and the Soviet occupying forces were among the oppressors. They took care that the periods of economic and cultural growth, when the long-suffering Magyars flourished and held their heads high, never lasted long. And today?

Tourism flourishes, as does the black market, but by no means in a fashion that allows people in Budapest to look forward to a secure and untroubled future. Hungary has 18 billion dollars' worth of foreign debts, and yet the plans for a joint World Exhibition in Vienna and Budapest in 1995 met with serious consideration on all sides before being dropped once more because of those very debts. The complaints about low wages, rising prices and inflation form the main topic of conversation in the innumerable coffee houses, and you find yourself wondering how is it possible that week after week the people of Budapest return in their thousands from Austria and West Germany, laden with video recorders and colour television sets, personal computers, deep freezes, microwave ovens and other highly expensive electronic and electrical gadgets. The stereotype figure of "Julischka from Budapest" is now only to be found in operettas. Her contemporaries are more interested in jeans and Michael Jackson.

Problems of communication are still considerable, though. Hungarian, one of the most interesting of European languages, is only understood by some 15 million people in the whole world. For many years Budapest has been among the most popular capital cities of the world – and yet hardly any of its buildings dating from the second half of the 20th century has any particular attraction. The main motive for travelling to Budapest is nostalgia, the attraction of a world still unfamiliar to Westerners. The spas of Budapest, too, offer more than the simple pleasures of bathing. And fortunately not all the magnificent coffee houses dating from the turn of the century have fallen victim to the bombs of World War II .

Preceding pages: Fishermen's Bastion with view of the Parliament buildings; the old city of Budapest; crowds in the inner city; market with plenty to offer. Left, detail of the Vörösmarty monument.

Pest a 17ik században

Budapest foldi Lajos Kiadása.

Üdvözlet ős Buda-Pestről.

1900/IV /17.

Buda a 17ᵏ században

Gruss aus Alt-Buda-Pest

...rtő" atyád Vilmos

Budapest lies in the centre of the Carpathian Basin and is the largest city in the catchment area of the Danube. The Danube, both of which has formed the national border between Czechoslovakia and Hungary since 1920, takes a southerly course about 47 miles (75 km) to the north of the city centre and divides the city into two unequal parts, which have undergone a historically independent development. The present city area covers 202.9 sq miles (525.6 sq km), with

the Martinovics tér (10th district) at latitude 47° 28' 56" N and longitude 19° 08' 10" E. Typical of Budapest, and unusual for a capital city, are the many springs, mostly on the west. The healing springs – 123 of them altogether – produce around 400,000 litres of hot water and 300,000 litres of lukewarm water every day.

At the last census (1983) Budapest had a population of 2,064,307.

Celtic and Roman beginnings: At the end of

66.9 sq miles (173.2 sq km) on the right western bank of the Danube, and 136.1 (352.4 sq km) on the left eastern bank. The former consists of Buda and Óbuda, the latter of Pest. In addition there are a number of smaller, originally independent communities. The western part of the city is dominated by low hills (Gellérthegy 771 ft (235 metres), Sashegy 843 ft (257 m), Nagy Hárshegy 1,490 ft (454 m), Széchenyihegy 1,581 ft (482 m), Jánoshegy 1,729 ft (527 m). The eastern part covers a level area 328-394 ft (100-120 m) above sea level. The geographic centre of Budapest is to be found in

1988 a hypothesis which had been in existence for some time was proven. Archaeologists revealed the remains of a fortified wall on the southern slopes of the Gellért hill. This was the final proof of the existence of a fortified settlement (*oppidum*). It was built decades before Roman rule – by the Eraviscans, a Celtic-Illyrian people who had migrated from the west around the middle of the 1st century BC. The site stretched from the present Gellért hill to the district of Tabán and contained many houses and temples. The actual founders of the city, therefore, were the Eraviscans, not the Romans. Even the name for the legion camp built in AD 90 was adopted by the Romans from the Celtic *ac-inco*, which means "plentiful water".

Geographic circumstances were the main reasons for the early development of human settlement here. Several fords to the south of Margaret Island made it possible to cross the Danube. This favoured trade on both banks of the river, but also made enemy attacks that much easier.

From 15 to 11 BC the Romans conquered the country between the Danube and the Sava, modern west Hungary, and established the province of Pannonia, named after the local tribe of the Pannonians, who were

Celto-Illyrians. At first the Eraviscan settlement continued, but was being gradually abandoned as early as the reign of the Emperor Tiberius (AD 14-37). A Roman legion camp was established to the north of the settlement, in the present III district. About 1½ miles (2 km) further north, the civilian town of Aquincum developed.

Its position near the border was of great

importance to the development of the city. The Danube was not only the border of the province, but at the same time the border of the Roman Empire. After the division of the province in 106 under the Emperor Trajan, Aquincum became the capital of Lower Pannonia and the seat of a governor (*legatus*). Trajan's successor Hadrian gave the city the right of self-government in 124 and thereby raised it to the status of *municipium*. Under Septimus Severus it rose to be a *colonia* in 198, the highest urban status in the Roman Empire.

Aquincum flourished in the 2nd and 3rd centuries. In those days it had as many as 60,000 inhabitants. A mixed Romanised population was created by immigration from all parts of the empire. Apart from the garrison and the civil servants, many craftsmen and merchants went about their business here. Imports from Italian provinces were gradually replaced by local goods; an important local type of ceramics (*terra sigillata*) developed. There is evidence of viticulture from the 3rd century on, accompanied by the rise of the wine trade.

The military importance and the flourishing economy of the city were reflected in the pattern of settlement. The roads were laid out in the characteristic chessboard pattern, the simple mud huts of the early period replaced by stone and brick buildings equipped with all the comforts of the Roman lifestyle – piped water, sewers, warm air heating systems, cold and hot baths. Among the important buildings, apart from the governor's palace, were the huge public buildings, the forum, a theatre and an amphitheatre, baths and temples.

Because of its location on the border, Aquincum was prone to attacks by enemies from outside the empire. During the final phase of Roman rule the Limes could no longer be held. The defence of the border was entrusted to auxiliaries from allied peoples. This move was also ineffective in protecting Aquincum from attack. The military town was burned in 250 and in 270, and the civil town was destroyed around the middle of the 4th century. Only a few of the people remained, living in the ruins and in the ramshackle repaired buildings.

In AD 1st century, after conquering the region that is western Hungary today, the Romans settled on the Danube on the site of modern Budapest. They set up a military outpost on the left bank of the Danube near the present Elizabeth Bridge. The remains of the walls of this outpost can still be seen in the Garden of Ruins in Március 15 tér.

The Romans named their province Pannonia. In the 2nd century they divided it into Upper (Pannonia superior) and Lower (Pannonia inferior) Pannonia, with the administrative centre at Aquincum. Incidentally, the first governor was the future Emperor Hadrian. The border of the province followed the course of the Danube.

The remains of some shrines to Mithras have also been excavated, and it is therefore assumed that the cult of this Eastern god was widespread among the legionaries in Aquincum. The remains of an ancient Christian basilica have also been discovered.

Aquincum's importance diminished with the decline of the Roman Empire in the 4th century. In the 5th century the Romans surrended the city to the Huns.

The Huns ended 400 years of Pax Romana. In 405 the rest of the Romanised population left the city and set out for Italy.

From 409 onwards the Huns took over the Danube basin and Aquincum. In 433 the province was ceded to the Huns in a treaty. In 437 Attila received the title of a Roman *magister militum*. For this reason, the ruins of the Roman camp entered legend – in the German *Nibelungenlied* among other tales – as the castle of the King of the Huns. As the realm of the Huns was inhabited by a colourful mixture of peoples, the depopulated Aquincum was resettled by various tribes. On the left bank of the Danube there is evidence of settlement by Sadagans, a Hunnish-Turkic people, from about 430 on. After the death of Attila in 453 his empire collapsed, and the Huns were followed in rapid succession by several Germanic (Ostrogoths, Gepids, Heruli, Langobards, Suebi) and Iranian tribes, all of whom nominally acknowledged the supremacy of the eastern or western Roman Empire. The Germanic tribes moved on southwards to Italy, where they conquered the western Roman Empire in 476, then on to southern France, Spain and even North Africa.

Into the area, now depopulated, of the Danube and Tisza basin came the Avars, a horse-riding nomadic people from the steppes of Asia, who were related to the Huns. For nearly 250 years (567 to 802) they ruled a vast region, with its centre in the Carpathian basin and reaching as far as the river Enns in the west. The Danube had lost its importance as a border river, just as it had under Hunnish rule, and the fort at Aquincum gained significance once more. The settlements dating from Avar times lay very close to it. A princely tomb discovered on Csepel Island supports the oral tale of a royal seat of the Avars.

Through several campaigns Charlemagne ended the empire of the Avars, who have since disappeared from history. His successors then set up a number of vassal Slavonic "dukedoms", which did not retain their loyalty to their Carolingian overlords for long. In 892 the Carolingian emperor Arnulf, attempting to subdue the Duke of Moravia, called on the help of a nomadic group, the Magyars. When the band of troops sent to help Arnulf returned, they reported that the plains on the other side of the Carpathians would make an excellent new homeland.

After an interregnum lasting about 100 years the Magyars took over the country around the year 900. This finally stabilised the precarious situation which had existed, with interruptions, since the time of the Huns; the Danube no longer separated two rival powers confronting one another, but flowed through one country, the kingdom of Hungary. The former city of Aquincum, once a border town, had developed into the centre of a new state.

Left, the legendary Turul bird is said to have guided the Magyars.

It would be easy to assume a continuous settlement of Buda from the wealth of grave goods that have been discovered, and even more so from the imposing ruins of buildings. This was not the case. Remnants of the Romanised population may have witnessed the beginnings of the Great Migration, but in any case they were absorbed into the cultures of the new peoples.

The geographical situation of Buda made this an area predestined for resettlement, particularly so in view of the impressive Roman buildings and their potential use as fortifications. From this point of view it is possible to speak of a continuity of settlement and of a topographical continuity, but not of a continuity of the inhabitants. Continuous settlement can only be dated back to just after 900 at the earliest.

The question of continuity also raises the matter of the present name of the city. First of all it should be pointed out that the name of the Hungarian capital is made up of two names: *Buda* and *Pest*.

Buda, on the right bank of the Danube, has a name that goes back to a man of unknown background. If you want to rely on oral tradition, this Buda (Bleda) was the older brother of Attila. The *Nibelungenlied*, composed around the year 1200, equates Buda with Attila's residence, giving it the name of *Etzelburg* (Attila's Castle). Even a chronicle of Frederick Barbarossa, who crossed Hungary on his way to the Holy Land in 1189, referred to Buda as *Czilnburg* (in Latin, *urbs Adtile*). This tradition was kept up by the German settlers, and was also used by the unknown author of the *Gesta Hungarorum* (late 12th century). He affirmed the Scythian origin of the Hungarians and tried to give the relationship between Huns and Hungarians some historical foundation. According to him, Attila renewed and refortified the city after driving out the Romans, and therefore it was known as *civitas Attile regis*, named Budavár by the Hungarians, Ecilburg by the

Left, King Stephen I (1001-38).

Germans. This refers to Aquincum, the origin of the later settlement of Óbuda (Old Buda).

The first mention of Pest in documents occurs in 1061. In Roman times a castrum stood on the site, a fortified bridgehead protecting the crossing of the Danube. The name is of Slavic origin. This is supported by a reference in the *Gesta Hungarorum*, which says that Prince Kurszán gave the task of securing the Danube crossing to the Ismaelites. The word means (lime) furnace. The German settlers, invited into the country by Queen Gisela the wife of St Stephen (1000-38), continued to arrive over the years, and referred to the settlement on the eastern bank as *Ofen* (Furnace) and to the one on the western bank as *Kreinfeld*. Not until after the Mongol invasion (1241-42) was the German name *Ofen* also applied to the settlement on the opposite bank, but it then remained in use for more than 700 years. The Ismaelites at that time first inhabited the former Roman fort, in today's 15 Március tér.

What was undoubtedly the more recent settlement was given the name of Buda, and the former Roman town which lay to the north had the prefix ó (= old) added to its name (*Vetus Buda*, 1261).

Growing from three roots: Without going into the details of the various individual settlements which had grown into larger units as early as the Middle Ages, it should be remembered that modern Budapest, as can be deduced from the information given above, developed from three separate towns. To put it in chronological order, the oldest settlement, with Roman origins, is Óbuda, the second oldest is Pest, and the most recent is Buda.

Despite their central position and their strategic and economic importance, neither Pest nor Buda became the first city of the nation. Prince Géza (972-997) preferred Esztergom, which was chosen as the seat of the Árpád dynasty. With the creation of the kingdom of Hungary, Székesfehérvár, where the kings were crowned, grew to be the first city. The civic charter of Székesfehérvár was accordingly considered to be the pattern for the privileges of other towns up until the beginning of the 14th century. The lesser importance of Buda and Pest is shown by the fact that, after the conversion of the Hungarians to Christianity, it was not those two towns but Esztergom, Székesfehérvár and Vác which became the seats of bishops. Not until the time of the Angevins (1308) did the twin towns serve as a formal capital.

In the early Middle Ages two urban cores existed, both important for future develop-

ments. In the northeast lay the former Roman city of Aquincum, now known as Óbuda and in part as Buda, with a priory and a palace in which the king stayed at times, for instance when dispensing justice.

King Béla III (1172-96) entertained Emperor Frederick Barbarossa here. Close to these buildings, craftsmen and merchants lived, and markets were already being held here. Pest stood on the eastern bank of the Danube. The Dominicans had built a monastery and a church here in the early 13th century. The present Inner City Parish Church dates back to the same period. Oppo-

site the church, on the western bank of the Danube, and lying to the south of present-day Óbuda existed a small settlement by the name of Little Pest. It was important for future urban development that the region around Buda and Pest became part of the royal estate. In this way the tenants of the surrounding demesnes came directly under the jurisdiction of the king.

The Mongol invasion (1241-42): The Mongols destroyed Pest after the decisive battle of Muhi. Once the Danube had frozen, they could deploy large numbers of troops to the western bank and destroy Buda. The Mongols disappeared as suddenly as they came. King Béla IV (1235-70) could then begin to think of rebuilding the nation, partly by re-settling certain areas. Loopholes in the system of defences made the king proceed more cautiously when extending fortified towns. It was his intention that Pest should take on an urban appearance. For this purpose the king proclaimed his *Golden Bull* in 1244. It was intended as a renewal of privileges which already existed, but in its effects it came close to being a founding charter. It was the start of the parallel development of the two towns, as Little Pest, later Buda, was included in some of the individual clauses of the charter.

The charter particularly stresses the rights of the *hospites* (guests, immigrants, settlers), guaranteeing them the right to keep their own language and customs. These urban policies of Béla IV, which are obviously based on older policies towards settlers, made it possible for the many immigrants who settled in Hungary during the Middle Ages to preserve their individual cultures until the 20th century.

On the high plateau of the future Castle Hill, the royal castle and the city of Buda were built. The centre of importance had shifted, a fact which was clearly underlined by the confirmation and extension of the city privileges by King Ladislas IV in 1276. This time the citizens who received the rights were not the inhabitants of Pest, but those of Buda.

Left and right, the first reliable chronicles date from the 14th century.

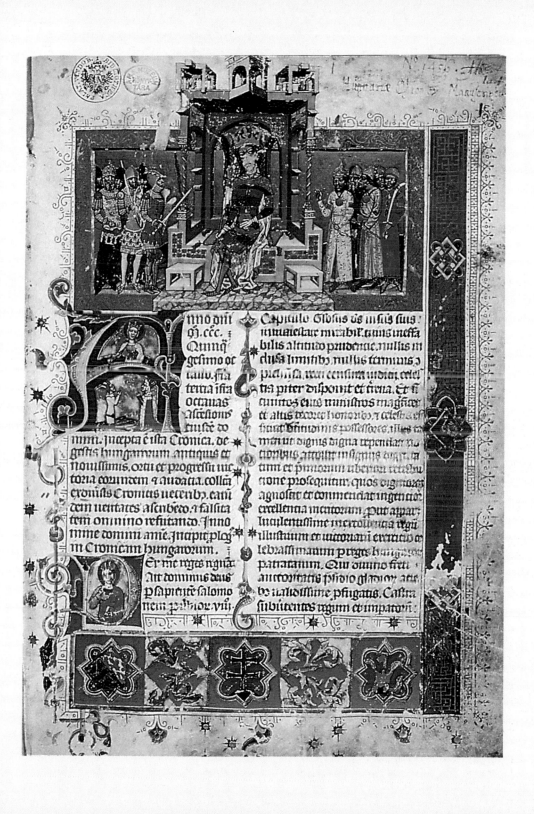

Thanks to its position as a bridging point and to royal support Buda developed politically and economically to become the centre of the kingdom of Hungary. The climax of its development in the Middle Ages came in the 14th and 15th centuries, and it continued to flourish until the beginning of Turkish rule.

At first, Óbuda was in the hands of spiritual overlords. In 1343 it became part of the Queen's estate but as early as 1355, the lordship was divided into three between the king, the queen and the cathedral chapter. Put in the shade by Buda, Óbuda lagged behind in its development, following gradually in the footsteps of Buda and only attaining the status of Royal Free Town (the highest form of urban charter) in 1514.

The fate of Pest was not much different. Because of the preferential treatment of Buda, Pest became no more than a suburb (*suburbium*), and its judge (*villicus*) took his orders from the rector of Buda. However, Pest was able to develop into a confluence of traffic routes crossing the Danube and a market town of the first order. An independent community from the early 15th century on, Pest became a Royal Free Town in 1470. The young city of Buda had a ground plan in the shape of an extended triangle with its tip to the south, where building began on the royal castle. Just as in Pest, a parish church was built here (for the German citizens of Buda), the Church of Our Lady, now known as the Matthias Church.

The monasteries and the churches of the Franciscans and the Dominicans gave greater emphasis to the urban character of the walled site. Apart from the Church of Mary Magdalene, both were daughter churches of the town's parish church. There were also three market places, another clear indication of the economic importance of the settlement.

Migration to the towns: Pest and Buda had a overwhelming attraction for the inhabitants of nearby settlements. Migration to these towns did indeed depopulate whole villages. Economic and also strategic considerations contributed to this "Great Migration" in the period following the Mongol invasion. Immigrants, particularly from the southern areas of Germany, flooded into the country. The three towns were home to a number of ethnic groups: Hungarians, Germans and Slavs (Slovakians), and there were nationalist tensions among them. In Buda itself, the Hungarians were the spiritual concern of the Church of Mary Magdalene, the Germans of the parish church. The Hungarians mostly lived in the northern quarter, the Germans to the south, with a mixed population in the smaller castle district. The predominance of the Germans is demonstrated by the fact that the castle district was also assigned to the German parish.

There is evidence of Jews living in Buda from 1250 onwards. In 1257 they received their charter from King Béla IV, which secured their legal and economic position. They were mainly concerned with the royal finances (in 1250 the Chamber Court was founded as a mint). The community was governed by a judge, assisted by a council of 12. Originally only men with four German grandparents were eligible for election to the post of judge. The Germans formed the majority on the council, too, as only two Hungarians sat on the committee of 12. Around the mid-15th century the position of judge was alternated annually between a German and a Hungarian candidate, and the town council was composed of Germans and Hungarians in equal numbers. This situation did not change until the Germans were driven out in 1529.

The growth of the economy: Economic development reflects the variety of trades carried on by the population. In the agricultural sector, livestock farming predominated on the Pest bank, viticulture on the Buda side of the Danube. Both therefore depended on imports of grain. In the late 15th century there were 79 trades in Buda and 32 in Pest which were organised in guilds. Only master tradesmen and merchants within the walls had rights of citizenship. Pre-eminent among them were the coppersmiths and goldsmiths and the so-called long distance traders (textile merchants), as well as the livestock merchants. This upper class, the patricians, had many relatives in the merchant houses of Vienna and Nuremberg, and had married into Hungarian noble families. Both secular and spiritual dignitaries held a special position.

Buda owed its incomparable rise to the court and to the central offices of the administration. At the beginning of the 16th century the town had a population of around 25,000: 12,000-15,000 in Buda, around 10,000 in Pest and 1,000-2,000 in Óbuda. King An-

had the castle extended further and partially rebuilt in the Renaissance style. The court at Buda was considered to be the most important centre of Renaissance culture north of the Alps. Artists and scholars too met here frequently; Italians and Germans contributed to the glories of the city and the castle. Although the first book was printed in Buda in 1473, King Matthias preferred the handwritten codices, which formed the famous *Bibliotheca Corviniana*.

Pest and Buda under Turkish rule: Even though stagnation set in during the Jagello era (1490-1526), the two towns continued to occupy a leading position in the country.

dreas III (1290-1301) had moved his court there, but the Angevin king Charles Robert (1308-82) had chosen Visegrád at the bend of the Danube to be his residence. It was his successor Louis I (1342-82) who finally moved the royal court to the castle of Buda. The castle was generously extended in the Gothic style by King Sigismund (1387-1437) of the house of Luxembourg, who was also Holy Roman Emperor from 1410 onwards. King Matthias Corvinus (1457-90)

Above, Pozsony, now Bratislava, took over Buda's role in 1641.

After the disastrous defeat by the Turks at the battle of Mohács (29 August 1526) the whole country, including Pest and Buda, lay like a helpless victim before the Turkish armies. Sultan Suleiman had the treasures of the churches, monasteries and castles removed to Istanbul, among them part of the Corviana library. The unfortunate war of the succession followed, with the Archduke Ferdinand of the house of Habsburg disputing crown and country with the vaivode of Transylvania, John Zápolyai. Eventually, with Turkish help, Zápolyai was able to enter Buda in 1529 and hold court there. After his death

Suleiman II had Buda occupied in 1541. At this stage the first break in the development of the two sister towns took place – the royal residence became a Turkish provincial town.

The long period of Turkish rule led to fundamental political, economic and ethnic changes. The conquered region was under the control of a Beglerbeg, a governor, who also bore the title of Pasha. It was divided into new administrative areas, so-called pashaliks. The Beglerbeg, appointed by the Sultan, took up residence in Buda. The control of the urban administration was in the hands of the kadi, and the judges of the autonomous communities were also under

his control.

The German-speaking population of Buda had already left in 1529, before the Turkish occupation (Pest by that time already had a majority of Hungarian inhabitants). Apart from Hungarians, it was mainly Jews and gypsies who lived in Buda. In the following period the Muslims became dominant, and Southern Slav Orthodox Christians formed the second largest group. The Hungarians, split into Catholic and Protestant groups, were actually in the minority. The garrison, too – during the reign of Zápolyai the castle of Buda was made into a strong fortress –

consisted mainly of Southern Slavs.

During this period the towns acquired an eastern, Balkan aspect. The economy was now based on trade from the southeast, and Eastern and Balkan customs and traditions in the crafts and in trade dominated the streets. Although the Turks mostly moved into existing buildings, the mosques with their minarets towered over the houses. A new institution brought into the country by the Turks was their baths, some of which, e.g. the Rudas and the Király Baths, are still in use today.

After 145 years of Turkish rule, the counterattack from the West finally came. On 2 September 1686, after a siege lasting several weeks, Buda was taken by Christian armies under the command of Charles, Duke of Lorraine, who had led the imperial armies in the defeat of the Turkish siege of Vienna in 1683. Prince Eugene of Savoy led a series of campaigns which cleared the Turks out of central and western Hungary.

The siege had reduced the fortress and the city to a heap of rubble. The formerly splendid capital suffered such destruction that it had to be resettled by immigrants. Towards the end of the 17th century Pest, Buda and Óbuda together had a population of only 6,000.

A reminder of Turkish rule, apart from a few Turkish baths, is the district of Tabán (*Debaghane*, *Tabakhane* in Turkish), the tanner's quarter. Other medieval place names were forgotten. The modern names mostly derive from those of the German-speaking new immigrants (mostly Swabians who were encouraged to settle by the Habsburgs). These names were "Magyarised" in 1847.

A new beginning: The 163 years from the liberation (1686) to the siege and storming of the castle (1849) cover several different periods, but compared to 145 years of foreign rule they represent a process of organic development.

After new market rights were granted to Buda and Pest respectively in 1694 and 1696, both towns were once more raised to the status of Royal Free Towns in 1703.

Left and right, two views of the Tabán district.

Urban trade was regulated by these privileges until the abolition of serfdom in 1848. As these charters were based on earlier rights, it is possible for one to speak of a survival of medieval legal norms and social structures.

At this time the citizens were granted titles as a body (this had already been given to the citizens of Buda in 1531). The body of citizens counted as the fourth estate and was permitted to send representatives to the imperial parliament. Every 2 years, in the presence of a royal commissioner, the judge (or mayor) and the council of 12 were elected.

net were moved to Vienna, which was the base of the house of Habsburg, who provided the kings of Hungary from 1526 to 1918. Coronations took place in Pozsony/ Pressburg (now Bratislava in Czechoslovakia), and the estates also met there. The aim now was to equip Buda with the most important institutions. The first measure undertaken by Charles VI (1711-40) was to order the removal of the Council of Seven, the highest judicial authority, from Pozsony/ Pressburg to Buda. Further decisive steps were undertaken in 1784 by Joseph II (1780-90), such as the removal of the governorship, the royal cabinet and the military command.

In the early 18th century this was followed by the creation of the so-called Outer or Great Council – those members entitled to vote in elections. The number of members was fixed at 30 for Buda and 24 for Pest, but was soon raised to 100 for both.

Institutions of importance: In order to visualise the extent of the developments which now began, it should be remembered that the central administrative departments, and most importantly the royal court, had been forced to move out during the period of Turkish rule. In this way the most important offices such as the court chancery and cabi-

The castle itself had been so severely damaged in the storming of 1686 that rebuilding was essential. The Baroque building has strong associations with the name of Maria Theresia (1740-80). After laying the foundation stone in 1749, work was not completed until 1771.

Following the stylistic trend dominant at the time, Buda and Pest took on the aspect of Baroque cities, as was already happening in Vienna and Prague. Some clerical orders, particularly the Jesuits and the Franciscans, also led the trend towards rebuilding in the Baroque style.

In the field of education, there were two Catholic high schools, and a Protestant high school was built in 1823. The Jesuits began teaching in Buda as early as 1687; the Piarists founded their school in Pest in 1717.

The university, founded in the first half of the 17th century in Nagyszombat/Tyrnau (now Trnava in Slovakia), moved first to Buda in 1777, and then to Pest in 1784. Plays in the German language had been performed in Buda from 1760 onwards, and the Castle Theatre opened its doors in 1787, but the first Hungarian plays were not performed until 1790. The press underwent a similar development: The *Ofnerische Merkurius* (*Ofen* = main ethnic groups, there was a strong Serbian immigrant community who came from the south, but in fact all the ethnic groups living in Hungary were represented in the cities. The Jews played an essential part in this mixture of peoples, and their numbers increased rapidly. The dynamic economic developments – in 1176 the silk factory of Valero, the biggest industrial undertaking in the city, was founded in Pest; so was the Goldberger textile factory in Óbuda; in 1836 a shipyard was opened in Óbuda in 1784 – brought about an almost explosive expansion of the population. According to the 1784-87 Land Conscription (a kind of cen-

German name for Buda), 1730-39, predated the *Magyar Merkurius* (1788-89, in Pest), the first Hungarian language newspaper, by half a century. This information also serves to illustrate the fact that both towns were resettled mainly by immigrants from German-speaking areas. As late as the first half of the 19th century Buda/Ofen was mainly German speaking, while Hungarian predominated in Pest. Apart from these two

Left, Baroque, the definitive style of the post-Turkish age. **Above**, Lajos Kossuth; **above right**, Prince Eugene of Savoy .

sus), Buda had a population of 23,919, Pest 20,704 and Óbuda 5,804. In the years that followed Buda was outstripped by Pest. In 1828 the figures for both towns were 30,001 and 56,577 respectively; by 1840 Pest (86,800) had twice as many inhabitants as Buda (40,000). While the number of Jews living in Buda (705) was quite small, the number of those living in Pest (6,031) made up 7 percent of the population and in Óbuda (3,530 out of a population of 8,317) the proportion was well over 42 percent. The Jewish proportion of the total population of the three towns was around 7.6 percent.

Constricted by physical geography, the major urban development took place in the lowlands, while the Buda hills had since the early 19th century been particularly favoured for the building of villas and large houses. In Pest the built-up areas expanded beyond the city walls as early as the mid-18th century. The new district of Lipótváros (*Leopoldstadt* in German) was planned in the late 18th century and in the first half of the 19th century and its houses were held to be a model of urban expansion. In 1808, under the direction of the Palatine, a committee for improving the city was formed. Although its activities were much circum-

putable centre of the country. Various cultural institutions put themselves at the service of the renewal brought about by the Hungarian language. In 1802, after pressure from Count Ferenc Széchenyi, the National Library was founded, in 1805 the National Museum was built, in 1825 the Count's son István founded the Hungarian Academy of Sciences, and the permanent Hungarian National Theatre was ceremonially opened in 1836. Almost symbolic of the general trend of developments was the fire in 1847 in the German theatre of Pest (built in 1812). This theatre, which had been left neglected for years, was not rebuilt.

scribed at first, the disastrous floods of 1838, when about two thirds of the houses in Pest collapsed, were a blessing in disguise for the committee's purposes. The scope for urban planning was now much wider. The concentration of population and industry led to the formation of new settlements. In 1831, for instance, Ujpest was purposely founded as a business and industrial district.

Reform and national renewal: The period from 1825 to 1849, the so-called Age of Reforms, was one very much under the banner of national renewal. During this period Pest and Buda grew together to be the indis-

The centrally orientated policy of reform was also expressed in the efforts to link Buda and Pest with a permanent bridge. This objective was fulfilled with the construction of the Chain Bridge between 1839 and 1849. Both towns were also to be extended to form a major meeting place of various transport routes. The railway network was planned in such a way that all the routes ran towards this central point.

Revolution broke out in Pest on 15 March 1848. After more than 300 years parliament was convened in Pest once more on 5 July. Events embarked on a dramatic course which culminated in the catastrophe of Világos on 13 August 1849. The castle of Buda was occupied by imperial troops at the turn of the year 1848/49. After weeks of bloody fighting it was taken by the Hungarian Honvé army in May 1849, but lost to the imperial troops once more after only a few weeks.

Capital and royal residence: The first Hungarian government, which came into being in 1848, chose Pest for its seat. One of the last acts passed by this government, on 24 June 1849, was to unite the towns of Pest, Buda and Óbuda, declaring them a municipality and at the same time, the capital of Hungary.

Károly Gerlóczy. As a compromise, Hungarian was decided upon as the official language, which resulted in strong tendencies towards assimilation during the urban expansion in the following decades, and was also to be seen in the change of language of the Jewish community. Around the middle of the 19th century, the Jews were mainly German-speaking, but by the turn of the century most of them indicated Hungarian as their mother tongue, without ever having given up German, which was taught as a compulsory subject in schools.

Population and language: The rise in population and its ethnic mix illustrated the extent

The following period of Neo-Absolutism prevented this plan from being carried out. Not until after the Austro-Hungarian Compromise (Ausgleich) of 1867 could the plans for unity be realised; unification took place on 23 December 1872.

On 25 October 1873 the newly elected city council held its first meeting, in which the mayor and two deputies were elected. Their names are typical of the ethnic situation: Károly Ráth, Károly Kammermayer and

Left, gate to the castle gardens. **Above**, Museum of the Visual Arts.

of the changes of the Ausgleich years. The first official census (1869) showed a population of 200,476 for Pest, 53,998 for Buda and 16,002 for Óbuda. The results of the final census before World War I (1910) showed a population of 863,735.

Over 40 years the population had risen more than three and a half times. As far as language was concerned, the three largest groups were formed by the Hungarians, the Germans and the Slovaks; during the period from 1880 to 1910 the proportion of Hungarians increased from 55.12 percent in 1880 to 85.88 percent 30 years later. The proportion of Germans sank drastically from 33.26 percent to 8.96 percent, and that of the Slovaks from 5.99 percent to 2.31 percent. However, the proportion of Jews increased over the same period from 70,879 (19.66 percent) to 203,687 (23.14 percent).

The enormous expansion overwhelmed the city's existing capacity. The city expanded in leaps and bounds along its edges. The population of Kispest and Pesterzsébet in the southeast (both did not exist before 1869 and in fact were still independent communities for a while from 1887 and 1897 onwards respectively) had already passed the 30,000 mark by 1910. To the north the popu-

lation of Rákospalota expanded more than sevenfold from 1869 to 1910, with a final figure of 25,135. Ujpest was incorporated into the city in 1907; by 1910 it had a population of 55,175.

The unification of the sister towns of Pest and Buda was preceded in 1870 by the institution of the Council for Public Works. Its major responsibility was the regulation of the city. The image of the city was to be totally renewed, with plans submitted through public tender. Generous radial roads and a Lesser and Greater Ring Road were intended to relieve the growing metropolitan

traffic. Buildings, too, were the subject of consideration. Apart from the palaces and the apartment houses, the most important buildings – intended to rival Vienna – such as banks and theatres dated from that time, as is the Parliament building, ceremonially opened in 1902. The final touches were also made to the castle of Buda during these years.

Europe's first underground railway: Urbanisation now took over all aspects of civic life, from sewers to pavements to water and gas pipes. Public transport was also expanded to fulfil the demands of a contemporary metropolis. Pioneering work was done in this department: in 1896 Budapest began the construction of the first underground railway in mainland Europe (the project coincided with the Millenial Festival), and at the time it was completed in 1903, the Elizabeth Bridge was the longest suspension bridge in Europe.

In 1893 Budapest received the special status of capital-cum-royal residence. Those were the years when the kingdom of Hungary looked to its past. In Óbuda, excavations of Roman Aquincum began in 1880. In 1896 the Millennial Festival took place, a reminder of the so-called "Taking of the Land" in 896, with the opening of Heroes' Square (Hösök tere) and the Victory Pillar in Budapest as its climax.

However, the glories of the city centre were only a diversion to take one's mind off the misery of the suburbs. The more than obvious contrast between the capital-cum-royal residence and the rural areas, where even larger towns such as Pozsony, Szeged or Debrecen could no longer compete with Budapest, made the contradictions of such a completely unequal development all too plain. Budapest had become the political, economic and cultural centre of Hungary to such an extent that the rest of the country took on a completely subordinate role – a state of affairs which in actual fact has lasted to this day.

<u>Above left</u>, the Four Rivers Fountain in Deák tér. <u>Right</u>, coffee house scenario around the turn of the century.

The direct consequences of World War I, which buried Hungary's past beneath it, affected the urban population badly. Food and other supplies failed in the last year of the war, and general dissatisfaction prepared the ground for revolution.

Even before news of the final defeat had reached Budapest, the Hungarian National Council under Count Mihály Károlyi had been formed from members of various bourgeois and liberal groups. On 31 October

only lasted a while. The Entente nations, who had already sent troops to fight the Bolsheviks in Russia, were worried about the possible emergence of another communist state. Under pressure from the Entente powers, the experimental dictatorship of the people collapsed all over the country.

The occupation of Budapest by Romanian troops was followed on 16 November 1919 by the entry of the "National Army" under the command of Admiral Nikolaus von

1918 Károlyi was assigned by the Archduke Palatine Josef to form a coalition goverment

On 16 November 1918 the National Council declared Hungary an independent and autonomous republic. However, in the confusion caused by the downfall of the previous regime, neither the government nor the National Council was able to master the situation. The government resigned and handed over power on 21 March 1919 to a Revolutionary Governing Council comprising social democrats and communists. However, the soviet republic under Béla Kun, which aimed at the dictatorship of the proletariat,

Horthy, the last commander of the imperial Austrian navy.

Hungary was severely mutilated in the peace treaty of the Trianon of 1920. Its area was reduced from 125,000 sq miles (325,000 sq km) to 36,000 sq miles (93,000 sq km), its population from over 20 million to barely 8 million. Apart from the social problems, which were still as urgent as ever, these losses faced the country with almost insurmountable difficulties. Budapest had to cope with 325,000 refugees from the ceded areas. Housing problems grew immeasurably. Thousands of people had to be housed in railway goods wagons. It was a sign of consolidation when in the late 1930s around 30,000 people were able to find accommodation in the barracks of the Auguszta, Zita and Mária Váleria estates.

Budapest expanded like a balloon. The rural population had shrunk dramatically, and the city continued to expand. Nearly an eighth of the population now lived here in the smallest possible space. The official departments of the capital tried their hardest to find some way of easing the problems, which were accompanied by social tensions. In the 1930s the population of Budapest rose to more than a million. From 1920 to 1941 there was a construction boom; the number of buildings increased by 50 percent.

In order to carry out these projects the city council passed several plans for redevelopment (1925, 1926, 1937) and foreign loans were taken out to finance them. It was not just the replanning of individual districts (e.g. Tabán) that was undertaken. The building of small apartments was intended to relieve pressure on housing. Notable successes were achieved in the cultural field, and sport and leisure also received support. The following achievements date from the years between the wars: first broadcast by Hungarian radio, 1925; building of the main transmitter at Lakihegy 1927; opening of the international free port in Csepel, 1928; first sound film from the Hunnia studio, 1931; civilian air transport 1923; the building of the Budaörs airport, 1927.

In 1938, thousands of people watched the ceremonies of the Eucharistic World Congress in Budapest. This was a major success for Hungary in breaking out of its isolation. It fostered relations with Italy and then ever closer relations with the Third Reich in the hope of revising the treaties that had removed so much of its territory. The Third Reich invested heavily in Hungarian industry and provided a market for the country's agricultural produce.

The inevitable outbreak of war drew Hun-

gary deeper and deeper into conflict. Prime Minister Pál Teleki attempted to keep the country out of the war, but committed suicide when his carefully laid plans collapsed. Viewed with growing suspicion even by its "allies", Hungary was occupied by German troops on 19 April 1944. Hitler's dictates led to the forced resettlement of the Jews of Budapest and then to deportations. After the vain attempts of the Regent Horthy (15 October 1944) to disassociate himself from Hitler, the Fascist Arrow Cross Party took over the government as a willing Nazi tool. The city was heavily bombed during the last months of the war and was besieged for 6

ÁPRILIS 4

weeks. The Germans blew up all the Danube bridges and fought bitterly against the Red Army. In early 1945 Budapest had half a million fewer inhabitants than a year before. About 30,000 buildings out of about 40,000 were damaged or destroyed. About 2 million cu yds (1.5 million cu m) of rubble had to be shifted.

Under the supervision of the Allies and the Soviet occupation forces provisional committees were formed to organise the work of clearing up and to strengthen the will of the population to survive. Life in Budapest gradually returned to normal.

Preceding pages, the Red Army moving in. **Left**, memorial for those who fought in the Spanish Civil War of 1936. **Above**, 4 April 1945 liberation by the Red Army.

WALLENBERG THE BENEFACTOR

The man is stepping forward, his left hand deep in the pocket of his trenchcoat, his right hand stretched out before him in a gesture of denial, the expression on his face one of sorrow and compassion.

At the back of the pedestal of the memorial, the sculptor has added an engraving showing a man battling with a snake marked by the swastika.

The statue by the artist and member of parliament Imre Varga portrays Raoul Wallenberg, looking down the Erzsébet Szilágyi Avenue in Buda. Wallenberg, the son-in-law of a wealthy Swedish banking family, studied architecture in America, free of financial cares. He made a brief attempt to establish himself in the business world and lived for some time in Palestine. In July 1944 he took on the task, given him by the World Council of Refugees, of helping the Jews who were persecuted in Hungary by the Nazis.

Earlier that year in March, the Germans had invaded Hungary and installed a pliable governor in the form of Döme Sztójay. This was the beginning of the Nazis' persecution of the Jews in Hungary. Under the threat of the approaching Red Army Adolf Eichmann, the organiser of the Jewish deportation programme speeded up the forced transportation of Jews to the concentration camps.

Shortly after his arrival in Budapest, the calm, rather shy-seeming Swede became an earnest opponent of the Nazis. His weapons were a printing press and a fountain pen, with which he signed the documents he had forged for the Jews. He acquired thousands of Swedish identification papers for the persecuted Jews and also, in the name of the Swedish government, he bought houses and apartments all over the city, in which he sheltered Jewish families.

Tireless and not in the least afraid, indeed cunning, he tripped up the Nazi extermination machine again and again. He organised protection for the Jewish inhabitants of the city when violent groups ranged through the streets. Thanks to his intervention, the Budapest ghetto was not blown up. Wallenberg succeeded in saving the lives of about 100,000 Jews.

On 17 January 1945, when the Red Army had surrounded the last refuge of resistance in the city, Wallenberg was taken by the Soviet forces to the provisional capital of the time in Debrecen. There all trace of him vanished.

Although the Soviet foreign ministry declared in 1957 that Wallenberg had died as early as 1949 of a heart attack, the search for him never stopped. But even in these times of *perestroika* and *glasnost*, when the crimes of the past are no longer beyond investigation, no new traces of the man have been found.

Wallenberg's fate remains a mystery. There are numerous Wallenberg committees in existence, which have made it their task to find out all they can about his life and his disappearance, and whenever an important guest from the Soviet Union visits the West, he is asked about the fate of Wallenberg. Wallenberg is an honorary citizen of the state of Israel and also of the United States and Canada. A Belgian university has granted him an honorary doctorate.

After the war Phoenix Street, where most of the houses that Wallenberg bought had stood, was renamed after him. The surviving Jews donated a memorial which was to be erected in the park of St Stephen in Budapest. This was where the Nazis had gathered the Jews together before deporting them. The memorial depicted a man fighting a serpent tattooed with a swastika. This statue disappeared under mysterious circumstances, before it was even unveiled.

The engraving on the pedestal of the Wallenberg memorial, mentioned above, is a reminder of this vanished monument. Here Wallenberg is shown as a man of the modern age, confronted with a great number of possible paths which one could take to discover one's purpose in life. Raoul Wallenberg finally found his purpose by a roundabout method. He was called to help human beings in need.

50

Hungarian post-war history has been formed by the fact that the country, following the pattern of other east European socialist countries, entered into the sphere of influence of the Soviet Union. The same also applies to the fate of Budapest, the political and spiritual centre of the country.

On 11 February 1945 some 16,000 Germans attempted to break out of Budapest, which was besieged by the Red Army. On 4 April the last German troops left the capital, which had suffered extensive damage from the war.

Soviet occupation: The Soviet Union, whose army had occupied Hungary in the winter of 1944/45, had their military government in Debrecen. From there they supported the formation of a government, the "National Front", influenced by the Hungarian Communist Party. However, the National Front was at first under the control of the allies. The Soviet military government made sure that all the important posts in the government of the defeated nation were held by loyal communists. They relied mainly on those politicians who had escaped to Moscow in the 1930s.

In the November elections the "Smallholders' Party" ended up as the strongest party. They secured 57 percent of the vote and an absolute majority in parliament. The party owed its success to their extremely popular programme of land reforms. The Social Democrats managed 17.4 percent of the vote, and the Communists obtained 17 percent.

The monarchy was abolished and on 1 February 1946 the republic was proclaimed. Its first president, Tildy, was from the Smallholders' Party. The Paris Peace Treaty, signed on 10 February 1947, confirmed the Hungarian borders during the period between the wars.

Step by step: The Communist failure at the

ballot box was deceptive. Their real strength was based on three factors. They enjoyed the complete support of the Red Army and the administrative machinery of the occupying forces; László Rajk, an active Communist since the 1930s, held the important position of Minister of the Interior, which made it easier for the Communists to weaken the resistance of the population by using the newly-formed police, the ÁVO. Finally, a strong centralised government was neces-

sary to help restore the economy of the country once more.

By the middle of 1946, the Hungarian pengő had set a world record for devaluation, with an astonishing ratio of 1:1.4 billion to its pre-war figure. In contrast to World War I, which was not fought on Hungarian territory, World War II rolled across Hungary like a huge tidal wave which left great destruction in its wake. About 500,000 Hungarians died in the battlefields. In retreat, the German army took anything that could be moved with it, and destroyed all bridges that it crossed.

Left, Liberation memorial on Gellért Hill. **Above**, Socialist realism – Soviet generals at an auspicious occasion.

In November 1946 the big Ganz iron works and the Weiss steel plant were nationalised. The same happened in February 1948 to the bauxite mines and the aluminium works. In May the same year, the banks passed into state ownership.

In the meantime, the Communists had won over a great number of the supporters of the Smallholders' Party and gained their support for their policies. The Social Democrats had joined them in the newly-founded Hungarian Workers' Party. Given the divided opposition, the new coalition rapidly gained ground, and in August 1947 they presented a 3-year plan which was intended

oned as a result of false charges.

Purges and show trials: Mátyás Rákosi, who had spent a large part of the Horthy years in Moscow together with other Hungarian comrades, began to consolidate the power of his own Moscow Wing of the party. The first big show trials against the more nationalist Communists such as László Rajk began with false charges such as "high treason and spying for the imperialist powers".

For Rajk, loyalty to the Communist party was more important than anything else. He publicly confessed to all the crimes attributed to him and was then "legally" condemned to death, executed and finally buried

to help the country back on its feet in the economic field. A further plan for collectivising agricultural production, which did not meet with much support from the population, was put together in 1948.

By mid-1949 the Communist held executive power in the country, after the opposition had been cut down to a manageable size. The influential religious denominations, chief among which was the Catholic church, had also lost much of their power and, as it seemed, much of their social influence too. Cardinal Mindszenty had opposed state control of education and had been impris-

in an unmarked grave.

Rajk was not rehabilitated until 1956, when his remains were reburied in the famous Kerepesi cemetery in Pest, where he found his final resting place in the company of many of his colleagues, both friend and foe, who had died of natural or unnatural causes.

More than 250,000 people took part in Rajk's funeral, which took place on 6 October, 17 days before the revolution. The so-called purges by those loyal to Moscow lasted well into the 1950s. They fell on those Party members who had remained in Hungary or gone into exile in the West – among others, the soldiers of the famous International Brigades who had fought against the Franco dictatorship – while Rákosi had been in Moscow.

Resistance to Stalinism: In 1950 the ÁVO units were re-organised into the ÁVH by Gábor Péter. The field of action of this police force was broadened. A network of spies and informants kept the state informed about the so-called disaffected. Stalinist paranoia stretched out its claws to Hungary as well as other places, and the gates of the prisons were opened but only to put people in.

Behind the Stakhanovite placards depict-

tion of the government to win the people over to their side. After many years of being forced to tighten their belts, the Hungarian people were simply longing for a better standard of living. Consumer goods such as nylons and watches became hot black market items.

The people rise up: After Stalin's death in 1953, Imre Nagy took power out of the hands of Rákosi and tried to clear up the most obvious injustices. However, after 2 years, Rákosi succeeded in resuming the responsible role of leader of the country (his rule by removing the blatantly anti-Tito Rákosi was finally ended by Khrushchev's personal in-

ing the amazing productivity of the "heroes of labour" and the huge banners announcing the workers' paradise, dissatisfaction with socialist experiments such as the model city of Sztalinváros (Dunaúvaros since 1956) was seething. The farmers were tired of being continually forced to work on collective farms according to centralised plans. Also, "ideological" re-education and the brutality of the ÁVH undermined the inten-

Left and **above**, twice a year the state goes public: on 4 April (Liberation Day) and 20 August (Constitution Day).

tervention in 1956). Khrushchev tried to gain the political trust of Tito in Yugoslavia and place his reliance on a new man: Ernö Gerö. The criticism of Stalinism brought out by Khrushchev in 1956 had relatively little effect on the leadership of the Hungarian party.

In the autumn of 1956 the Communist establishment around the world shook but the events that followed made the world hold its breath. On 23 October there was a demonstration in Budapest, mainly by students, who gathered in front of the Parliament building demanding reforms. The government, led by Gerö who was out of the country at the time, tried to play for time, but finally ordered the forcible suppression of the demonstration. Two days after the troubles, the people rose up against Communist rule, and the insignias of Communism were destroyed all over the capital. The red stars were cut out of Hungarian flags, and the massive statue of Stalin in Budapest was dragged through the streets. Many members of the ÁVH were lynched.

Political prisoners, among them Cardinal Mindszenty, were released, and new political parties appeared on the scene. When the Hungarian army under General Pál Maléter

The long Kádár years: The political opportunist who was selected to lead the stubborn Magyars after 1956 was called János Kádár, a former comrade in arms of Imre Nagy. As he was directly appointed by the Kremlin and literally set up in Budapest in the cloud of exhaust fumes from the Soviet tanks, he was met with suspicion from the start. He soothed the USSR by making himself a spokesman for their foreign policy. It was Kádár who saw to it that two Hungarian divisions were sent to Czechoslovakia in 1968 and took part in the bloody suppression of the Prague Spring.

Once Kádár had shown enough proof of

deserted to join the rebels, the Soviet Union intervened. It took only a few days to suppress the revolution. Some 3,000 people lost their lives, and the number of executions is unknown. Nearly 200,000 Hungarians fled the country. Nagy took refuge in the Yugoslavian embassy but was persuaded to come out. After refusing to denounce his policies in public, he was condemned to death in a trial, the outcome of which was determined in advance, and was hanged on 16 July 1958 as a so-called counter-revolutionary (for a more detailed account of the events of 1956, read "The Tragedy of 1956" on page 60).

his vassal's loyalty to the Eastern superpower, he could start trying to improve relations with the West. For a long time the western Hungarian border has been considered the most open of any in the Eastern block. Kádár's good relationship with his Austrian neighbours, whose government at the time was led by Bruno Kreisky, had many Hungarians talking of a new Austro-Hungarian Empire (the initials for the Empire had been K. u. K – *Kaiserlich und Königlich* = Imperial and Royal; K. u. K. now refers to "Kreisky and Kádár").

Tourism gained in importance as the policy of opening up to the West developed, and the standard of living of the Hungarians rose quite noticeably. In the West the idea of a Hungarian "goulash communism" began to circulate, which had succeeded in satisfying the needs of the population in a limited way within the framework a socialist planned economy.

On the occasion of his visit to the Vatican in 1977, Kádár attempted to clear up the differences of opinion between the government and the Catholic church of Hungary, which was still very strong. These tactics of compromise and dialogue have proved successful. Hungary has been spared the sharp conflict search of better employment led to Hungary's currency reserves melting away. The 1960s, therefore, remained lean years generally, though Kádár's famous words in 1962, "He who is not against us is for us," led people to hope for a better and more liberal future.

Economic elements: From 1968 on a new economic policy allowed limited business in the private sector and permitted various state controlled concerns a remarkable degree of autonomy. Economic results were now the measure of success and not political subservience. Farmers could market their own produce to a limited extent, which partially

flict between church and state, which has for instance led to decisive political changes in Poland. In Hungary both parties have come to an arrangement.

As far as economic policy was concerned, Kádár stuck to the old ways. He forced through the collectivisation of agriculture and concentrated on increasing industrial production. However, bad harvests and the migration of farm workers to the towns in

Left, freedom of religion is guaranteed. **Above**, the leadership in the spring of 1989.

solved the problem of food distribution. The rise in the prices of oil and other raw materials in the 1970s put new pressure on the economy and fuelled inflation. In many respects, though, the experiment with limited free markets within the socialist economy was a success.

New problems: The relative prosperity of the Kádár period has strengthened the desire for more private initiatives in the economy and for political reform. *Glasnost* and *perestroika* have also shaken the Hungarian establishment. Many representatives of party and state bureaucracy see it as a threat to their positions, but for others it's already old hat.

The prosperity of many Hungarians and the attractive displays of many of the shops in Budapest cannot hide the fact that the economic position of Hungary has become precarious in the extreme. In recent years the standard of living in Hungary has sunk to 1973 levels and unemployment (estimated at 3 percent) has again become a problem. According to official mid-1989 figures Hungary's foreign debts amount to nearly 18 billion dollars, and the estimated rate of inflation is 20 percent. The income from tourism around Lake Balaton is not even

enough to pay the interest. It remains to be seen whether the frequently renewed plea to the Hungarians to tighten their belts just a bit more will continue to be successful, and whether the new non-Communist government elected in 1990 will be able to find any new solutions

The changing attitude of officialdom: The whole theme of the year of 1989 in Budapest was the official change of attitude to the events of 1956. The slogan was "The atttitude towards the uprising shows the attitude to Hungary's future."

Leading representatives of the reform wing of the Hungarian Socialist Workers' Party carried out the political and legal rehabilitation of Imre Nagy, executed in 1956. The latter had shown the way to overcome the dictatorial one-party system by the inclusion of non-Communist politicians in his 10-day government. The Hungarian Prime Minister Miklós Németh in fact explained in a newspaper interview that Nagy had tried to "renew socialism under the sign of democracy and national feeling".

On 16 June, the 31st anniversary of the execution of Nagy and four of his important colleagues, the Heroes' Square in Budapest saw a memorial service for the "extraordinary statesman" Imre Nagy and his comrades in arms, organised by the Commission for Historical Justice (*TIB*). A quarter of a million people took part. The ceremony lasted more than 11 hours altogether. There were 13 memorial and funeral speeches and thousands of wreaths and flowers were laid. The ceremony ended with a funeral procession, several miles long, from Heroes' Square to Rákos Kerestúr.

New freedom: By the late autumn of 1989 the time had come. As the Communist Party of Hungary dissolved itself and the legislature replaced the old constitution, which was based on Stalinist precepts, with a new democratic one, the newspapers proclaimed triumphantly: "Parliament topples the One-Party State!" The first domino had fallen, the one which was to topple the governments of east European countries such as the German Democratic Republic (East Germany), Czechoslovakia and Romania.

On 23 October 1989 there was a demonstration to commemorate the uprising of 33 years earlier, and this event was not brought to a close by violent intervention, which had been the case only the year before. However, a certain amount of sobering up has dampened the euphoria over newly-gained freedom. A political change will of course do nothing to alter Hungary's economic problems – at least not immediately.

Left and **right**, Imre Nagy's daughter at his funeral in 1989; display of patriotism in red, white and green.

Ünnepélyesen kikiáltották a Magyar Köztársaságot

Az Október 23-a [

Istentisztelet a Bazilikában — Gyűlések a Corvin köz

On 23 October 1989, the day on which the Hungarian uprising began 33 year before, Mátyas Szurös, in his capacity as provisional president of the country, stood at noon on the balcony of the Parliament building and proclaimed the Hungarian Republic. About 100,000 people gathered in the square in

zottság megemlékezései

, a Kilián laktanyánál, a Rádiónál, a Műegyetem előtt és a Bem téren

front of the Parliament to witness the historic moment. With cheers and an ovation lasting several minutes, they greeted this decisive constitutionally protected step by Hungary along the road to a democratic system of government.

The events of the period from 23 October to 4 November 1956 did not, at first, show any signs of an intention of restoring an earlier social order. When the protest march had formed on the afternoon of 23 October, the crowd of demonstrators were demanding neither the overthrow of the government nor the destruction of its fundamental socialist principles, not even the restoration of the republic based on private ownership. By removing the despotic institutions of Stalinism

ashes of László Rajk and other executed comrades from the edge of the cemetery to a tomb of honour.

At about this time those anti-Fascist and social democratic politicians who had played an important part in the rebuilding of the country from 1945 to 1949, but after the complete and exclusive takeover of power by the Communist party had been removed from public life, even imprisoned in large numbers or interned, were freed.

and its representatives, they wanted to restore the values of their fathers, who had paved the way for socialism.

As early as the beginning of that summer they were secretly discussing the open and courageous speech which Nikita Khrushchev had held on Stalinism in a secret sitting of the 20th party conference of the Soviet Communist party. They wanted open discussions, initiated by some of the Communist intelligentsia. Every day they read in the newspapers about the gradual rehabilitation of the victims of the show trials. On 6 October a deeply moved nation removed the

In the meantime the top party leadership insisted stubbornly that lessons had been learned from these revelations, and that leading persons could, with the exceptions of a few scapegoats, remain in their positions. Imre Nagy, who had been considered the leader of anti-Stalinist renewal from 1953 onwards but could not hold on to his position against the power of Mátyás Rákosi in 1955, strolled calmly through the streets of Budapest, a private person excluded from the Party, respected by the people...

The condition of society: The centre of political power in Hungary was thoroughly shaken in 1956. What was the condition of society? Neither the great mass of industrial workers nor the farmers, forced into collectives, viewed this government, which exercised power in their name, as in any way representing them. They suffered under its dictatorial aspects just as much as the former members of the aristocracy and upper middle classes, who were at that time still living in the country in very large numbers. The majority of the non-Communist intelligentsia was definitely opposed to the new system – partly as a result of their pre-war education, partly because of the treatment they had been subjected to since 1949, when

of possibly going to war. Later, during the final phase of the tragedy, it became clear that even the Communist Imre Nagy held such illusions. It was he, at any rate, who broadcasted an appeal on the radio begging the UN to intervene.

Many important moments in the unfolding course of events still have to be examined carefully. Many political parties had just been founded or were rising from their ashes. It is of course impossible with hindsight to establish an "inventory" of these numerous political groups who had grasped what was permissible or tolerable, and to what extent, in the framework of the Europe at that time.

the one party system was introduced.

The influence of the West: A decisive factor for the later course of events was probably this: the non-Communist but opinion-forming classes at that time believed only the Western mass media. Radio stations – those mainly under American control – gave the impression that Washington was seriously considering waiving the Yalta agreement and taking political risks, even to the extent

Left, the 1956 uprising – the royal coat of arms surfacing once more. **Above**, bullet holes, evidence of the uprising.

It is a fact that in the last days of October lynch mobs ruled the streets and political demands were made which were unacceptable to the Soviet leadership. On 3 November Cardinal Mindszenty held a speech on the air in which he stated that the socialist system had lost any claim to legitimacy, and as this was the case it was necessary to return property ownership to the situation before land reform and before nationalisation of industry had taken place.

Suppression by the Soviet military: The General Secretary of the Soviet Communist Party, Nikita Khrushchev, was staying in

Brioni. On the advice of Marshal Tito, he decided to restore the status quo in Hungary with the help of the Soviet army. The USA kept to the then current standards for keeping the balance in world politics. The Western world gave no signs at all of breaking "letter or spirit" of the Yalta agreement, although their propagandists had previously misled Hungarian listeners on this point. Imre Nagy was made Prime Minister, but even he was unable to get the Party to support him.

The role of Janós Kádár: It is now clear from those documents which are available that when János Kádár, the new Party leader, spoke to the people on the radio in the early

branded a supposed supporter of Tito and imprisoned in 1950. As soon as he was able to get back into political life, he backed Rákosi's most merciless opponent. In the summer of 1956 Kádár gained a seat on the Party's top level committee, but was not a member of Imre Nagy's circle. Once Kádár took over the leadership of the Party on 25 October – in other words, while the battle was already raging – the Hungarian Socialist Workers' Party was proclaimed shortly afterwards. From the beginning Kádár had no illusions about what could be done within the framework of the geographical and political order which had developed in Central Eu-

morning of 4 November, it was no "Soviet puppet" who put himself into the public eye of his country and the world. It has by now become well known that he did not take this decision alone. Kádár was one of the small number of Hungarian Communists who did not return from emigration to Moscow in 1945, but had lived and fought within the country all the while. For this very reason Rákosi, who favoured only those Communists who had been in exile with him in Moscow, had put him on the "blacklist", although Kádár had been among the top leaders of the Communist Party. Kádár was first

rope and what could not. On the other hand, he knew his compatriots extremely well. It may be for this reason that his senses reacted in a somewhat more reliable way than those of other politicians.

Hostility towards the new leadership: The new leadership was in a difficult situation. The majority of its potential partners, those Communists and left-wing sympathisers who wanted a bourgeois renewal, instead of socialist one, remained effectively paralysed or hostile and stayed out of public life, as they could not come to terms with the trial and execution of Nagy.

The government of János Kádár had to be very wary of the help offered by not a small number of its supporters. After all, its aim was not to restore the abuses of the despised Rákosi system again. It wanted to and had to distance itself just as unmistakably from the anti-Communist "counter-revolutionary" aspects of events.

A great part of the intelligentsia turned its back on the bleeding country in 1956. Over 200,000 Hungarians fled the country. Other intellectuals were taken "out of circulation" in various ways for longer or shorter periods. Farmers left the collectives in large numbers, but otherwise there were no political

the Soviet leadership was supporting a certain degree of renewal and not insisting on a Stalinist restoration. In 1962 Kádár's famous "He who is not against us is for us" speech led people to hope for a better and more liberal future. Another factor which helped in the process of consolidation was that many Hungarians had realised that it was an illusion to place any hopes on the West.

People who had taken an active part in the show trials during the years of Stalinism are now not allowed to be members of the police force or the judiciary. Yet many sadists who tortured political opponents in 1950 and

demonstrations in the villages.

Positive developments: Nonetheless, there were positive developments after 4 November. In the midst of a deep national crisis people noticed that the Party leadership under Kádár was not looking for confrontation, but rather for compromise. Up until 1962, however, severe punitive measures had an inhibiting, at times even paralysing, effect. It was soon noticeable, though, that

Left, plot No. 301 – the last resting place of Imre Nagy. Above, Nagy's funeral in 1989 was intended to reconcile the nation.

afterwards are now living in freedom as respectable pensioners, because no evidence can be obtained and no charges have been laid against them.

Recent events in the Soviet Union and in Hungary have now opened the way for more research. The abdication of Kádár, the other political changes which led to the election of a non-Communist government in 1990, and the ceremonial funeral given to Imre Nagy, executed in 1958, and to other comrades, will definitely lead to an objective verdict on the events, perhaps one which can be accepted by all those who took part.

If you needed any further proof that Budapest is an international city, a walk along Váci utca, the renowned quarter mile of the Hungarian capital, would convince you. Among the cheerful crowds who throng the pedestrian precinct between Kossuth utca and Vörösmarty tér, Hungarian voices are relatively rare. German is the dominant language, especially the softer modulation of Hungary's Austrian neighbours. There is quite a strong sound of Viennese dialect wherever the tourists gather – in Váci utca just as up in the castle quarter of Buda, where you can find the best shopping opportunities and where – alongside Adidas, Ricci or Salamander – German, Austrian and other Western companies have opened shops.

It's not surprising. After all, at 7.45 a.m., you can get on the Lehár Express at the Südbahnhof (Southern Railway Station) in Vienna, which will bring you to Budapest in comfort and within 3 hours. In the first-class coaches, the adjustable reclining seats, the buffet with steward service, even the television (undoubtedly these trains are the most luxuriously equipped on Austrian soil) are provided by, of all people, the Hungarian State Railways. And all this for a price that's so low that it almost makes you blush. A provocative price, admittedly, as the objective is to lure tourists into the country (meanwhile, the prices have been raised by 30 percent; it is not necessarily the cheapest fare any longer).

Easy entry regulations: Unheard of in Eastern bloc countries is the border control on the trains, with entry permits handed out on the spot (at least for Austrians entering the country, though other nationalities require visas in advance when travelling by train). The Hungarian customs officials, too, have become very relaxed – with a few exceptions –

Preceding pages: all roads lead to the capital; Elizabeth Bridge – without a traffic jam for once; the cakes in Budapest are world-famous. Left, these two are among the 19 million tourists who visit Hungary every year.

and sometimes display an almost "Western" attitude. After all, they have to get into the practice. Both Budapest and Vienna have applied for the hosting of the World Exhibition of 1995 and are expecting a massive influx of Western tourists for the event. *Pressinform*, the Budapest information office for foreign tourists, claims that 10 million visitors are expected.

Admittedly, it is much nicer to travel to Budapest in the late afternoon on the equally priced, i.e. equally cheap, *Arabona*. Unfortunately, you don't arrive on *Nyugati pályauvar*, the Western Railway Station, a steel construction envisaged by the ingenious industrial architect Gustave Eiffel, dating from the 1870s.

Whatever time your journey to Budapest, you will arrive in a city where the whole revolutionary mood of the "Hungarian Spring" has been made visible, where people move more proudly, more freely, and the young people are in fact more fearless and wilder than in the other socialist states of Europe.

The Budapest "economic miracle" is of course a secret of the Hungarian economy. But they always were skilled in making deals, being neighbours of Austria. It's only that they just weren't allowed to for many years. Money may be desperately short all over the place – the country had debts totalling some 18 billion in 1989 – but the buildings are still coming up. The hotels, for instance.

Accommodation: The "City Gate" hotel is now being built, with Austrian help again. Another hotel, partly Finnish financed, is being built near the Danube shore opposite Margaret Island.

However, despite the many hotel buildings and despite thousands of private accomodation possibilities, the capacity is still too small. For this reason a separate department has been created within the Hungarian Ministry of Trade in order to pave the way for future economic cooperation with companies from the USA,

Antiques and hard currency: One branch of trade could be very much an up and coming thing, if it were not for the pitfalls of Hungarian economic bureaucracy. The antiques trade is beginning to flourish in the places where the tourists go, and in Budapest particularly it has by no means reached its limits. If this trade could only really get going, and if dealers had the possibility of rummaging to their heart's content in many a dream of a Budapest art nouveau or art deco furnished household, what deals could be struck then! This would be a form of business that would surely also interest the Americans and the Japanese, not least because of the bargain prices. However, the

clothes, Western in design and of acceptable quality, at very low prices.

For guests from Western countries, Budapest offers an additional attraction - the well-supplied Western currency shops, where with cash or with credit card you can buy anything from salami to cigarettes and from alcoholic drinks to the Herend porcelain which is much in demand – all of it very good value.

Some of the prices are lower than those in the duty free shops of some airports. However, tourists don't just come to Budapest for the shopping – at least that's what many of the Austrian visitors say, trying to distance

cause of the bargain prices. However, the pressure on the Ministry of Trade to disallow too many hard currency shops in Hungary is growing. Whether such measures would be any good in preventing illegal sales via the blackmarket is doubtful, however.

Budapest is a European metropolis, in which, for the equivalent of a few US dollars, Deutschmarks or Austrian Schillings, you can spend all day being driven around in one of the 3,000 taxis, and where the use of public transport is almost free; where food and drink cost about a quarter of those in the Western world; where you can also get

themselves from the shopping fever of the reciprocal hordes from Hungary, who recently have been descending on Vienna and snapping up everything for sale in the way of Western electronic goods, favoured status symbols in Hungary. (The tale that, on the other hand, thousands of Austrians put up with hours of sitting in traffic jams in order to stock up their larders with ridiculously cheap food in Hungarian border towns, is probably mere slander.)

Facades, renovations and cleaning up: But of course there is the other Budapest, the Budapest that recently approached the

Council of Europe for the title of a "capital of European culture" – knowing very well how many tourists such a label would bring in.

It is, in fact, quite a unique experience to walk through the empty streets of the city centre of Budapest, between the Parliament and Lenin körút, on a weekend, and to see why Budapest was always known as the "Paris of the East".

Slowly, the gloomy, dark, weathered and blackened appearance of the city is giving way once more to a visible core of decadent beauty. The dirty grey facade of state socialism, additionally damaged by the exhaust fumes of Eastern two-stroke car engines,

with various shell and bullet holes as reminders of the October revolution of 1956, is gradually being retouched out of existence...

Polishing and painting continue through Saturdays and Sundays. This can hardly be interpreted as revitalising the centre, it's more a matter of repairing the facades. All the same, a fantastical world suddenly appears, a fairy-tale labyrinth opens up before you. Jugendstil never displayed such picturesque forms elsewhere as it did in Budapest. Its apologist, Ödön Lechner, competed with his famous Viennese colleague Otto Wagner, as to who had the greater skill and imagination.

New entertainment: Finally, there is the Budapest of young people, who has created new restaurants of more refined cuisine, new fashionable bars and new discos. Nightlife is becoming more intense, as alternatives to the cheap and cheerful Eastern bloc routines in the various hotel nightclubs are developing. It is difficult to say whether it is this that attracts more tourists or whether the traditional Budapest would fare better. It is probably true that people travel to a city to see the buildings, the sights, for shopping opportunities and for the "experience" (which is how the tourist industry jargon very discreetly describes the entertainment scene).

At any rate, the figures for accommodation, whether seen relatively or absolutely, have been rising steeply in the Hungarian capital over the last few years. In particular, the much-wooed Americans with their dollars, who went through the shock of Chernobyl in 1986 and stayed out of Central Europe in droves, are coming back. From 1987 to 1988 the number of US tourists in Hungary (the majority of them visiting Budapest only) increased from around 81,000 to 102,000. In the autumn of 1988 Budapest was the successful host to the annually held ASTA congress of nearly 6,000 American professionals in the tourist industry.

It happens more and more frequently that tourists, especially those not from mainland Europe, fly direct to the Hungarian capital and make a short excursion to Vienna from there instead of organising their trip the other way around.

The sidelong glance towards Vienna, the ambition to do one better than the former imperial city, goes back a long way in Budapest. To outshine Vienna – perhaps not. To achieve equal status – definitely. The former royal residence of Budapest has grown into a serious rival of the imperial city of Vienna. It is also trying to defeat its teacher from the capitalist West with the latter's very own weapons.

Left, After the shock of Chernobyl, tourists from the USA are beginning to come back. **Right**, claimed to be the "Paris of the East".

It is not size alone, sheer numbers and population figures, that makes a city a metropolis. There is more to it. A metropolis is the beating of the heart of a country. In such a city the country's life forces are concentrated as if by a lens; political, economic and cultural, they diverge far beyond the borders. This is where all the strings are gathered together; this is the nerve centre that sends out signals. This is where the time is set, and the clocks of the country follow accordingly.

If you looking from this angle, the metropolis is the calling card of a nation. From its appearance, the situation of the country can be quite easily deduced.

A metropolis defined: Probably no-one has ever seriously questioned the fact that Budapest is indeed a metropolis. The conditions are better met in this capital than in most others of Europe, except perhaps in Paris: the geographical position, which is at the centre of the country; the way in which all transport routes, road and rail, lead to the capital; the absence of any rival cities – in Hungary there is Budapest the capital, the rest is provincial – and consequently, the focus of all activities from all walks of life in the capital.

Dominated by the Danube: Except for Prague, no city in Europe is dominated by a river as much as Budapest. The Danube flows through the capital for nearly 19 miles (30 km) and divides it into two very unequal halves. Buda with its many hills is considered upmarket, while the other side of the Danube has lost much of its former splendour. During the daily rush-hour, traffic jams on the six bridges, though unavoidable, apparently get on every road-user's nerves.

The motorists in Budapest – only those, of course, who can afford it – are fanatical drivers in every sense of the word. A typical citizen of Budapest jumps into the car to nip round to the tobacconist's. And there are surprisingly many who allow themselves this obvious luxury – even those who can't afford it at all. However, Hungarians have always been good survivors (you could probably call them "fatalists"), and have always succeeded in extracting the silver lining from the apparently most wretched circumstances – at any price.

The volume of traffic in the city centre of Budapest is definitely of international proportions, but if you have a good nose, you will soon notice that you are in the Eastern bloc. Above the traffic jams hovers a cloud of the unmistakable smell of two-stroke mixture, coming from the exhausts of the countless East German *Wartburgs* and *Trabants*, the Polish *Fiats* built under licence, the Czech *Skodas* and the Soviet *Ladas*, which form the bulk of motorised transport in the country.

All roads lead to Budapest: Every route into and through the country runs via the capital of Budapest – international heavy goods traffic is no exception. Every hour, hundreds of container trucks thunder through Budapest in the direction of Bucharest, Sofia and Istanbul.

As far as motorway statistics are concerned, the Hungarian capital may be far behind, but historically speaking at least the Hungarians are in the lead: they can boast of having built the first underground railway on the mainland of Europe.

The year of 1896 was the height and the apotheosis of the splendour of Budapest. About a century later, the plaster is beginning to crack. Budapest building firms simply cannot keep pace with the restoration of the eclectic and occasionally kitsch opulence of the turn of the century. Sadly, the beautiful facades of Budapest are rotting from within.

Every self-respecting metropolis has a centre – or several of them. On Castle Hill, once the centre of rule over the kingdom, it is tourism that rules today. Political power has moved to the other bank of the Danube. State television, the National Bank and numerous ministries have settled in a separate government quarter around the Neo-Gothic Parliament. A few hundred yards downriver from this political enclave lies the busy business centre of the Hungarian capital. In the famous Váci utca the visitor can discover more than just beauty salons and boutiques. Some Western companies, banks and insurance companies also like to display this upmarket address.

The black market has its headquarters next to the Eastern Railway Station (*Keleti pályaudvar*), a magnificent functional building completed during the late 19th century which is constantly having to do duty as the backdrop to historical films.

Coffee houses and espressos: What would a genuine Central European metropolis be without coffee houses? Like the little knots in a net that still survives, these magnificent temples of contemplation, impregnated with smoke, link cities and countries which history would possibly have kept apart for centuries.

In these times of burgeoning democracy, the old cafes of Budapest and the newer espressos are experiencing a Renaissance.

Left, keeping fit with aerobics seems to be (almost) everyone's business nowadays – even in this metropolis! **Right**, modern steeds and riders of the puszta.

Revolutions have been proclaimed in the coffee houses of Pest, and it was quite natural for the Smallholders' Party, the most formidable political power in the country until the Communist takeover in 1948, to choose the cafe "Pilvax" to reconstitute themselves in December 1988, after an interruption lasting 40 years. In the spring of the revolution of 1848, students and intellectuals gathered in the "Pilvax", to plan the revolt against the Habsburgs who were eventually suppressed with much bloodshed.

Desires and hopes: The aim of all coffee-house politicians, yesterday's and today's, was and is to escape from the isolation that

has been forced upon them for so long. The real objective of their desires and hopes, well known to every visitor to Budapest, is not so very far away from all these meeting places: the Neo-Gothic Parliament building on the banks of the Danube.

Quite deliberately, the building was constructed (about a century ago) to be a few yards longer than its counterpart in London. However, in contrast to the British House of Commons, a truly democratically elected gathering of the people's representatives has never met in this Hungarian showpiece of a building, not once in all its history.

All the strings that hold the country come together in Budapest. This is where the administrative, economic and also the cultural power of Hungary is concentrated. Budapest has a population ten times that of the second largest city in Hungary (Miskolc) and it has many more cultural and scientific institutions than all the other cities taken together. If you want a good view of the Hungarian cultural scene, Budapest is the best place for it.

Nationalistic or cosmopolitan: If you try to grasp the fundamental characteristic of Hungarian culture, you will – whatever form of culture may be under discussion – come to the realisation that it is an indubitably and unmistakably national culture, while at the same time being – in the best sense of the word – a European culture. Its most interesting feature is its very ambivalence, the dual aspects which enrich and complement one another; the continual tension between the international, intellectual movements which offer integration, on the one hand providing a stimulus for discussion, but on the other hand arousing markedly nationalist ideas which emphasise on and encourage differences. The strength of these opposing poles which are characteristic of the Hungarian culture has varied in the course of its history and they are also present in very different quantities in various forms of the arts, but their dual nature is certainly its evergreen characteristic.

For a thousand years the Hungarian culture has had a continuing reciprocal relationship with the intellectual life of Europe. It is most closely connected to the parental body of European culture by a rich network of capillaries, and it is a firm and independent part of the total culture of Europe. Hungarian culture has received much that is valuable from Europe and has provided not a little towards the development of European culture. Goethe's work, which has been translated by

the best Hungarian poets over the last 1½ centuries, is as much part of the literary life of Hungary as Bartók's music is part of the musical language of Europe.

However, despite the unbroken reciprocal relationship, past and present, of exchange between Hungarian and European culture, other countries have learned little about the intellectual life of Hungary – with the exception of a few masterpieces and their creators. This is due mainly to the peculiarities of the Hungarian language, which had the effect of making all those works which exist because of the language inaccessible to other countries, as they still are partially today.

Language and literature: In forming the national characteristics of a culture and creating a national identity, language plays an important part, especially with less numerous and therefore endangered peoples. This applies to Hungarian culture as well, and especially to the Hungarian language.

About 200 years ago, Johann Gottfried Herder prophesied in his essay *On the Origin of Languages* that the Hungarian language would briefly disappear from the surface of the earth as if it had never existed. If the process had been left up to historical circumstances, his prophecy might even have been fulfilled. However, it did not come about: if the language had become extinct, Hungarian nationality would also have ceased to exist.

Language is the elixir of life for a people or a nation – so says a quote from the great Hungarian poet of the 20th century, Gyula Illyés: "The language is the nation."

Linguistic cohesion determines a nation, keeps it together, and keeps it alive. As long as the language survives, the nation lives on.

Fortunately Herder was wrong, but we cannot help noticing again and again how isolated the Hungarians are by their unusual language, both within and outside their borders. This has come about for historical reasons. Ever since the 9th century, when the Magyars settled in the Carpathian basin, they have lived in the middle of Europe as if on a linguistic desert island. Those who speak our nearest related language are far away – more than 3,000 miles (nearly 2,000 km) – in Finland.

Hungarian is a Finno-Ugric language, one of a group that split off from the larger family of Uralic languages in about 4,000 BC. Speakers of Finno-Ugric languages are widely distributed; the areas they inhabit the stretch from northern Norway to the river Ob in Siberia and south to the Carpathian Basin. Hungarian forms the largest (over 14 million speakers in Hungary itself and in the neighbouring nations) group, but is also linguistically the most isolated – the nearest Finno-Ugric speakers are to be found on the shores

guages try to learn Hungarian will find it particularly difficult. This is because the structure of Hungarian is radically different from that of all other European languages. In Hungarian there is no grammatical gender, there are no prepositions, no declensions, and there isn't even a fixed word order. In contrast, there are innumerable endings, which added to the word determine the number of nouns and their role within the sentence, which change the meanings of words and determine the number and the person of the action, which extend the meaning of a word in a special way and thus enriching it. Word order within a sentence is

of the Baltic, in Estonia and Finland. It is perhaps the dispersion of Finno-Ugric language speakers that has led to a wide range of differences in individual languages. Finnish and Hungarian, for example, are about as similar as Russian and English (which are both members of the Indo-European family). The openness of the Magyar culture towards outside influences can be seen in the extensive borrowing that Hungarian has made from other languages, including those of the Turkic, Iranian and Slavic groups, as well as German, Latin and the Romance languages.

Foreigners who have learned other lan-

relatively free, but by changing the order of the individual words the meaning of the sentence can be changed in a variety of ways. The Hungarian language is extremely rich in fine nuances, which are hardly understood by a non-Hungarian, however well he may speak the language, and which can only be translated with much effort and in a very weakened form into other languages.

Another peculiarity of the Hungarian language is that many moods can be expressed by relatively short sentences or single words (e.g. "I love you" is *szeretlek*). On the other hand, as many suffixes can be added to a basic word, you can get the most monstrous word conglomerations (e.g. *legmegvesszte-gethetetlenebbeknek*, which means "for the incorruptible ones"). All these characteristics combine to make access to Hungarian literature, especially poetry, almost impossible for those with a different mother tongue. This means that the deepest and most sensitive emotions of the Hungarian soul, the works of the great poets of the Hungarian language such as Sándor Petőfi, János Arany, Mihály Vörösmarty, Endre Ady and Attila József must remain closed, for the most part, to readers from other countries.

Theatre: Any attempt by foreign visitors to

so close as to be almost erotic, and on the other hand because they enjoy being impartial observers in situations of conflict. Hungarians have a lively imagination. It is not difficult for them to identify themselves with the nice hero up there on the stage and to recognise their enemies, unloved neighbours, or even their friends (of whom they are secretly jealous) in the stage role of the villain, the plotter, or the clumsy clown.

The theatre in Hungary – in Budapest particularly – has wide-ranging traditions, not so much in the way of actors and acting as in respect of the plays themselves. In the early decades of this century there was a

be acquainted with the very lively theatre scene in the Hungarian capital is also bound to suffer from this language barrier.

Hungarians have a natural inclination towards the theatre – and, it must be said, all too often towards the theatrical. On the one hand, they love the theatre because it is an extension of the expressive power of the language, to which they have a relationship

Left, young people have few problems understanding the language of pop. **Above**, a rather compelling performance in one of the city's dozen theatres.

whole "regiment" of popular Hungarian writers – from Franz Molnár to Ladislaus Bus-Fekete – who year after year provided the stages of the world with new successful comedies, sketches and burlesques (later on, they were equally successful in Hollywood). Many of the Hollywood "greats" – Cukor, Fox, Korda, the actor Tony Curtis – were of Hungarian origin.

It would appear that after World War II the comedy writers disappeared together with the old social order – after all, their works were written for that very order (one need only think of Molnár). In the socialist world the theatre is seen as the reflection of social circumstances and the fate of human beings in realistic surroundings. The example of the Soviet Union has proved that this ideological framework need not exclude great achievements in the field of directing and of acting; but it has not been until the last few years that Hungary, i.e. Budapest (outside the capital theatre groups of some fame and more than regional importance probably only exist in Szolnok and Kaposvár) has been able to hold its own.

Nearly every performance of the József Katona Theatre is full to bursting point. The theatre is named after József Katona, 1791-

a reputation in theatrical circles throughout Europe. Its success is due to the artistic professionalism and honesty of expression, an openness and tolerance which occasionally leads to works of world literature being "rubbed up the wrong way".

This has nothing to do with extreme forms of direction according to Western models. In the Katona-József-Színház up is still up and down is down, but the freshness and originality with which the new wine is poured into old vessels could persuade even someone who does not understand Hungarian to take a look at a Budapest theatre from the inside.

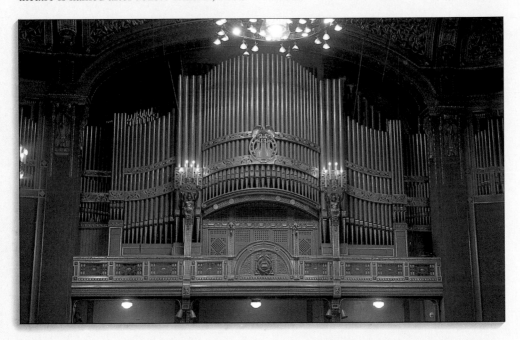

1830, a lawyer and a playwright. He wrote the play *Bánk Bán*, which later became a great success with Hungarian audiences, and was made into an opera by Ferenc Erkel, but which was virtually ignored during Katona's lifetime.

The audience comprises mainly students who are (or have to be) satisfied with standing room or at best an improvised seat on the steps of the auditorium. The young ensemble, under its director Tamás Ascher, was founded in 1982 as an experimental offshoot of the National Theatre and in its brief period of existence has already gained

Music: Visitors to Hungary are bound to have heard quite a lot about the famous fiery and temperamental Hungarian gypsy bands, usually heard as an accompaniment to lavish meals of *pörkölt* or *gulyás*, highly seasoned fish soup and good Hungarian wine. Unfortunately, you may be disappointed. Whatever you hear on such occasions may not be Hungarian folk music. What is it, then? Gypsy folk music? Not even that! They are simply songs written for listening and dancing, products of popular Hungarian music which has a history dating back only about 150 years, and which is performed by professional musicians and entertainers, usually gypsy bands.

The music of the gypsy bands indubitably has its place in the broad spectrum of Hungarian culture, but what the primás and his colleagues are offering has little to do with the folk music of peasant origin which has survived to the present day and is cultivated in the so-called urban dance house, *táncház* (pronounced "taants-haas") in Hungarian.

What does a *táncház* look like? A small group of musicians – a violin to lead the melody, a double bass to keep the rhythm, and one or two additional instruments – provides the musical background.

been inspired by Hungarian themes. In the 19th century Franz Liszt, composer, virtuoso and ladies' man, used his talent to make Hungarian artistic music internationally famous too. In the 20th century Béla Bartók and Zoltán Kodály made use of the original sources of Hungarian music, the folk songs, in their works.

This is where we come up against a fundamental problem to do with the position and importance of the Hungarian people and their culture within Europe. Taking account of the supposed or actual positive and negative features of the national characters, we have to discuss the question as to whether the

Ever since the late 1960s one development has become noticeable, especially in the towns: young people have discovered folk music for themselves.

Where does the interest in Hungarian folk music come from? For more than 200 years its fiery rhythms, its lilting melodies and its curiously exotic nature have stirred the imagination of the composers of the West. The greatest European composers – among them Haydn, Beethoven and Brahms – have

<u>Left</u>, **Franz Liszt founded the Academy of Music.**
<u>Above</u>, **there's music in the air.**

Hungarians have a "Western" or an "Eastern" style culture within Europe. On the one hand there is the uncritical acceptance of Western European cultural models, on the other there is the passion for Eastern cultures; there is the uncertainty that comes from a position between the two opposing directions, and the feeling of loneliness caused by linguistic isolation, which can go as far as a certain arrogant revelling in being different. Speaking relatively, it would indeed be possible to describe the Hungarian culture as one that has arisen at the meeting place of routes from every direction.

The music that is commonly known as "Hungarian" goes back to the so-called *verbunkos* music (the name comes from the German word *Anwerbung*, i.e. recruitment) from the second half of the 18th century. This mingled Hungarian folk songs and old dance tunes with themes from Romania and from the Balkans and with folk tunes from the West, come mainly from Vienna. Verbunkos brought Hungarian music out of its isolation: it now became a matter for the whole nation. Right from the beginning there were attempts to put verbunkos music on the same level as concert music. However, it developed in two different directions. While

1843 he became Director of Music at the court of Weimar. He was also famous as a conductor – he conducted the premiere of Wagner's *Lohengrin*, for instance – one of a long line of famous Hungarian conductors that continues to the present day (Solti, Sebestyén, Szell, Doráti). In his *Hungarian Rhapsodies* Liszt made the folk songs of his country famous all over the world. His great achievement in his re-working of Hungarian music, popular at the time, was to bring it out of the narrow limits of folklore; endowing it with the dignity of the concert hall, he made it, so to speak, fit for high society.

Ever since the early decades of this cen-

csárdás music spread throughout the country, the forms of dance music were preserved by the folk-based songs. *Verbunkos* music also appeared in the more sophisticated national art forms, such as Hungarian opera (Ferenc Erkel's *Bánk Bán* is one example), symphonic and chamber music.

Hungary's first composer of national, indeed of worldwide, importance was Franz (Ferenc) Liszt, whose work anticipated many of the movements of the 20th century and opened up new avenues for music. Franz Liszt (1811-86) gained fame as a virtuoso piano performer as well as a composer. In

tury music from Hungary has triumphed on operetta stages all over the world. Franz Lehár, Emmerich Kálmán, Paul Abrahám are among the greatest and most famous of the talented composers who devoted themselves to the light-hearted muse. Franz Lehár (1870-1948) set the scene for a new style of operetta with *The Merry Widow* in 1905.

The situation was similar to that on the ordinary stage: entertainment in the theatre, whether in words or music, was firmly in Hungarian hands.

A long way from the bustle of everyday life and untroubled as to whether the mass of people applauded them or not, the two great personalities of the 20th century were working to lay the foundations of the link between Hungarian and European music. Béla Bartók (1881-1945) started compiling his folk music collection after finishing his studies at the Academy of Music in 1903. Hungarian folk music also influenced his own work during his most productive period (the 20 years following World War I) as a composer and concert pianist. He published many works of Hungarian folk music and some of Romanian and Slovakian music. Bartók's near contemporary Zoltán Kodály (1882-1967) began to collect Hungarian folk songs

The work of Béla Bartók and Zoltán Kodály was not only of immeasurable national value, but also most important for musical education. The decisive factor in the work of Bartók and Kodály was that they met folk song in the places where it still survived: in the villages and in the farms of the puszta. Education was the fundamental idea and the aim of Bartók's and Kodály's concept of music. Those who learn to treasure the folk songs will also enjoy the culture and the national traditions.

Architecture and monuments: If you were to visualise a bird's eye view of Budapest, noting its essential architectural features,

for his thesis on the topic in 1906. He then became teacher of theory and composition at the Academy of Music. He published collections of folk songs with Béla Bartók. His own work was mainly influenced by Hungarian folk music: best known perhaps being the *Psalmus Hungaricus* (written for the 50th anniversary, in 1923, of the union of Buda and Pest), his comic opera Háry János and the Hungarian dances for orchestra.

Left, the renovated opera house basking in its new glory. **Above**, the courage to experiment with new forms of architecture is lacking.

you could easily recognise the central role of the Danube. The river is of enormous importance: both the appearance and the urban structure of the city are decisively influenced by the river that runs through it.

The Danube is the main north-south axis of Budapest and of its transport network. At the same time it is the boundary line between different landscapes. On the right bank, almost reaching the river, lies the varied scenery of the Buda Hills. On the left, or Pest, bank, there is a broad level plain. Roads from the various parts of the country, leading in to the capital, run to the Danube and its bridges, as do the ring roads laid out around the turn of the century. This makes the network of main streets within Budapest easy to grasp and useful in its structure, but nonetheless they are extremely overcrowded due to the huge increase in traffic.

Budapest, a city of 2 million inhabitants, owes its urban structure to a long historical development. Within the area of present-day Óbuda there was already a Roman city (Aquincum) 2,000 years ago. In the Middle Ages, Buda was one of the most important cities of Europe. And yet the period which is responsible for the present-day appearance of the city did not begin until about 120 years

motifs of folk art, but paid attention to vernacular buildings, attempting – like Finnish Jugendstil – to create a national style of architecture in this way.

The need for conservation: Now, at last, it seems that the preservation of Hungarian cultural heritage and monuments is gradually coming to the fore. There are, of course, examples of the opposite tendency. For instance, a popular presenter of a programme on Hungarian television entitled "What Our Grandchildren Will Never See" examines in each programme a few buildings or facades which are in urgent need of restoration but are being allowed to decay or even demol-

ago, after the Austro-Hungarian Compromise of 1867.

With the exception of the castle district and a few public buildings in the Classical style, the city was created towards the end of the 19th century in the Historicist style. Around the turn of the century many buildings characteristic of Hungarian Jugendstil were added, most importantly the works of Ödön Lechner, who wanted to devise an original Hungarian style and used elements of folk art, but also of the ornamental style of Mogul architecture. Another movement of Hungarian architecture did not take up the

ished because of lack of money or simple apathy. Every time one sees the programme, one is impressed by the painstaking way in which it follows up matters that may seem of no importance whatsoever to outsiders and are yet of the greatest value.

The need for preserving historic buildings in Hungary, and especially in Budapest, is being given ever increasing importance when the old building stock is being renewed. At the same time, the field of activity for the conservationists is constantly being expanded. A very fine example of this is the growing attention paid to the need to preserve more than individual buildings, to save groups of buildings and even whole districts.

The changeable history of the country has resulted in few historic urban cores being preserved. During World War II, in all the protected areas of Budapest, buildings sustained severe damage. However, although this may sound like a paradox, this very damage was responsible for the discovery of many details of the buildings, painted, covered or walled up over the years, which only came to light again during restoration work after the war and which are now among the witnesses to our past.

The problem arose in the case of the for-

Széchenyi National Library in the Baroque and Neo-Baroque wings of the palace. The people of Budapest have now got accustomed to (or are reconciled with) the sight of the Hilton Hotel – despite having completely rejected it at first. Although the whole Castle Quarter (on the UNESCO list of world cultural heritage since 1988) is under strict architectural regulation, those in charge of ancient buildings consented at the time to the construction of a large modern hotel. The ruins of the former Ministry of Finance, unused for 30 years, were resurrected to life. The late Baroque facade of the old Ministry and the remains of the Gothic church of St

mer medieval castle and royal palace of Buda, one of the buildings that dominate the appearance of Budapest. The use to which it should be put was, for a long time, a matter for long and heated debate – as was the case with the Hilton Hotel. Eventually the Budapest City History Museum, a local museum, found a home in the medieval castle, as did the National Gallery, the Historical Museum of recent times and the

Far left and left, Jugendstil is the dominant artistic style. Above, tympanum of the art gallery in Heroes' Square.

Nicholas and the Dominican monastery were incorporated in an acceptable fashion into the expensive new building.

Hungarian conservationists are of the opinion that it is important not only to preserve and maintain valuable historic buildings of the past for future generations, but also to discover sensible uses for these old buildings, to harmonise the preservation of the cultural heritage with the architectural requirements and human needs of both the present and future. In general, the basic assumption is that the further development of districts which are protected should not be halted by sterile solutions. On the contrary, by caring for historic buildings, these should be given sensible uses, which permit the organic survival of the buildings in question. This line of thought is already being put into practice in many places today.

Museums: What do the museums of Budapest have to offer guests who are interested first and foremost in culture? What is the thinking behind the exhibitions, and what features do the different museums have?

Budapest has a whole series of interesting museums, from which visitors can find much worthwhile information. The majority of the big museums in Budapest are national

survival of the Hungarian nation, it is often over-emphasised. Visitors will notice just by scanning the list of names of the Budapest museums how often the word *nemzeti* (national) appears. This is no accident, but it has a deeper meaning and says much about the nature of the institutions. In many respects these are almost without exception museums of the nation. There can hardly be another country in Europe where the term "national" is so frequently used when naming cultural and official institutions as is the case in Hungary, and if there is one, it must certainly be another small nation whose existence has often been in danger during its history. Inci-

institutions, i.e. their exhibits are not locally based or composed of interesting trivia for a small number of specialists. Whatever is on show is of national (and often of international) importance, and the exhibits speak to the whole nation.

National institutions: The nationalist aspect plays an important part in many ways (the motivation and the reason behind the founding, the function, the aim of each institution, the name, etc). It is strongly stressed for historical reasons. For a foreigner who does not know enough about Hungarian history, about the centuries-old struggle for simple

dentally, there is a constant tendency in Hungary to include the word *nemzeti* into the names of various institutions, even when there is no obvious reason for it – probably to give the institution in question more weight. Often this leads to quite comical and complicated combinations, e.g. Nemzeti Uszoda (National Swimming Pool), Nemzeti Lovarda (National Riding Stables), Nemzeti Baromfifeldolgozó Vállalat (National Poultry Processing Company).

A temple for the nation: The founding of the Hungarian National Museum dates back to the year 1802. The basic stock of the museum goes back to an aristocratic collection, a gift to the nation by Count Ferenc Széchenyi. In the first half of the 19th century, museums were being built in many European capitals to make royal or aristocratic collections accessible to a broader spectrum of the public. The motivation for the building of the great museums in Western capitals was the fact that large collections of exhibits had been gathered together and that a steadily increasing section of the population was showing interest in them. The plan was to display these collections in a systematic way in large buildings designed for the purpose. These museums, such as the British Museum in

national independence, a manifestation of the awakening of the national consciousness and the will of the people, so long suppressed. The National Museum was the symbol of the nation that was forming, and above all it wanted to prove that this nation had the right to exist. This basic need for national affirmation, combined with the aim to extend the collection and to secure its presentation to the nation, simply demanded its own, impressive, worthy framework. For the awakening national spirit, Classicism was the best architectural form, because this was openly and most clearly able to express the nostalgia for a famous past.

London or the Old Museum in Berlin, all had far less of a nationalistic character than the National Museum in Budapest. In Hungary the motivation was quite different. The size of the collection in the museum at that time – mainly consisting of gifts from the nobility – hardly required that a large building be constructed to house it.

The building of the Hungarian National Museum was, in the first instance, an act of

Left, there are nearly 80 museums competing for the favours of the public. **Above**, the overblown foyer of a cinema.

The construction of a building according to plans by the most famous architect of Hungarian Classicism, Mihály Pollack, was decided upon. The building, with its magnificent pillars and its tympanum, is reminiscent of a Greek temple. An imposing flight of steps leads up to the Greek-looking front, to the solemn vestibule, which also contains a few Roman elements, and to the ceremonial hall. Here is a true temple to the nation! At the time, about 150 years ago, the building was constructed too large for contemporary use, and even today there is still plenty of space in order to display Hungarian history and archaeology in a suitably modern and impressive manner.

As long as it has been in existence, the National Museum building has several times been linked with important events of the Hungarian nation. If you asked ten Hungarians at random their thoughts when you mentioned the National Museum, at least seven would mention the bourgeois revolution and the liberation struggle of 1848/49, together with the name of Sandór Petőfi. When revolution broke out on 15 March 1848, the garden of the museum was the place where the revolutionary youth gathered. From this point the country-wide popu-

would have been nearer, and separated only by a strip of sea from Asia – but to Pope Sylvester II in Rome, i.e. to the West and to Europe). In the decade or so since the crown was returned more than 5 million Hungarians, half the population of the country, have made the pilgrimage to the Ceremonial Hall of the National Museum to see the crown named after the first Hungarian king.

Other museums: With the passage of time and with the growth of the collections, some specific collections of the National Museum have moved out into their own museum buildings. This was, for instance, how the Ethnographic Museum was created. From

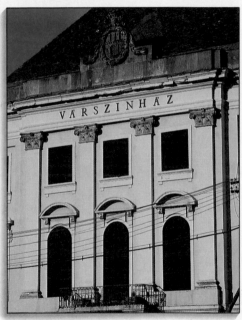

lar movement developed. At least five of the ten people you approach would point out that the Hungarian royal crown, 1,000-year-old symbol of the Hungarian nation and sovereignty, is on display in the Ceremonial Hall (in January 1978 the royal crown together with the coronation regalia, which had been taken out of the country at the end of World War II, was returned to Hungary from the USA). St Stephen's Crown is, at the same time, also a symbol of European continuity in Hungarian history (for when the first Hungarian king, St Stephen, requested a crown, he did not turn to Byzantium – which

the beginning, the collections of this museum concentrated on cultural artifacts from peoples all over the world, including the peoples of the Carpathian Basin, which in concrete terms equals the area covered by Hungary's historical, pre-World War I borders. The museum also has a valuable, extensive and important collection covering the way of life of the Hungarian people, past and present, and their artistic activity. The biggest of the permanent exhibitions is the one of Hungarian national costume.

As a building, the Museum of the Applied and Decorative Arts is certainly one of the most beautiful and also the most interesting of the museums of Budapest. This museum was built by Gyula Pártos, according to plans by the main representative of Hungarian Jugendstil, Ödön Lechner, for the Millennial Celebrations in 1896. Using both Hungarian and Eastern motifs, Lechner developed a style with a very individual, nationalistic character. He borrowed elements of decoration from Persian and Islamic Indian architecture, among others, as he felt they were related to Hungarian folk art. Lechner produced a harmonious whole from these very different units. He used modern glass and steel construction and for his facades he used

lections cover furnishings, glass, ceramics, textiles, pictures and jewellery.

The most beautiful of the radial streets of Budapest ends in Heroes' Square (Hösök tére). In this square, opposite one another, are the two most important museums of the visual arts: the Müsarnok gallery, a permanent exhibition hall of modern art, and the Museum of the Visual Arts (Szépmüvészeti múzeum), the biggest Hungarian collection of visual arts in the world. The gallery of old masters contains many important works by famous names. Italy and Spain are particularly well represented. Art historians with an interest in Spanish painting are often heard to

pyrogranite and majolica tiles from the Zsolnay porcelain factory in Pécs. The colourful splendour of the facades combines with the jagged lines of the openings and applied ornamentation, in a wealth of colours and shapes at the edges and ridges of the roofs and at the peaks and lanterns of the domes. A visit to Budapest, for those who love this style of art, is worthwhile if only to look at this one building. The museum col-

declare that outside Spain there is no Spanish collection anywhere that is as grand as the one in Budapest. Among the most beautiful and valuable treasures in the collection are surely the works of El Greco and the Goya Room.

As mentioned above, Hungarian culture is unmistakably a national phenomenon, i.e. it has never been moved right off the course of its development by foreign influences. However, as can be seen from many of the exhibits in the museums of Budapest, many of the stimuli for further development have come from outside the country.

Far left, Victor Vasarely's op art. **Left**, the Baroque Castle Theatre. **Above**, modern art is not given enough recognition yet.

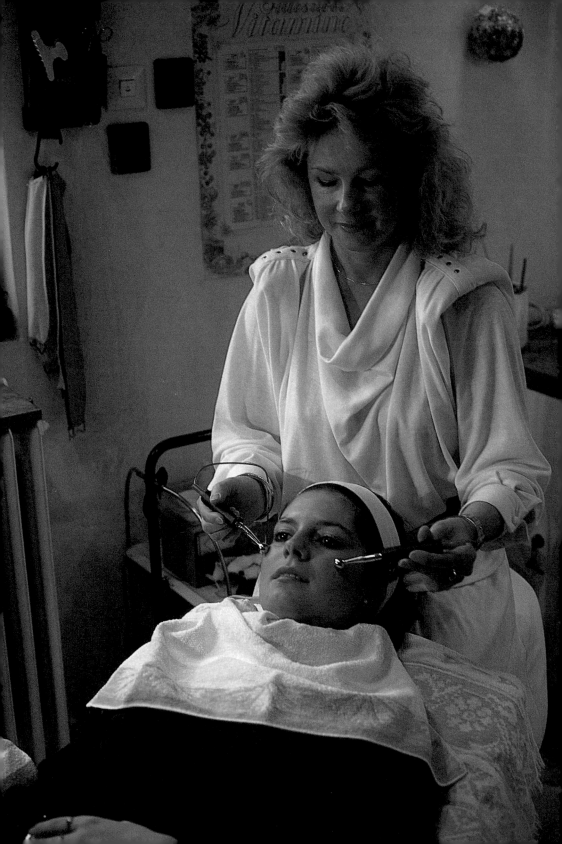

Officially, *la dolce vita* shouldn't exist in a country which according to its treaties is obliged to promote socialism. However, some citizens of Hungary can enjoy quite a good life in their country. Foreigners can live particularly well, especially if they come from the West. Guests from the "fraternal socialist countries", too, know how to value the good life in Hungary. Many visitors from the Eastern bloc believe that the Hungarians live in the land of milk and honey. Even though average Western standards do not always apply in matters of accommodation or eating out, the Magyars are quick to learn. Ever since their government gave them the chance of setting up their own businesses, many would-be entrepreneurs have seized the opportunity and displayed quite unexpected initiative.

It is probably a well-known fact that Hungary was once a hospitable country. Because of the long period of state-controlled tourism, many of its human qualities – friendliness, personal effort, personal initiative, the ability to speak foreign languages, cleanliness – disappeared. These lean times now seem to be partially over, and not the least thanks to Western help. Today one can expect, in those centres of tourism that mainly cater for Western guests, a level of service that boasts of international standard.

The Queen of the Danube: What are the attractions that draw foreign visitors into the land of the puszta? Mainly a sense of romance, the nostalgic cuisine and a whiff of *dolce vita*. Hungary can now boast 17 to 19 million foreign visitors every year, but it should be remembered that before World War II, Hungary was a classic travel destination. Central Europeans who could afford it came to spend the summer by Lake Balaton, and the capital Budapest was also a magnet for visitors. An advertising brochure dating from 1937 praises the Hungarian capital to German-speaking readers as the "Queen of the Danube". It continues: "Because of the

Left, visit to the beauty parlour – a daily affair.

multitude and variety of medicinal springs, Budapest is the world capital of spas."

Since then the water supply, which was once enriched by minerals with therapeutic effects, has been muddled up by the building of the underground railway. Budapest has lost its fame as the "capital of spas".

Nowadays Budapest is not visited mainly by people looking for relief from their aches and pains by taking the waters, but by sightseers, tourists who only stay a few days and therefore only bring home with them a fleeting and necessarily superficial impression. Yet even they fall victim to the charm of the Danube capital.

Hotels in Budapest: In 1945, during the final days of the war, it was not just a conservative view of the world which was destroyed in Budapest, but also the world's external and architectural expression then. Most of the hotels along the Danube embankment were piles of rubble and cinders. The subsequent years of hermetic isolation of the very world from which hotel guests could possibly have come was not exactly conducive to the growth of tourism. Of the 40 privately owned and well-managed hotels which had enjoyed an international reputation before 1938, only a few have returned to their original function.

The three spa hotels – especially the one on Margaret Island – were run down, and of the five luxury hotels on the banks of the Danube (Bristol, Carlton, Ritz-Dunapalota, Hungária and Gellért), only the last one, a relic of *fin-de-siècle* splendour, had been spared to some extent during the turmoil of the war. The Carlton got a new name, and, as the Hotel Duna, it reminded one of the former incomparable chain of hotels along the Corso. But the new age permitted a rediscovery of tourism as an economic factor and provided a boom for the construction industry. One of its first achievements was the Budapest Hilton. The Budapest champions of local patriotism saw it as sacrilege, but it proved a hit with the public. The Hilton gave the city, awakening from its death-like trance, a new emblem. The hotels which were built for Western hotel chains along the Danube banks became incredibly popular with the tourists and the more privileged inhabitants of Budapest as well.

Fortunately, the patriotic critics who vehemently fought the building on the site of the ruined Dominican monastery within sight of the Matthias Church did not win their case. The Budapest Hilton, then, became the precursor of a new wave. Four billion schillings were liquified by Austrian investors. Thanks to this credit of 300 million dollars, Austrian construction companies have built new hotels in Budapest and in

son, Hungária and Erzsébet, all bear testimony to the new collaboration between East and West.

The expectations of the more wealthy visitors may be fulfilled by the five-star hotels (on average, about 60 percent of their rooms are usually booked), but the range of cheaper accommodation looks rather more meagre.

In 1988, there were only about 250 hotels with 48,000 beds in Hungary, a rather modest capacity which only puts Hungary in 23rd place in Europe.

Food and drink: The liberalisation which has made the inhabitants of other Eastern bloc countries jealous of Hungary for a long

the provinces, with an additional capacity of 7,234 beds. Ever since 1978 building has been going on apace. Hotels built by the Hungarian architect József Finta have become part of the city and they fulfil the most demanding expectations. Most of them belong to Western hotel chains but are run by Hungarian managers. The facades of the Forum, Duna-Intercontinental and Atrium-Hyatt dominate the modern view from the Danube. But the Danube Corso is not the only place where there are new hotels. Elsewhere are those such as the Novotel, Penta, Taverna, Astoria, Flamenco, Béke Radis-

time has begun to bear fruit in the very area where foreigners are likely to make contact with Hungarians: whetting the appetite with good food and drink.

During Stalinist rule the many little restaurants specialising in local dishes, which had been restored by their hardworking owners after the destruction of the war and had a good reputation among gourmets, were demoted to "catering outlets."

When the borders opened and visitors came looking for the pleasures of the palate, it was soon seen that these places no longer possessed either flair or originality and were not exactly conducive to furthering the good reputation of Hungarian cuisine. The old masters were permitted to return to the catering industry and to take up the leases on reputable establishments. The next step was the wave of re-privatisation. Cautiously at first, but in a more determined manner after 1982, the opening of private restaurants was permitted. A great number of the 14,000 restaurants, patisseries, coffee houses and *csárdas* (traditional inns) are now in private hands. Until recently eating out in Hungary was not only decidedly cheap for Western tourists but also affordable for local people. However, since the introduction of value

charged cuisine of the Magyars has its followers among gourmands who like heavy meals and spicy dishes. If you're hoping for nouvelle cuisine, you'll be disappointed. But first, a few mistaken beliefs about Hungarian cuisine need to be cleared up. Actually, there is no such thing as "Hungarian cuisine", but only a range of local dishes, restricted to particular regions and dependent on local circumstances. These dishes include many elements from the cuisines of neighbouring lands which have been brought into the country. To undermine the statement that there is no particular cuisine that is common throughout all parts of Hungary the follow-

added tax, things have changed. Since the beginning of 1988 the Hungarians have had to watch every forint. A result of competition is that the restaurants compete for a smaller number of guests by offering better service and improved quality, even if the meals are at soaring prices.

A common cuisine: The tasty, varied, but first and foremost incredibly calorie-

Far left, "Madame the first violinist awaits your pleasure!" **Left**, the renovated National Hotel. **Above**, the most successful branch of McDonald's in the world!

ing are some examples.

When the Magyars invaded eastern Central Europe about 1,000 years ago, they were a warlike, nomadic people. They cooked dried meat in cauldrons. This habit of the Magyar warriors was the origin of *gulyás*, now firmly established on the menus of East and West, perhaps the only genuinely "Hungarian" dish. The name of this delightful dish has been taken over from Hungarian cuisine, but usually, when it is served outside the country, it would be unrecognisable to Hungarians. In Hungary goulash is not a strongly paprika-seasoned, braised and thickened dish of veal, pork or beef, but more of a soup. The "goulash" which has made its way onto the menus of the whole world from Vienna – i.e. a thick, paprika-seasoned stew in which meat predominates – is known in Hungary itself as *pörkölt* (which translates as "singed meat").

Now we have made the acquaintance of two of the four original specialities of Hungarian cuisine. The fact that paprika was not added as a seasoning to the meat soup in the cauldron until much later is another matter. Lean cubed meat of all kinds for frying (similar to *boeuf Stroganoff* but finished off in a goulash sauce) is the main ingredient of *tokány*. Finally, there is *paprikas*, a stew, which has among its ingredients not only meat but also fish, game (in separate versions, of course) and also potatoes and mushrooms. This almost completes the list of original Hungarian dishes. There is one further Magyar culinary specialty: the *tarhonya*, a form of pasta. This accompaniment to meat is a sort of egg noodle, originally meant to be put into soup, which is prepared by the farmers' wives before cooking (much as *cous-cous* is among the Arabs).

The development of Hungarian cooking: Once the marauding hordes of riders had settled in what had been Pannonia, the Hungarian cuisine was enriched by the eating habits of their neighbours. The Slavs provided everything which could be made out of grain, and the Turkish occupation, which lasted for nearly 1½ centuries, left permanent traces in Hungarian cuisine. Paprika, maize, almonds, hazelnuts, pumpkins and many other vegetables were taken over from the Turks. Legend has it that a Magyar girl who escaped from the Sultan's harem first introduced the Hungarians to paprika. How the Turks came to use paprika, though, is still a mystery. The plant grows wild in Central and South America, and was probably brought to Europe by Columbus. It may have been imported from Spain, from India or even direct from South America.

The social structure in what was a purely agricultural country also left its mark in the kitchen: the lower agricultural classes, farm labourers and serfs ate nothing but what was left over after their dues had been paid.

Almost up until modern times, bread and bacon were the mainstay of the diet of the hardworking rural population. The nobility and the rising middle classes copied everything that came from the "court", i.e. from Vienna, and so the lighter French-Italian cuisine gradually began its triumphal progress through Hungarian kitchens. A classic example is the salami, which originally came from Verona, and has become, via a diversion through the puszta, a Hungarian specialty and is even exported as such.

There are two peculiarities of the true Hungarian cuisine. Paprika combines most easily with lard to make a successful marriage of flavours, so cooking is generally done with lard, thickening is done with flour and lots of sour cream is used to refine the flavour. (Say hello to the calorics!)

The Hungarians have always been great meat eaters. The statistical average is 80 kg of meat per annum. This puts Hungary in third place in the European table of per capita meat consumption, behind Denmark and the Netherlands. This is not much when measured against the legendary 300 kg of Argentina, but even then!

Exact statistics on cereal production put paid to a widely held erroneous belief. Although about 70 per cent of the total area of the country is in agricultural use, Hungary is by no means the "bread basket" of Europe. Rather, it is in the middle range of European countries as far as cereal production is concerned, and even Austria and West Germany produce more.

Wines and spirits: However, Hungary sadly does have the distinction of being placed first in the list for alcohol consumption. About 52 billion forints (nearly double the budget deficit of 34.4 billion forints) is spent annually on alcoholic drinks!

The most important of the 16 large and small wine-growing regions of Hungary are those around Lake Balaton, even though the "king of wines and wine of kings", Tokay, comes from an area far from Balaton. Most wines are now grown and produced on a large scale on state-owned farms, but Tokay is still made by painstaking traditional meth-

Right, the romantic face of socialism.

ods. The secrets of the region are the Furmint grape and the autumn climate of alternating mist and sun, which produces the noble rot of the grapes used to make the superior Tokay Aszú. The Hungarians have the Romans to thank for their wine industry. About 2,000 years ago the Romans introduced the vine into Pannonia and yet another region was converted to the worship of Bacchus. This is why wine is at home in the Buda Hills and around Sopron, where Roman legionaries had planted their vines.

Today more than 370,500 acres (150,000 hectares) of wine is cultivated in Hungary. Seventy percent of the total are white wines, 20 percent red and the rest are dessert wines. Hungary is one of the major wine exporters of the world; 8.5 million bushels (around 3 million hectolitres) of the essence of the noble grape are exported. The most famous varieties are Kéknyelü (Blue Stalk), Szükebarát (Grey Friar), Hárslevelü (Lime Leaf), Ezerjó (Thousand Blessings), Lányka (Little Girl), Mezesfeher (White Honey), and the Olaszrizling from Mount Bad-acsonyi, the Bikavér (Bull's Blood) from Eger (made from Kadarka, Kékfranos and Merlot grapes) and the Kékfrankos (Austrian Blaufränkisch, a relation of the Gamay) from Sopron. Hungary is a producer of classic aperitifs: the Prince of Wales, later King Edward VII, popularised the apricot brandy barack. Of no lesser quality are cseresznye (cherry spirit), vilmos (made from Williams pears) and szilvapálinka (plum brandy). However, you will search in vain for a native vodka in Hungary. This is not for political reasons, but because potato and barley based spirits do not go too well with the highly seasoned local dishes. Incidentally, in Hungary a wide range of vodkas from Poland, the USSR, the CSSR and even from Mongolia and Vietnam is available.

Inns and restaurants: When Ferdinand de Lesseps, the builder of the Suez Canal, was invited on an official visit to Budapest about a century ago, he is said to have pulled a scrap of paper out of his pocket immediately after his arrival. He gave it to his hosts. Written on the slip was a single word: "Gundel."

So much for the legends of Hungarian gastronomy. What about the reality? The traditions of the inns are linked to the names of famous restaurants – especially to that founded by the Gundel family, immigrants from Bavaria in the last century.

Humble origins: Budapest was not recognised as a capital city until after the Compromise of 1867 between the house of Habsburg and the rebellious Magyar nobility. The magnates, the original rulers of the country, did not feel at home either in bourgeois Buda or in peasant Pest. Their palaces were in Vienna or Bratislava, so they held court and entertained their visitors in those cities. The nobility rarely visited Buda. For this reason, plain inns were enough for the common run of travellers in Buda, and the range of dishes was designed for the needs of a clientele of modest means. Beer taverns were the most sophisticated thing on offer, and broiled beef was regarded as a delicacy.

Not until Budapest began to rival the imperial city of Vienna in wealth, elegance and culture did the finest hour of the great chefs and bakers arrive. These had come from the West and they transplanted the skills they had learned in Paris, Zurich or Vienna to Hungary. The Spolaritsch, Kugler and Gerbeaud families were shining examples to the catering trade, and Matthias Baldauf, also of German descent, gave his name to the well-known *Mátyás-pince* (Matthias Cellar).

There are a number of beer taverns in Budapest, but no wine taverns such as the Austrian *Heurigen* (a tavern in which young wine is served). Unfortunately, it is impossible to recommend a single wine bar with some local colour, in which it might be possible to sit after supper over a few glasses of wine and enjoy the unique view of the Danube and the panorama of the capital.

Coffee house culture: However, Budapest's coffee house culture is definitely superior to that of Vienna, the rival city in the West. In this field Hungary's capital has probably displaced its model Vienna from the first position for all time. Among the first-rate coffee houses are the former haunt of the literati, the "New York" (now the Hungária), the Jugendstil Belvárosi/Lidó, the historically important Pilvax (which played an important part in the 1848 revolution), and the oldest restaurant in the city, Százéves – all these establishments apparently have a regular clientele.

The patisseries of Budapest are quite exceptional on their own account. An absolute must when staying in Budapest is a visit to the venerable establishments Gerbeaud in the inner city and/or Ruszwurm on Castle Hill. The Lukács patisserie, which preserves the name of its founder János Lukács, also boasts very elegant surroundings.

If you like ice cream, we recommend a visit to the almost unpronounceable Különlegességi in Népköztársaság útja, or the

important feature of these establishments. There are, however, a number of bars where the artistic scene meets, such as Pipacs, Balettcipö or the espresso bar Miniatür. There is a cultivated atmosphere and certain whiff of excitement about the Casino in the Hilton Hotel, but there is one reservation: you will remain in the company of foreign tourists. Permitting the people of their own country to visit capitalist "gambling dens" – at present such generosity is still beyond even Hungarian ideas of liberalisation.

Shopping for good buys: What items are worth bringing home from Hungary? If you are interested in the pleasures of the table,

"arty" meeting place Müvesz (meaning artists' cafe) near the Opera. The establishments we mention are all protected buildings because of their interiors, which date from the turn of the century, and so are worth seeing not just because they offer pleasures of the palate.

However, if you prefer nightlife, it would be better to avoid the Hungarian capital. Budapest by night is very tame and totally provincial. The bars in the international hotels and the revue-cabarets Orfeum, Maxim and Lidó offer a revue programme. That statement alone sums up the most

you should definitely make a visit to the "Belly of Budapest", the central market halls. Even visiting high-ranking officials are invited to the market, which, in a European social and historical context, have taken on the role of the former Parisian *Halles*.

Huge quantities of fresh and preserved food can be seen there: ranging from salami (not always the very best quality) and spices (even if they don't have the same great variety as in the bazaar of Istanbul) to livestock and preserved delicacies. A bit of advice for your shopping trip: dried mushrooms, a wreath of paprika, cheese, hand-made egg noodles, cloves of garlic and of course *foie gras* are specialties which make particularly suitable gifts for the folks back home. The items can be bought here and are of excellent quality. Such gourmet special-ties can be had at a low price with Western currency. Your luggage on your homeward trip would be incomplete without salami, sheep's cheese, spices, wine and fruit bran-dies, although there are customs limits on the amounts you can take out of the country.

Another tip: Quality Western goods are – though this may sound strange – cheaper in the East! Lacoste tops, Benetton clothes,

as Prague used to be) an El Dorado for antique collectors is definitely over. The export of antiques is tied to permits, and the times when one could snap up at giveaway prices the treasures of the middle class or even the aristocracy which had been washed away by the waves of social change – those times belong to the mists of a nostalgic past. Even collectors of old rural furniture can no longer find enough, although "treasures" do sometimes turn up in the fleamarkets.

Worthwhile souvenirs are the industrial-ised products of folk art: tablecloths, blouses, wooden dolls, ceramic and pottery wares, vases and plates. It is worthwhile

Dior and Adidas products (all manufactured in the country), and in particular select for-eign perfumes in their original packaging can be obtained at duty-free prices in Hun-garian shops for foreigners. Smokers, too, can find what they are looking for: the Havana cigars, produced under licence, are inexpensive.

The golden age when Budapest was (just

Left, taking a break on the Corso by the Danube. **Above**, many antiques are at affordable prices. **Following pages**, hearty Hungarian sausages and ham.

making use of the services of the Intertourist shops. There are about 100 of these foreign currency shops all over the country. They only accept Western currencies, but offer a range of goods of outstanding quality. However, you would do better to buy porce-lain, especially Herend ware, in the West. Whatever on offer in Hungary is sometimes only second grade.

For a visitor from the West, a stay in Hun-gary does have some aspects of *la dolce vita*. However, Hungary is fast catching up with the changes that go on around her – a trend which is already influencing price levels.

When we speak of the specialties of Hungarian cuisine, the majority of these are the creations of famous chefs or pastrycooks. Many of such dishes were named after famous people or after those who created them. The actor Ede Ujházi liked a particular chicken soup, and a bean soup was given the name of the novelist Mór Jókai (who wrote the work on which the *Gypsy Baron* was modelled). A creamy cake is dedicated to the former Count Palatine of Hungary, one of

the Esterházy princes; the pastrycook Dobos from the northeast Hungarian town of Eger (home of the red wine Bull's Blood) baked a gateau which is named after him. The multi-talented Gundel not only invented the nut and chocolate pancakes named after him, but also dishes using fogas (pike-perch), ribs of veal, tokány and salad à la Gundel.

The famous sauerkraut dish (wrongly named after Szeged), is called *székely-gulyás* in Hungarian. However, it has nothing to do with the Székler people, who are Hungarian-descended inhabitants of Transylvania. The name comes from the Budapest lawyer Dr Székely, who was so fond of this dish that he ate this dish every day. Here are two recipes from the Hungarian kitchen. You should try the originals when in Budapest.

Székely-gulyás (the original recipe of Dr [jur] József Székely, 1825-95):

Ingredients:
300 gm very tender pork (shoulder, hand, neck, possibly breast)
300 gm equally tender beef
300 gm bacon
100 gm pork dripping
250 gm onions (red onions)
15 gm paprika spice (mix the sweet and hot flavours)
1.2 kg sauerkraut
160 gm paprika pods
20 gm flour
½ litre sour cream
salt, one clove of garlic, cumin, finely chopped dill.

Preparation: Cut the meat into cubes 2-3 cm across. Mix the beef with onions sautéed briefly in dripping. Lightly brown the pork and the bacon. Turn down the heat and quickly stir a little cumin, paprika spice and the squeezed clove of garlic into the dripping with the onions, which should not be too hot. Add the meat (do not add salt!) and brown. After adding water do not boil, but let it simmer in the juices. Wash the sauerkraut but keep the drained water for adjusting the flavour later on. When the meat is half-cooked, reduce till only the frying fat is left. Add the sauerkraut and the paprika pods, cut into small cubes. Mix well, add ¼ litre sauerkraut water or bone stock, cover and simmer. Do not overcook the sauerkraut. Mix the flour with a little sour cream to thicken the sauerkraut with it. Bring to the boil, pour over the rest of the sour cream and sprinkle with finely chopped dill.

An old kitchen tip also applies to *székely-gulyás* – warmed up the next day, it still tastes good, maybe even better...

Somló Pudding (*Somlói galuska*):

In the last few years, the delicious *somlói galuska* has become the "in" dessert in Hungarian restaurants. As there is hardly a cookery book that describes this dessert, we will reveal the recipe from a lady chef in one of Hungary's top hotels.

Ingredients:

Sponge mixture or sponge fingers
Vanilla and chocolate cream
100 gm chopped walnuts
100 gm raisins
a little apricot preserve
1 teaspoon cocoa powder, whipped cream

For the punch sauce: 125 gm sugar
2 dl water, 1 dl rum
Vanilla, lemon and orange peel
For the vanilla cream: ¼ litre milk
1 packet vanilla sauce powder
1 tablespoon sugar
one egg yolk, chocolate cream
Cook all the ingredients together and put in the fridge to cool.
Sponge mixture:
6 egg yolks, 6 egg whites
180 gm sugar
120 gm flour
80 gm edible starch (cornflour, arrowroot or similar)

Preparation: Beat the egg yolks in a bowl until frothy. Add the sugar. Beat the egg whites until stiff and fold them into the egg yolk. Mix the flour and the starch and also fold into the egg yolk.

Put the mixture into a baking container lined with greased greaseproof paper and bake in a preheated oven. Baking time: 40 to 45 minutes (set the electric stove at 160-200 degrees).

Take a bowl and line it either with the cooked sponge mixture or with closely packed sponge fingers. Sprinkle about a third of the punch sauce and spread a third of the vanilla cream on top. Sprinkle half the chopped nuts and raisins on top. Lay another third of the sponge or sponge fingers on top and sprinkle with punch. Add nuts and raisins on top.

The topmost layer is the rest of the sponge, which is sprinkled with the last of the punch. Then spread the apricot preserve on top and sprinkle on cocoa powder. Put into the fridge. Before serving, spread the whipped cream on top and pour the chocolate cream over.

Liberation Square, Budapest, V District – this is definitely the most beautiful, most harmonious and most magnificent square in the centre of the city. It is shaped like a long drawn-out oval and every building along it is a work of art in itself. On the southern side of the square there is a building with a massive pillared facade. Here, at nos. 8-9, is the home of the Hungarian National Bank.

For some time now the Hungarians have been concerned more with material than with ideological processes. There is no more whispering behind hands when the talk is about gold, currency, or business.

This was the spirit behind the extensive bank reforms 1 January 1987, which resulted in the creation of the first currency bank in the history of socialism.

Independent business is the magic formula of the Hungarian reforms. With reference to the National Bank, this means individual initiative, money as the most important regulator of individual and collective trade, independence and self-sufficiency of the bank in its relations with the state.

Bankers who know something about their business, who take money seriously and consider dealing with money to be their vocation, are still objects of admiration in Hungary. János Fekete, deputy president of the National Bank, has been promoted almost to the status of national idol. His achievements in international currency dealings and at the IMF were the foundation of the legends which have grown up around his success.

If money in Hungary after almost 40 years becomes an independent institution again, it will be a step in the right direction towards a society which postulates the right to self-determination. The state still has its hands on the controls of a complex and complicated artificial system of distribution. Every business undertaking is dependent on the state. The founding of an independent currency

Left, the past and the present meet on a higher plane.

bank opens up new horizons for a self-regulating money and goods economy.

On 15 March 1848 Sándor Petöfi voiced this vision: "We demand an independent Hungarian national bank."

Not until 1867, after the Compromise with Austria, did the age of modern currency dealing dawn on Hungary, due to the founding of the Hungarian General Credit Bank by the Austrian Rothschilds and an Austrian bank, the Wiener Creditanstalt.

This Austro-Hungarian bank was the direct predecessor of the Hungarian National Bank, which had two head offices, one in Vienna and one in Budapest, each with a managing director. The common currency bill, the krone, was printed in German on one side and in Hungarian on the other. Each head office had the printing masters for one side only.

However, after World War I – Hungary, as part of the Austro-Hungarian Monarchy, had fought on the losing side – Hungary lost huge sections of its territory, a large part of its population, and the economic infrastructure of the monarchy. The most disastrous consequence of the Treaty of Trianon in 1920 was that the suddenly and unexpectedly independent much-reduced rump of Hungary was torn out of the economic unit of the monarchy and became extremely dependent on foreign trade. The war, the regime of Béla Kun, and the Romanian occupation had exhausted resources. The new frontiers cut factories off from their accustomed supply sources and from established markets. The underdevelopment and the lack of competitive ability of the Hungarian economy were demonstrated instantly and dramatically. Debts rose continuously, the balance of payments was chronically in the red. The problems of the national economy and state finance have proved to be long-lasting and have outlived all political changes of power.

The Hungarian National Bank was founded in 1924 under these inauspicious circumstances. A loan agreed by the League of Nations gave some sort of a base for financial stabilisation, though it brought with it a heavy burden of repayments.

The name of Sándor Popovics is linked with the issue of the first independent Hungarian currency, the pengö, in 1926. Three years later the situation prophesied by the bank president Popovics in his warnings and protests came about. As only a small proportion of the loans had been productively invested (they were mainly used for sophisticated projects which the state could not afford to pay for but urgently needed for prestige purposes: the similarities in today's situation are unmistakable), there was no chance of systematic repayment. National bank-

Czechoslovakia. There was now no hope of having the national borders revised, the dream of the revival of past glories had to be finally buried. This did not mean that hardheaded realism was now the major virtue of the ruling party of Hungary. The policies of the Communist Party, which held the dictatorship of the proletariat from 1948 on, were no less irresponsible than those of its bourgeois predecessors before the war. Within a short while the bank was unable to act, because it had been incorporated into an allpowerful state machine.

Stabilisation and the issue of the forint in 1946 were expressions of a functioning

ruptcy could only be avoided by the support of several European currency banks. In the summer of 1931 the National Bank ceased making repayments of foreign debts altogether. In 1933 it introduced a regulated and centralised system of currency dealing and created the currency monopoly which it still possesses today.

In one respect the second collapse after 1945 was even harder for Hungary to bear than that of the first in 1918 and 1920. The new peace treaty, signed in Paris in 1947, reimposed the frontiers of the Treaty of Trianon, with a further rectification in favour of

banking system which was generally considered reliable. But then the bank, which had previously been in the hands of shareholders, was nationalised together with the other major banks. The protests of many middleclass members of parliament did not find much support among the Hungarian public.

The first draft of the 5-year plan was already counting on unusually high sums for investment. After a short while this sum was increased to the irresponsible level of 82 billion forint. In protest, the acting director of the National Bank, Ferenc Jeszensky, called the leading managers of the National

Bank and the directors of the bank branches together for a crisis meeting in early January 1952, when he tried to explain what a serious mistake the 5-year plan would be. Not long afterwards he was relieved of his post as general director of the National Bank.

For a long time Mr Jeszensky's revolt marked the end of an independent National Bank. Important financial decisions were taken without the bank even being asked, and when state authority said it needed money it was simply printed. The bank scrved in the first instance in carrying out the technical aspects of projects in the planned economy. As an extension of the long arm of the state, it was controller and source of credit in one for businesses. Businesses had to carry out all financial transactions via their single account with the National Bank, their contacts with each other were restricted. Nonetheless, the control exercised by the bank was fairly ineffectual, as it was always the bank that had to pay.

However, even the new banking reforms have only slightly loosened state domina-tion. No more than 10 percent of business finance goes through the five newly-founded banks. The remainder stays part of the state planned economy and is controlled by the budget. A particular weak point of the reforms is that the new private businesscs do not yet enjoy equal status with the state industries when it comes to financing invest-ment, and still have to finance themselves by means of private loans. There are no laws that would guarantee the independence of the bank, and no parliament or administra-tive body that would ensure the laws were kept – even if they had been made in the first place.

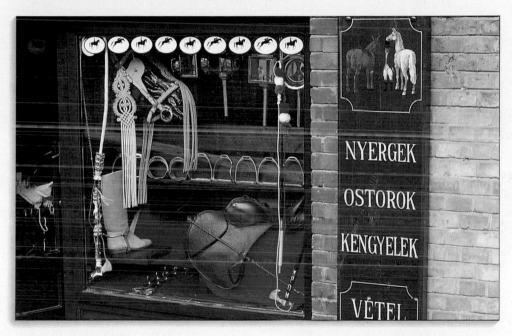

In addition, society in Hungary is in a condition of moral schizophrenia. On the one hand, people such as the deputy presi-dent of the bank, Fekete, are admired as cxperts, but on the other, many others are en-vious of their high salaries. In school and at home young Hungarians are still state be-neficence rather than using the initiative to make something worth of possessing.

On this point, hopes linked to the bank reforms are justified. A new generation of bankers, should it one day remember the traditions of this old bank, can look forward to a great future.

Left, every third Hungarian is living below the poverty line. Above, material pursuits of the country's 50,000 millionaircs.

Ferenc Jánossy is a businessman. Among the lessons he learned at school was that one day communism would defeat capitalism. Economics was out of place in the school curriculum, and even at university Marxist subjects took precedence.

Ferenc is a practical man. Given the choice after completing his studies of going into a state-owned business or continuing his theoretical studies at university, he chose a third alternative: he started his own business. The businesses were brought within the framework of the law, probably to save the Hungarian economy from total collapse. Ferenc Jánossy and thousands of his colleagues went ahead and founded companies and carried on their business quite legally. The former taxi driver put his whole family to work and founded the "High & Deep" construction company, which specialised in the renovation of water towers and radio masts. Today Mrs Jánossy sits at her micro-

occupation of independent businessman did not exist in Hungary in the early 1970s, but anyone who was really determined found ways and means of earning money illegally without paying taxes. Jánossy drove his Soviet Lada through the city centre of Pest and stopped in front of nervous passersby who were trying in vain to flag down one of the state-owned taxis. As a sideline, this clever ex-student also used his car to transport building materials and food, i.e. he knew where such items were to be found and where they could be resold at a considerable profit. In the early 1980s these illegal small computer, mother-in-law does the book-keeping, and father is responsible for the supply of materials. There are tens of thousands of Jánossys in Hungary now: quick-thinking businessmen who make a profit, and who by now are no longer ashamed of their prosperity. The private companies seek out the multitude of little gaps in the planned economy where lack of state provision fills the purses of skilled "organisers."

A third of the Hungarian GNP is now created by non-state enterprises. In the autumn of 1988 parliament opened the very last set of floodgates for private businesses. New laws permit the founding of private companies with up to 500 employees. Western companies are lured into the country to set up joint ventures, with tax concessions and guaranteed investments offered. However, the Hungarian "economic miracle" praised by some journalists is no such thing. Its foundations are extremely shaky. Western consumer and luxury goods, which today fill Hungarian shops, have always been and still are being bought on credit. Hungarians are consuming more than the average wage, according to statistics, would ever permit them to do.

In the state-planned economy, full of shortcomings, there are always goods which are desperately needed somewhere or other. If you can find out which factory has stopped production because the director was unable to obtain, by honest or dishonest means, some ball-bearings; and if you can discover from a colleague where this much needed spare part is to be found, you can multiply your income several times over by the simple expediency of making three or four telephone calls. The continual bottlenecks in currency exchange, in particular, force Hungarian businesses to fall back on the services of professional "brokers."

Every other Hungarian is already self-employed in some way or another. People take on extra jobs to supplement their incomes. Secretaries take work home with them after the office closes, builders work several shifts to build their own houses on the side, and the taxi drivers in Budapest are usually middle school teachers by day or who have some academic qualification. Among this number trying to improve their standards of living, a small elite, favoured by the tax laws and a clueless economic police, has been able to pile up millions of forints.

The wealth of this small circle of successful businesspeople is considerable. Every pupil knows the story of the world-famous university lecturer Ernö Rubik, who devised the Magic Cube to teach his students to think in three dimensions. In a radio interview Rubik, whose net fortune was estimated at about £1 million (an absolute fortune given the average income of £60-70 per week!) he could place himself on the list of Hungarian millionaires. With supreme self-confidence Rubik placed himself among the top fifty capitalists in the country. A bank manager who was also in the studio denied this. Rubik, he claimed, was "not even among the top 300 rich people" – and that was just going by private deposit accounts.

In the few years since economic reform began the handful of unorganised "founding fathers" of private enterprise have become a wealthy upper class which has replaced the Communist Party elite. Anyone with social aspirations lives in a house on the south side of Rose Hill in Buda. By now the price per square metre of luxury apartment in this area has reached a thousand dollars. The children of the nouveaux riches are sent to schools which are considered good and exclusive. Among these are the few remaining Catholic institutes and old, respected state schools.

Social life is carried on in a few tennis and riding clubs in the wooded country around Budapest. Western clothes, travel abroad and Western cars are considered almost obligatory in this social group, where material wealth is no longer suspect and people are no longer shy of showing off what they've got to their friends. The high society in Budapest prefers to meet in the disco of the Novotel hotel. Less popular meeting places are the "Vienna Coffee House" in the Forum Hotel on the Danube quayside, the "Gerbeaud" patisserie on Vörösmarty tér and a series of private arty clubs or secluded late night bars in the centre of Pest.

It may in the past have been easy to flout the rules of the state-planned economy, but the new tax laws which came into operation on 1 January 1988 have made the Hungarian millionaires more cautious. A special unit of tax inspectors raided the state-owned video hire shops late one evening and went through the files. All those who had hired video cassettes had to show the official departments in exact detail where and when they had bought their video recorders – and where the money had come from.

Left, waiting for guests – the Vadrozsa restaurant. Following page, Liberation Bridge over the Danube.

STREET RODEO

If you drive through Budapest, please keep in mind the battle of Mohács, where in 1526 the Hungarians attacked a numerically far superior Turkish army and were – of course – put to flight by the same. It is well known that critical commentators on current events have come up with this formula: the way a nation goes to war is the way its inhabitants drive their cars.

In the case with Hungary, the formula can be reduced to a few words using the following concept: fast, without consideration and extremely poorly equipped. Western-assembled and the better class of Eastern-assembled cars are no longer an unusual sight in Budapest, but the majority of privately-owned cars are of the modest kind. However, going by their style of driving, most Hungarian motorists seem to believe that they are sitting in armoured vehicles.

If you also consider the wretched condition of most of the (far too narrow) Hungarian roads, the situation becomes quite clear. Motorists, indeed those who take part in the flow of traffic in the land of the Magyars, lead a dangerous life. The extremely high accident figures (on par level, by the way, with the surprisingly high suicide rate) speak for themselves.

Although the highway code has set a speed limit of 37 mph (60 km/h) in the capital, the people of Budapest just do not seem to be able to keep to it, especially on the broad main streets such as Németvölgyi út and Hegyalja utca, which appear to function as race tracks. On Erzsébet Bridge you meet masses of stunt drivers – every single one of them self-taught, of course.

At night the people of Budapest drive even more reckless than in the daytime. The taxi drivers are the undisputed rulers of the streets. They race through the streets, turning into bumpy side roads; they see the pavements as an additional traffic lane, to be utilised as such when necessary. Most Budapest taxi drivers are also loquacious and sociable people, who feel that it is important to entertain their passengers. You can imagine how much undivided attention they give to the traffic.

Like every other modern big city, Budapest has suffered from a dramatic increase in the volume of traffic. The local public transport system is good – there is the metro, there are buses and trams – but all the same, countless car-driving masochists hurl themselves into the daily chaos of traffic.

Still, let's be fair, there are no grounds for criticising traffic – on some of the main roads, it flows without any problems. There are only two periodically recurring events that often confuse the flow of traffic in the city. In spring, the Danube floods its banks and the streets running parallel to the river are closed to traffic. Also, in the summer, the annual flood of tourists swamps the city with cars and coaches.

Newcomers driving in the city are overwhelmed with a number of obstacles which they sometimes believe have been created especially for them. The nightmare of every driver new to Budapest is that while cruising along one of the main roads, the driver suddenly has to turn right (or left) because that's where the museum is, the one that's open for one hour only. First of all such drivers have to keep their eyes peeled for the appropriate signpost; then they must not lose sight of it while jammed in the chaotic traffic. They have to stick to the limit of 37 mph (60 km/h), while the others are boxing them in at speeds of 45 or 50 mph (70 or 80 km/h). In moments like these, it is not always easy to break out of the tactical position in the central lane!

Parking in Budapest is no less of a problem. Car parks do exist, but many of those who keep magnificent family-sized cars have difficulty finding a parking space. Do take care; foreign number plates are no protection against being towed away! The city has garages available for visitors where the latter can leave their cars relatively in safe hands. Breaking into cars is fairly common nowadays, but the removal of Mercedes badges is even more popular.

The appearance of Budapest, a city of two million which is home to one Hungarian in five, has been determined by the architecture of a relatively short period: a period of barely 50 years which preceded World War I. A feverish construction boom broke out in 1867 after the Compromise with Austria, whereas even in the 1840s, the poet Sandór Petöfi could hear frogs croaking near what is now the National Museum.

St Gerard, Gellért in Hungarian, raising his cross to bless the city from his lofty perch on Gellért Hill, looks towards the east. This makes him one of a rapidly disappearing minority in Hungary. But after all, Gerhardus wasn't even Hungarian, he was a Venetian bishop...

The majority look westwards – and vice versa. "Western" flair, the absence of the traces of grey Communism in the streets of the city, has proved a powerful attraction for tourists. They stroll past the shop window displays of cosmopolitan Váci utca, enjoy the evening view of Castle Hill with its palaces, and dine in hotels which have every imaginable luxury on offer. Life in "the most cheerful camp of the Easter Bloc" (which is crumbling anyway) has its good points.

Let's return to the National Museum. This is a monument of national resistance to Habsburg imperial Baroque. The rising middle classes found the nobility to be on their side as far as profit-making construction was concerned. Suddenly everything was possible and everything was allowed. Ancient classical architecture was used at first, then expanded to take over the whole of history, leading to the development of the magnificent Historicist style of Budapest (which nowadays often looks very much over the top). There are tenement blocks in the "Gothic" style, palaces in "Renaissance" taste, and public buildings according to the ideals of a completely new, overblown "Baroque" which piled massive edifices one on top of the other. It is enough to stand in Lajos Kossuth Square and look at the Parliament building, and at the Ethnographic Museum which was built at the same time, to get a feel of the desire for greatness which bordered on the megalomaniac.

Budapest – a city of monuments? The spirit of the city – its petit bourgeois aspects and its elegance, its business sense and its desire for pleasure – was not formed by the middle classes alone. You can find it in the wine taverns of Pest and in other places, where debates are held about the state of the world, with or without socialism, in the legendary baths with their medicinal springs that have for generations been one of the main attractions of Budapest, or in the cafes dating from the 1920s, shrines of nostalgia which form the charm of Budapest.

Preceding pages: the Chain Bridge in festive illumination; a place of traditions – the coffee house; concert in the Conference Centre; nightlife is still considered tame. Left, youthful joys, ancient background.

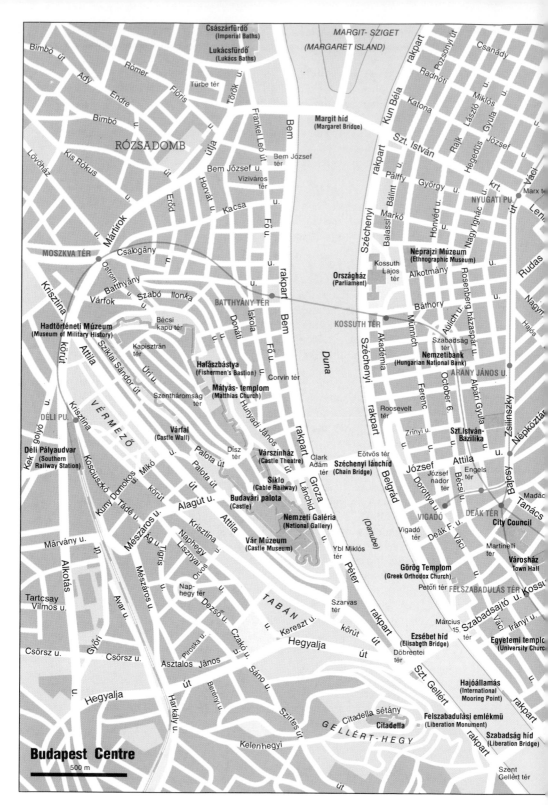

Budapest Centre

500 m

CASTLE HILL

From whichever side you approach Budapest, and whatever means of transport you use, as soon as you reach the Danube, which divides and (of course) also unites the city, the first thing you notice is the **Castle Hill of Buda**.

Castle Hill is actually a mile-long ridge which rises gently on its northern side but otherwise drops quite steeply. It provides a wonderful view of the Danube and the chain of the Buda Hills which surround the city to the west. The silhouette of the castle is impressive, too, seen from the left, level bank (the Pest side) of the river. For this reason no car-driving visitor to the city should miss the chance of taking two drives down one of the Danube *rakpart* (quays), one by day and one by night, especially as the Castle Quarter and the bridges are often floodlit. The miles of road along the river banks give you a

**Left,
Plague
Column in
Trinity
Square.**

sense of the size of the Hungarian capital, of the generously planned city of 100 years ago; they give something of an impression of the great power of the former Kingdom of Hungary until the end of World War I, i.e. until the collapse of the Austro-Hungarian Empire and its monarchy.

The towers and bastions, the long facade of the Baroque castle and palace (by far the most extensive building for accommodation purposes in the country), the other great buildings bounded by the Gothic tower of St Matthias' Church, which provides the contrasting vertical emphasis for the picture, the ornamental lines of the Neo-Gothic white marble Fishermen's Bastion in front, followed by the dark facade of the Hilton Hotel – taken all together, the scene is quite unique, and makes an unforgettable impression on the observer. In early 1988 UNESCO added the Castle Quarter of Buda to the *World Heritage List,* which lists the cultural and natural heritage of the world.

Connections by public transport to Castle Hill are quite good. There are some bus connections from the centre of the city. From **Clark Ádám tér** at the head of the Chain Bridge you can also take the nostalgic **Sikló** (cable railway) to travel up Castle Hill. The entire **Várnegyed** (Castle Quarter) has been barred to cars for some years, with a few exceptions (such as guests of the Hilton Hotel, visitors to the casino); car access only goes as far as the car park in the castle precincts. For this reason alone, it is a good idea to use cheap (24-hour tickets are available at very reasonable rates) public transport. It is not only younger people who find it fun to get to the Castle quarter along romantic byways, using the steps.

At the top, if one is disabled or if one does not want to take photographs, one can take a comfortable ride in a cozy minibus just for a few forints or in a horse-drawn trap for a few hundred forints. As most visitors arrive in Budapest by car, on the Buda side, it

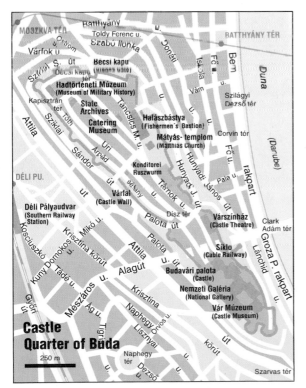

Castle Quarter of Buda

250 m

makes sense to begin a tour of the city on Castle Hill.

Trinity Square: Where is the best starting point for a sightseeing tour? The best place is probably right in front of the Matthias church, in the generously spacious **Szentháromság tér** (Trinity Square), which gets its name from the more than 46-ft (14-m) high plague pillar to the Trinity, built in 1713 as a gesture of thanks by the survivors of the plague, in its centre and is, in a sense, the centre of the castle district. The former **Town Hall of Buda** – today the seat of the Linguistic Institute of the Hungarian Academy of Sciences – is a not too ostentatious Baroque building with decorative oriels, built in the early 18th century. Also worth seeing are the gateway, the inner courtyard and the beautiful staircases.

The Matthias Church: The observer is bound to be fascinated most by the **Matthias Church**, formerly the Church of Our Lady. The cathedral was named after King Mátyás Hunyadi

Corvinus, whose coat of arms can be seen under the window of the third storey of the octagonal 263-ft (80-m) high main tower.

This church was mentioned as early as 1258 as the Church of Our Lady, the parish church of the German citizens, who made up the majority of the city's population up until the first half of the 19th century. It was turned into a mosque by the Turks in 1541, although they did not alter the structure of the building at that time. The church suffered serious damage in 1686 during the conquest of Buda by the imperial Habsburg troops. The church was then rebuilt in the Baroque style, and its present form dates from the second half of the 19th century. At that time the architect Frigyes Schulek aimed to give it a Gothic character.

Of the original medieval building, only the lower part of the main tower, the base of the main walls, one or two interior pillars and parts of the portal of Our Lady on the south side have sur-

Matthias Church reflected on the panels of the Hilton Hotel.

vived. Everything else is the work of Schulek, who has made a relatively convincing success of what was effectively a redesign job, of the interior in particular.

At times the Matthias Church is also referred to as the Coronation Church, but this is an exaggeration, as in the Middle Ages, Charles Robert of the house of Anjou was the only one to be crowned King of Hungary (1307-42) here. Esztergom and Székesfehérvár were earlier royal centres where the Hungarian kings were crowned. More than half a millenium later, in 1867, the imperial couple Franz Joseph I and Elizabeth were proclaimed apostolic monarchs of Hungary here, and in 1916 it was their successor Charles I of Habsburg – King Charles IV to the Hungarians – who was crowned here, the last Hungarian king of the imperial house. A requiem mass, arranged by the Habsburg family, was celebrated by the Primate of Hungary in the Matthias Church in the spring of 1989 for Charles's queen Zita. Despite its crypt, the Church of Our Lady has little importance as a burial church, either. The sarcophagi of King Béla IV and his wife Anne de Chatillon, dating from the end of the 13th century, are the only ones to be found here, and they were only moved here in 1848 from Székesfehérvár, where most of the Hungarian kings are buried.

The Church Museum: The **Church Museum** in the gallery of the Matthias Church and in the passages leading to it houses magnificent vestments and liturgical objects dating from various centuries, including monstrances and chalices dating from the Renaissance and Baroque periods, together with souvenirs of the coronation of Emperor Franz Joseph I and Empress Elizabeth as King and Queen of Hungary. The so-called **St Stephen's Crown** and the **royal regalia** on display are, however, replicas. The originals of these crown jewels can be seen in the National Museum in the centre of Pest.

Detail of the Fishermen's Bastion.

Although much of the Matthias Church is neither original nor historic, from the end of the last century up until present times it has stood in the national consciousness of the Hungarians as a symbol (indubitably dominant and of great significance) of the former greatness, decline and rebirth of the nation from the ruins to new importance.

The Fishermen's Bastion: Right behind the Matthias Church – on the eastern edge of the Castle Hill – is the famous **Halászbástya** (Fishermen's Bastion). It is not as a fortification that it has become popular, as its construction is far too frivolous to be of any defensive use, but rather as a viewing terrace which gives a marvellous view of the Danube, its bridges, the Parliament building, the Basilica and the other large buildings on the left bank of the river. It consists of a complex of steps, passages and towers of white marble, partly in a Neo-Romanesque, partly in a Neo-Gothic style, designed by Frigyes Schulek (mentioned earlier) at the beginning of the 20th century. In the Middle Ages the fishermen were supposed to have been responsible for defending part of the city walls, hence the name Fishermen's Bastion.

The square is dominated by the bronze statue – cast in 1906 by Alajos Stróbl – of the founder of the state and converter to Christianity, István or St Stephen.

The Hilton Hotel: Hess András tér adjoins Szentháromság tér. Here, next to the Matthias Church and the Fishermen's Bastion, is the Budapest Hilton Hotel. This new building was the subject of much argument and resistance for many years and also criticised at first. By now people have got used to the fact that the building which combines the remains of the old Dominican monastery with innovative modern architecture, has been well integrated into its historic surroundings.

The square is named after the German printer Andreas Hess, invited to Hungary by King Matthias, so that he could print books there – in Latin, as was usual at the time. A relief next to the hotel entrance shows the traditionally popular Renaissance monarch, who came from an ancient Hungarian noble family. The original sculpture, which dates from 1486, is to be found on the city gates of Bautzen (East Germany), and there is a replica in Old Szeged, in the south of Hungary.

In the Middle Ages the church of St Nicholas and a Dominican monastery stood on the site of the present Hilton Hotel. Remains of both, the base of a tower and parts of the cloisters, were incorporated into the modern building. The restored statue in the little car park portrays **Pope Innocent XI**, to whom in 1935 the Hungarians gave belated thanks for his diplomatic and spiritual support for the campaign to free them from Turkish rule, a quarter of a millenium before.

The streets of the castle quarter: The two squares described above are starting points for walks through the streets

Romantic atmosphere in the Castle Quarter of Buda.

of the **Várnegyed** (Castle Quarter), which are full of atmosphere at any time of the day. There are four streets, three of them running strictly parallel to each other, and only the fourth, the **Táncsics Mihály utca**, forming a semi-circle. Only a few small and narrow alleyways link up the four main streets.

It is hard to say which street is the best. **Uri utca** (Lord's Street), **Országház utca**, **Fortuna utca** and **Táncsics Mihály utca** all have their own individual charm. In the latter Baroque and Classical houses predominate although most of the buildings have foundations dating from the Middle Ages.

The Synagogue: During extensive restoration work to house no. 26, which dates back to the 15th century, a former synagogue of the Jewish community of Buda was discovered. The community was important in the Middle Ages and also during the Turkish occupation. A few Jewish tombstones dating from this time can be seen in the gateway.

Fortuna utca: Further to the west, **Fortuna utca**, named after the Fortuna Inn (house no. 4) which still exists today, runs through the castle quarter. The street was also once known as French Street, because many French merchants and craftsmen lived here with their families. Looking at the houses, you can see the extensive rebuilding work necessary after the destruction brought about from the two fateful years of 1686 (the coming of the Habsburgs) and 1945 (the retreat of the German Wehrmacht). Remains of medieval times – such as niches sitting in the gateways and Gothic door frames – have, however, survived, despite facades in the late Baroque/early Classical style. This can be seen quite clearly in the Fortuna house, which was created at the beginning of the 18th century from the remains of three medieval houses. In this house, above the Gothic wine cellar and the restaurant, is the **Kereskedelmi és Vendéglátóipari Múzeum** (Museum of Trade and of Catering).

Restaurants
– foreigners
only?

Gothic traces: Architecturally speaking, you can say the same of the two longer streets which run further west parallel to one another, **Országház utca** (National Assembly Street) and **úri utca** (Lord's Street). In the former, take note of the palais which contains the **Alabárdos restaurant**. In the courtyard, there are arcade arches dating from the 15th century, and the Gothic origin of the rooms of the restaurant itself can also be recognised. The large building (house no. 28) was built in the second half of the 18th century for the order of Clarissan nuns, but after their dissolution by Joseph II, was later refashioned into the High Court and National Assembly building, which met here between 1867 and the building, three decades later, of the new Parliament on the left bank of the Danube.

A coffee house from 1827: At the point where there is a connection across from úri utca and Szentháromság tér is the very popular **equestrian statue of Andreas Hadik**, one of Maria Theresia's generals. In this narrow alley there is also a patisserie with a grand old name: **Ruszwurm cukrászda**, which has survived all the revolutions and wars since 1827 intact and is still popular today.

Historical pathos: All four of the lengthways streets of the Castle Quarter run into the two squares **Kapisztrán tér** and **Bécsi kapu tér**, which run into each other, although each has its own individual atmosphere. The memorial between the tower, which now stands alone, of the former Church of Mary Magdalene and the Museum of Military History portrays the man after whom the square was named: **John Capistranus**, saint, Franciscan monk and fiery campaigner against the Turks. Of all the earnest and would-be uplifting monuments in the Hungarian capital, this one probably has the most pathos. Pressing down on a fallen Turk with one foot, the Franciscan monk waves the Christian banner and leads the armies of King János Hunyadi forward into the

St Stephen
guards the
Fishermen's
Bastion.

battle of Belgrade, which in 1456 was a victory for the western (Christian) lands. Incidentally, Pope Callixtus III then passed a decree that the bells would be rung at noon in every church throughout Europe in memory of this event. The Church of Mary Magdalene itself, with its Gothic nave dating from the 13th century which was destroyed during the battles in Budapest in the last months of World War II, was the only Christian church on Castle Hill during the Turkish period (what was then the chief mosque is now the Matthias Church). For 1½ centuries, Catholics and Protestants had to stop their religious feuding and share the church. While one congregation went to mass in the choir, the other prayed in the central aisle of the nave.

The Museum of Military History: Weapons, uniforms, flags and military maps as well as other warlike equipment from the 11th to the 20th centuries can be seen in the **Hadtörténeti Intézet és Múzeum** (Museum of Military His-

An oasis for pedestrians – the Árpád Tóth Promenade.

tory). The items in the collections are mainly from the past, from the wars against the Turks and the "wars of liberation" against the Habsburgs, which produced the Kuruz rebellions and the charismatic leader Ferenc Rakóczi, and were in large part motivated by religious differences.

Bécsi kapu tér means "Vienna Gate Square." The gate itself does still exist, one of the few remaining city gates of Buda, but it was much rebuilt in the period between the wars. On its southern side the square is lined by a row of wonderful houses with late Baroque facades, but the Protestant (Lutheran) church dates from the end of last century. The Neo-Romanesque building opposite dates from the beginning of this century and houses the **National Archives**.

Starting from the northwestern corner of the Castle Hill and running along the fortification walls to the castle itself lies **Tóth Árpád sétany**, the promenade named after the lyric poet. In three

places along this walk lined with trees there are projecting bastions and roundels which offer a view into the valley of the park of the **Vérmezö** (Field of Blood) and the **Déli pályaudvar** (Southern Railway Station). The Vérmezö owes its name to the fact that this was the spot where, in 1795, the Hungarian Jacobins were executed, starting with their leader Ignác Martinelli. The Déli pályaudvar is also the terminus of the east-west line of the metro. Trains from this station mainly run to southern Hungary and to Lake Balaton, but there are also some international trains to the West, primarily in the direction of Vienna.

On your way from the promenade towards the castle you will pass Disz tér, where your eye will immediately fall upon the bronze statue of a Honvéd officer. This statue is a memorial to the fighters of the 1848/49 revolution against the Habsburgs. The statue next to the Korona patisserie, on the other hand, is dedicated to the famous Hussars. It portrays one of these martial figures thoughtfully testing the blade of his sabre. The building that is no. 3 in this square was once the town palais of Count Batthyány; it is one of the few palaces built by the top rank of the Hungarian aristocracy on Castle Hill.

The link between the Matthias Church and Disz tér is provided by Tárnok utca, which still has a few restored sections of houses dating from the Gothic period to show. Number 16 is an example, which is now the inn **Arany hordó vendéglö** (Little Golden Barrel), as is no. 15, which is now the **Tarnók espresszó**. The **Patika Museum** (Pharmaceutical Museum) a few steps further on dates from the 18th century.

Before moving on to the castle, you should note that over the last few years, with the ever-increasing flood of tourists, the number of boutiques, antique shops and galleries in the streets of the Castle Quarter has also grown considerably. There would be no point in list-

Idealised revolutionary forces of Béla Kun near the Déli pályaudvar: sculpture by Imre Varga.

ing individual establishments – they often disappear as quickly as they spring up.

Vászínház (Castle Theatre): If you go from Dísz tér to the castle, you will first pass the **Vászínház** (Castle Theatre), which – like the Castle Theatre in Vienna – was founded during the reign of Emperor Joseph II. Previously this had been the site of a Carmelite convent, which was dissolved by Joseph, a son of Maria Theresia. During the battle of Budapest in the winter of 1944/45, the theatre was burned to the ground. It was completely rebuilt in 1978, with a late Baroque facade appropriate to the period in which it was founded. It is an interesting sight and an off the beaten track for tourists.

The Tunnel: A continuation of the 1,247-ft (380-m) long bridge created by Adam Clark between 1853 and 1857, which was destroyed in the last war, is the *alagút* (Tunnel) under Castle Hill, also the work of Adam Clark. Nowadays it has become one of the nodal points for the traffic of this city of 2 million inhabitants. For some years toll was even charged for its use. A similar toll today might persuade some of the notorious car drivers to make the switch to public transport…

Ferdinand Gate: If, after visiting the Castle Quarter, you have nothing else planned, leave it in a southerly direction. You will pass steps, courtyards and fortified medieval passages and the mighty **Buzogány-torony** (Club Tower) on your way to the Ferdinand Gate (renovated between 1835 and 1848 by the command of the Emperor Ferdinand V), through which you pass to get to the Elizabeth Bridge.

Tabán: A park lies between Castle Hill and Gellért Hill. Up until the 1830s a picturesque part of the city lay here, with little houses and narrow twisting alleys – Tabán. It was a settlement of Danube boatmen, who fled here at the end of the 17th century from those areas to the south of the Danube which had remained in Turkish hands.

In the 1830s, this romantic but socially backward district of the city fell victim to the sledgehammer. Only the medicinal baths dating from Turkish times have survived Rácz füdö and Rudas fürdö – as have the **Tabáni plébánia templom** (parish church of Tabán), a Baroque building dating from the beginning of the 18th century, and the triangular Szarvas-ház. The building has an arcaded courtyard which contains the restaurant **Aranszarvas vendeglö** (The Golden Stag), which specialises in game dishes.

The Castle: Buda, referred to in most older books by its German name of Ofen, was once a bourgeois city. Not until the middle of the 13th century did it develop under the protection of a royal castle. And it was not until the turn of the 14th and 15th centuries that the Hungarian kings made it into a permanent residence. This was done during the reign of King Sigismond, later Holy Roman Emperor. In the 15th century Buda shone in its full royal glory under

The 350-m tunnel (dug in 1857) under Castle Hill – the needle's eye of the capital.

the rule of Matthias Corvinus and his wife Beatrix of Aragon, who made their court into a centre of art and science in Central Europe. However, around the royal palace Buda remained a bourgeois city even if state officials and the nobility did build their houses and small palaces here towards the end of the Middle Ages.

From 1541 on – as has been mentioned in another connection – no Hungarian king ever resided on the Castle Hill of Buda again. At first the Turks occupied it for 145 years. Even after they had been driven out in 1686, no ruler came back to the half-destroyed city. The emperors of the house of Habsburg ruled, even as kings of Hungary, from Vienna. Even the Hungarian National Assembly and the Hungarian administrative departments remained, till the mid-19th century, in Pressburg/Pozsony, now Bratislava in Czechoslovakia, which became after 1541 the *de facto* as well as the *de jure* capital of Hungary. The Emperor Charles VI and the Empress Maria Theresia may have had a Baroque palace with more than 200 rooms, which were extended in the last century, built on the ruins of the medieval royal castle of Buda, but even this impressive building was only the residence for a Palatine (viceroy). For this reason the Hungarian magnates did not build their great palaces here, but usually had them built in imperial Vienna. An exception is the palace of Count Batthyány mentioned above.

The bronze equestrian statue of the **Prince of Savoy**, triumphantly facing the Danube, has been able to survive all hostility towards the Habsburgs. During the last months of World War II, Castle Hill, the palace and even the houses, in which German troops had dug themselves in, suffered heavy damage. The process of rebuilding is by no means finished, although the facades of the buildings seem intact.

The destruction brought by the war also had its positive side. On the one hand, it made possible the discovery and excavation of previously buried parts of the medieval royal castle, and on the other Gothic structures were discovered in the streets of the town, in houses where they had disappeared behind later facades from the Rococo and Baroque periods. The museums give visitors a good impression of these.

The Hungarian National Gallery: A visitor entering the palace precincts (Várpalota) from the castle quarter will see the large complex from the following point of view: the northern wing houses the **Museum of the Hungarian Workers' Movement**, and the entire east wing is taken up by the **Hungarian National Gallery**, the most important art collection in the country.

The Castle Museum: The Castle Museum on the south side of the palace is one of the foremost sights of Europe. Its structure alone is extraordinary. It covers several floors, just as the individual parts of the medieval castle, all built at different times, and the attached courtyards, gardens, dungeons and bastions

Rider from the Hortobágy puszta in the castle courtyard.

all lie on different levels. The entrance to the museum is on the level of today's inner palace. From here, you literally descend into the depths of history.

A historical sensation: In the individual rooms you can see everything that has been discovered and excavated during the process of rebuilding the castle after the war: all that has been found so far of the buildings and furnishings which belonged to the kings of the houses of Anjou, Luxembourg and Hunyadi. This is not a small achievement, when you consider that up until rebuilding started no-one was even sure of the exact site of the medieval castle, never mind what the interior was like. However, nothing in the chambers, halls, libraries, chapels and workrooms has remained undamaged or in its original condition; not even any of the remains of the legendary Renaissance palace of King Matthias Corvinus. Wherever Hungarian archaeologists, historians and architects have found sufficient basic elements, which were enough, with the help of contemporary descriptions, to give a precise picture of the rooms in question, reconstructions have been undertaken which have been quite successful in recreating the style and the atmosphere of the times. This is especially true of the late Gothic Great Hall, a double naved room with cruciform vaulting dating from the time of King Sigismond, the first King of Hungary to reside in Buda. Here some of those Gothic statues on display were a sensation in historical circles when they were discovered in 1974 in a filled-in pit. They are all made of the same material, soft, white limestone from the western edge of Buda, and artistically speaking very attractive. They portray knights, courtiers, noble ladies, but also heralds, men-at-arms and girls of the common people. The most beautiful thing about them is perhaps that they have been left as they were found, even those that were damaged or mutilated. Nothing has been added, repaired or reconstructed. The same treatment has been given to the

The biggest building in the country – the castle of Buda.

"spiritual" busts – madonnas, apostles and bishops – which were found in the same pit and can now be seen in the castle chapel. Only the lower part of the originally two-storey chapel was slightly damaged when it was discovered. The Gothic windows and the pointed arches have been restored.

The Renaissance Hall is no remnant of the famous palace of King Matthias Corvinus, but a recently built addition to the museum, in which all the discoveries from the times of that monarch have been put on display. There are fragments of window and door surrounds, mostly made of so-called red marble (actually a red limestone from the Esztergom region), and of the balustrades of the loggias of those buildings which surrounded the trapeze-shaped courtyard of the palace. The capitals of pillars and the friezes are the creations of Italian masters. Coloured majolica tiles, which once covered the floors, and parts of a coffered ceiling are further scraps of the past which help visitors gain an impression of the former magnificence of the palace.

The royal couple: The way in which artists of the time saw the royal couple Matthias Corvinus and his third wife Beatrix of Aragon (also famous for her patronage of artists and musicians) can be seen in the double relief made of white marble, the work of the Italian artist Gian Cristofero Romano. It has survived the 500 years between its creation and present times, among other reasons because it had been moved to Vienna before the Turkish invasion, from where it was returned to Hungary in 1933. Another reminder of the royal couple is the double coat of arms at the Beatrix fountain, which is to be found in the small courtyard with its lovely atmosphere. To the right is the coat of arms of the king, to the left that of the house of Aragon, both surmounted by a stone crown.

Of all the sights in the Castle Museum, the stove tiles also deserve mention. They are on display in the treasure

The power and the glory – the inner courtyard of the castle.

chamber. These are unusually original works of art from the time of the kings Sigismond, Ladislas Posthumus and Matthias Corvinus, with finely worked figures of heralds, knights and courtiers, carried out in an extraodinarily rich range of colours. Matthias has been immortalised for posterity seated on his throne, with crown, sceptre and imperial orb.

The Hungarian National Gallery: The palace and castle, which after their restoration no longer house any official departments, have been used purely for museum purposes since the end of World War II. Well worth a visit, of course, is the **Magyar Nemzeti Galéria** (Hungarian National Gallery). It gives an overall impression of Hungarian painting and sculpture from the Middle Ages till well into the 20th century. The halls of the ground floor are reserved for medieval art, and this is where you will find some very impressive **Gothic altarpieces** from the 14th and 15th centuries. Famous outside the

borders of Hungary are the "beautiful madonnas" on exhibition, which date from around 1400. They can certainly stand comparison with any of the works of the so-called "soft style" which predominated in Austria and Bohemia.

Wide-ranging displays: The Baroque department on the first floor is well equipped with portraits and statues of saints from the palaces and the collections of the aristocracy, which became state property after World War II and the Communist takeover of power at the end of the 1940s, without appropriate compensation being offered. Well represented is the portrait painter Adam Mányoki, who studied in Paris but also worked in Germany, particularly in Berlin and Dresden. Perhaps the best known of his works is the portrait of the rebel leader Ferenc Rákóczi II, the Prince of Transylvania, who led the revolt against the Habsburgs in 1703, which can be seen here. No less well represented on the same floor are the well-known 19th century artists, start-

ing with the landscape artists and portrait painters of the Biedermeier (early 19th century) period, such as Károly Markó and Miklós Barabás, going on to the historical artists such as Viktor Madarász and Gyula Benczúr and ending with the Romantics such as Mihály Munkácsy.

The Impressionists: Works by the artists of the "School of Nagybánya", which was strongly influenced by the French Impressionists and was responsible for the breakthrough of Hungarian painting into the modern age around the turn of this century, can be seen on the second floor. Here you can also admire the best known works of the most important Hungarian representative of the Viennese "Secession" style, József Rippl-Rónai.

Special exhibitions: The National Gallery often arranges special temporary exhibitions of individual artists or particular periods, drawing on its large stock. Visitors to Budapest who are interested in art should keep themselves informed of these special exhibitions, which are well worth seeing. Contemporary artists mainly exhibit in small, mostly private, galleries. There is as yet no really suitable state museum of modern art, despite the initiative across all national borders of the German art collector Ludwig, who left a very respectable collection of modern works to the city of Budapest.

Víziváros (The Water City): From Castle Hill you can go down to the Danube via the winding flights of steps – emerging either at the western bridgehead of the **Lánchíd** (Chain Bridge) or in the historic community of **Víziváros** (the Water City), the district between Clark Ádám tér and Bem József tér.

The Water City lies parallel to the Danube. The main street is the **Fö utca**. In this street the Turkish **Király Baths** are an interesting sight. They are open on alternate days for men and women. Not far away is the **Buda Redoute** (Budai vigadó), famous as a concert hall and also popular with foreigner visitors.

Survivors from Turkish times: the Király Baths dating from the 16th century.

Batthyány tér: The centre of this district, however, is **Batthyány tér**, where among other things there is a very busy market hall. Because of its metro station and because it is the starting point for the HÉV light rail route to Szentendre, as well as for several bus routes, this square plays an important role in the capital's public transport system, which hardly disturbs the contemplative atmosphere of the square, and **Víziváros** has many other little corners with a pleasant atmosphere. The square, with its monument to **Ferenc Kölcsey**, the poet who wrote the national anthem, is dominated by the airy facade of **St Anne's Church**, and is ranked one of the most beautiful Baroque churches in the capital. The former "White Cross" inn now houses the "Casanova" nightclub.

A Pole and a national hero: To the north **Bem József tér** marks the boundary of **Víziváros**, where with a little imagination you can still get the feel of the world of the craftsmen, tradesmen and fishermen who once lived between the castle and the slopes of the Danube banks. This square is named after a man whose monument stands here. The monument portrays General Bem, one of the great figures of the Hungarian revolt against the house of Habsburg in 1848/49. He, however, was not a Hungarian, but a Pole. In the first half of the last century he was involved with all sorts of rebellions, revolts and revolutions, before he ended his life as a pasha in Turkey. However, the Hungarians considered him to be one of their own, and his life history, like a popular adventure story, seems to be infectious. When the political pot is coming to the boil in Hungary, as it did in 1956, this square is always in the centre of the action. A huge demonstration was held here on 23 October 1956, in sympathy with the people of Poland and their struggle for reforms, and it developed into the Hungarian uprising.

Rose Hill: Above **Víziváros** lies the most exclusive residential area of the capital, with quiet streets, fine houses surrounded by gardens, and a few cultivated restaurants – this is **Rózsadomb** (Rose Hill). This is where the upper political echelons live, as do the snobs, countless leading businessmen and famous artists. Many diplomats also have their residences here. If you want to be part of high society, you need to have your house built here, the most famous of the Buda Hills. **Rózsadomb** also has links with Turkish times. The name alone points in that direction, for in the 16th and 17th century the Turks are supposed to have converted the area into a sea of flowers. Here is the tomb of the man who, according to legend, brought roses to Budapest: Gül Baba, the "Father of Roses."

His final resting place is the octagonal *türbe* (tomb and chapel) built of sandstone blocks, crowned by a dome of copper sheets, and surrounded by flowerbeds full of roses.

"Gül Baba" did in fact exist, but he is unlikely to have introduced the cultivation of roses. He died only a few days after Sultan Suleiman took possession of Buda. The Sultan gave orders that he should be interred in a *türbe*, for Gül Baba, a dervish of the Bektashi order, had repeatedly distinguished himself during the Sultan's campaigns.

After his death he was honoured as a saint and his *türbe* became a place of pilgrimage. The importance accorded to him can be seen in the picture hanging on the wall of the tomb which shows the sacred shrines of Islam. The Kaaba in Mecca is in the centre, but among the holy sites surrounding it is the *türbe* of Gül Baba.

Finally, we should not forget to mention that Hungary owes something "typically Hungarian" to the Turks – paprika. The Turks brought it to southern Hungary, where it was known as "Turkish pepper."

However, the Hungarians did not cultivate it on a large scale until the 20th century, when they made it into a national symbol and an export.

TURKISH BUDAPEST

Budapest – or, to be more precise, Buda and Pest – was (or were) ruled by the Turks for 145 years, from 1541 to 1686. However, they have left little trace of their long occupation in the city and in the culture of the people, except for the delightful baths.

Sultan Suleiman the Magnificent, incidentally, had no need to conquer the castle of Buda. It came into his hands through trickery. Queen Isabella, the widow of John Zápolyai, the last king of Hungary who was not a Habsburg, had sent her year-old son Sigismond with a ceremonial escort to the tents of the Padishah below the castle, in order to do him honour. While the ceremony was going on, the janissaries sneaked into the castle, rapidly disarmed all the gate guards and occupied all the important defensive places. Buda was then in Turkish hands; Queen Isabella and the child Sigismond received safe conduct to Transylvania, which remained free of Turkish occupation. But the castle of Buda, for nearly a century and a half, was the residence of Turkish pashas, governors of the central region of Hungary which now belonged to the empire of the Crescent, under the rule of the Sultan in Istanbul.

Budapest is different from Pécs or Eger in that there is no mosque or minaret dating from those times on its skyline. The churches which the Turks turned into mosques when they entered Budapest, among them the Matthias Church and the Inner City Parish Church in Pest, were rapidly reconverted into Christian churches, and other mosques were destroyed during or immediately after the re-taking of Buda and Pest by Austrian imperial forces.

Nothing in the Matthias Church remains as a reminder of the years in which the name of Allah was praised there, but in the **Inner City Parish Church** near the Elizabeth Bridge there

Rose Hill, the most prestigious address in Budapest.

is still a *mihrab*, a prayer niche facing Mecca, with an Arabian inscription.

In the castle the names of two **bastions** keep the memory of the Turks alive: **Véli bég bástya** (Veli Bey Bastion), for instance, and the Kassim Pasha roundel, which is also known as the **Fejérvári rondella**. Finally, on the Anjou bastion at the northern edge of the Castle Hill, there is the monument to the last Turkish governor to rule over Hungary, Abdurrahman Pasha. He commanded those Turkish troops who defended the castle of Buda against the Habsburg force, and he died in battle on 2 September 1686, just before the imperial army conquered the city and the castle.

Óbuda: To the north of Rose Hill lies the oldest settled historical district of the country's capital. The military and civilian towns of Roman Aquincum were built on this site, replacing an earlier Celtic-Illyrian settlement. Under the Árpád princes Óbuda was much more important than Buda and Pest, but later it was overshadowed by these two cities and led the life of a small town. It is supposed to have had its own individual charm, though. Not much of that is left today, just a little around **Fö tér** and the **Zichy Palace**, where there are still some of the old houses and pubs – mostly much restored. Apart from these places, Óbuda is a hyper-modern socialist residential area with high rise apartment blocks, multi-lane highways and department stores, but unfortunately very few green spaces.

Apart from the Classical synagogue and a beautiful Baroque church below the Árpád Bridge, places which should be mentioned (and visited) include the two museums dedicated to famous artists: that of Victor Vasarely, born in Pécs in 1908, who lived for many years in France, and that dedicated to the leading sculptor of our times, Imre Varga. He was, incidentally, the creator of the statue of Raoul Wallenberg, which is described elsewhere (page 48) in this book.

The Turks are no longer hated.

ROMAN BUDAPEST

Previous excavations have provided evidence for a Roman presence in three places. The military town lay in the centre of Óbuda, with the civilian city of Aquincum on the northern edge of Óbuda, along the present-day road to Szentendre (Szentendrei út).

Coming from the city centre towards Óbuda, you first reach the remains of the **amphitheatre of the military town** (corner of Korvin Ottó utca/Nagyszombat utca). This was the amphitheatre which served the legionaries stationed in Aquincum – the civilian town had its own facilities. It must have been a large arena, measuring 430 ft (131 m) long, 351 ft (107 m) wide, with seating arrangements for an audience of 14,000 to 16,000 people. However, only the foundation walls of the impressive building can be seen, and a few sections have been restored.

The other discoveries that have been made during the excavation of the military town can be seen in a special museum (Táborvárosi Múzeum) in Korvin Ottó utca 63. There are fragments of houses dating from the 2nd to the 4th centuries and objects of everyday use dating from those times.

On the way to the civilian city of Aquincum it is worth making a diversion to see the so-called **Hercules Villa** (Meggyfa utca 19-21). It must have been the home of a wealthy Roman of high social status of the 3rd century. Archaeologists have named it after the mosaic that has been excavated there, which shows Hercules pursuing a centaur which has carried off a maiden. This mosaic and the fragments of others can be seen in protected rooms which have been specially designed to house them.

Experts consider the mosaics of the Hercules Villa to be the most beautiful ever to be discovered on Hungarian soil. However, they are unlikely to have been

The baths of Budapest offer more than watery pleasures.

manufactured in Pannonia. It is considered more likely that they were designed in the Hellenistic regions of the Mediterranean and merely pieced together in Aquincum.

The best way of getting to the **civilian city of Aquincum** would be to take the suburban light railway (HÉV), which runs, starting at Batthyány tér in the **Víziváros** (Water City), from Buda to Szentendre. Get off at the "Aquincum" stop and you will find yourself right opposite the site of the excavations.

Here, in an area of 1,312 ft by 1,968 ft (400 by 600 m), the civilian population of the Roman city lived. Opinions differ on the size of the population: people more or less agree on the number of legionaries stationed in Aquincum, which is estimated to be at 6,000 to 10,000 men, at any rate during the period when the Roman province flourished most.

Only about a quarter of the city has been excavated to date. From the walls and the street paving that has come to light it can be seen that the streets ran at right angles, that piped water and sewers existed and that there were public baths and a market hall. The civilian town, too, had its amphitheatre, but it was smaller than that for the soldiers. Visitors can still see its remains to the left of the railway in the direction of Szentendre.

The discoveries from Aquincum can be seen in the museum with the Classical facade on the site of the former civilian town. Here you can see the pottery bowls in everyday use, the jewellery, the sacred objects, the tools, coins and weights. Copies and reconstructions are used to give an impression of the daily life of Romans on the fringe of their empire. Tombstones and statues can be seen in the pillared hall surrounding the museum. Remains of wall paintings and mosaic floors are visible in a special room in the southern part of the excavation site.

Among the sites of Óbuda, apart from the excavation site of **Aquincum**, is the **Kiscelli Múzeum** (Little Zell Museum), which is part of the Historical Museum of the Castle. This department shows the development of Buda and Pest from the end of Turkish rule in 1686 up until modern times. It is attractively situated on a hill above **Bécsi út** (Vienna Street).

The building which houses the museum is well worth seeing. It is a Baroque monastery building dating from the mid-18th century. The museum also has a famous collection of works by Hungarian artists of the 20th century. It is named after a little chapel which once housed a copy of the venerated picture in the pilgrims' church of Mariazell in Austria.

Among the possible routes down off Castle Hill is the one on the north side through the **Bécsi kapu** (Vienna Gate) down to **Moszkva tér**, one of the most important meeting points for public transport routes in Budapest. There is a metro station here, and many bus and tram routes cross at the square.

Shade and slumber under the remains of the Roman civilian town of Aquincum.

THE HILLS OF BUDA

Using the rack and pinion railway, which has its valley station in the avenue of **Szilágyi Erzsébet fasor** opposite the round building of the Hotel Budapest, you can make an extended trip to the **Széchenyi hegy** (Széchenyi Hill). The railway covers a difference in height of 1,034 ft (315 m). From this point you can already get a splendid view of Budapest. Then you can carry on using the **Úttörö Varsút** (Pioneer Railway) a narrow gauge railway operated by members of the Communist youth organisation.

A labyrinth of caves: In the hills of Buda, apart from the famous hot springs and artesian wells, there are many interesting caves. They were created by earthquakes in the layers of limestone and dolomite, and also by the erosive effects of water trickling upon the rock. Under the Castle Hill, too, in the layers of limestone tufa, a cave system stretching for many miles has developed, making a widespread network of double cellars. You can get into the labyrinth of caves directly from the cellars of some of the houses. The **Pálvölgyi barlang** (Pálvölgyi cave) with its miles of passages and its lovely stalactites and stalagmites make an interesting attraction of the sort you hardly expect to find in the big city.

In the nearby woods there are a few very good restaurants to be found, and you can drive up the winding road to the 1,691-ft (497-m) high **Harmashatár hegy** (Three Borders Hill), from which point you will have a wonderful view of Óbuda and its surroundings.

If you want to approach the big city from a different route and obtain a different set of impressions, you can return to the city centre in an hour and a half on foot. But then again, who has that much time available? It is interesting to remember, in this context, that Budapest, by European standards, is one of the half

Left, two ages, two different styles of building. **Below**, rambling in Budapest – why not?

dozen most popular places for visits and holidays.

Gellért Hill: If you stand in Március 15 tér and look southwest across the Elizabeth Bridge, you will be able to see the 427-ft (130-m) high Géllert Hill rising steeply from the bank. With its rocky cliffs and steep drop down to the river, the hill dominates the scene in this part of Buda.

As far as the people of Budapest are concerned, the hill is more of a decoration than a tourist attraction. It is customary not to climb the hill more than once in a lifetime – usually when young and in love – as high up as the monument to St Gellért just above the western bridgehead of the Elizabeth Bridge, from which point you have a beautiful view of the Danube, the Parliament building and the Castle Hill of Buda. Past the **Gellért Memorial** there are much more comfortable and steeper footpaths leading upwards, and from the southern side, where the slope is more gentle, you can even drive up by car or by bus.

The name of the hill is linked to a legend. The Venetian bishop Gerardus, known to the Hungarians as Gellért, suffered a martyr's death here. In the 11th century Gerardus was supposed to have been a missionary among the Magyar tribes, but was captured in the area of present-day Buda, put into a barrel studded with nails and thrown into the Danube from this hill, which bears his name. At the place where the deed was said to have been done stands the memorial, by Béla Jankovics, dating from 1902.

In German legend and folk tale Gellért Hill occupies a position analogous to that of the Blocksberg in the Harz mountains. It was a meeting point for witches, who were believed to have celebrated their extravagant feasts, such as the one on Walpurgis Night (30 April), here. The beautiful water queen Lau is supposed to have let herself be lured to one of these witches' sabbaths, and it was only thanks to Doctor Faustus

Tourists caught up with the view from the Citade,l up on Gellért Hill .

that she was saved from the claws of the devil.

The Citadel: After the crushing of the 1848 revolution and the revolt against the house of Habsburg, the emperor Franz Joseph I had a fortress built on the plateau of the hill, a kind of castle intended to keep down the restless natives. After the so-called Compromise of 1867 the Hungarians repeatedly demanded that the Citadel, the "Bastille on the hill," must be removed. In 1897 this finally came about. The Austrian troops withdrew, the fortress was sold to the city administration of Budapest, which then in a symbolic act had some portions of the thick walls torn down and removed.

Gellért Hill and its fortress last fulfilled a military function in the winter of 1944/45, when German troops in the battle for the capital fired on Soviet troops on the other side of the Danube. Up until the 1980s the People's Army would hold a big fireworks display on the hill on 20 August, the day of the constitution.

Another reminder of the battle for Budapest is the **Liberation Monument**, which can be seen at a distance. It was put up in 1947 and is the work Zsigmond Kisfaludi Strobl. A female figure stands on a massive pedestal, holding a palm branch as a symbol of peace. At her feet stands a Soviet soldier. Carved into the pedestal are some of the names of the Soviet soldiers who died in the battles around Budapest, some of whom had to fight a war on two fronts: against Hungarian as well as against German troops.

Otherwise, the plateau at the top of the hill is a peaceful place. In the citadel there is a plain hotel for tourists and a restaurant, and there is a wine cellar in the former barracks, where a gypsy group plays great music every evening for the visitors.

On the southern side of Gellért Hill there are districts where the only thing interesting for a visitor to Budapest would be the roads that run through

them. The motorways from Vienna to Györ and from Lake Balaton run into **Budärsi út**, and you then have the choice of reaching the city centre either via **Erzsébet híd** or **Szabadság híd**. If you just want to drive through Budapest, the best route is to follow the signposts leading to the **Petöfi híd** (Petöfi Bridge), where you will then be directed to the southern motorway in the direction of Szeged. However, only 19 miles (30 km) of this motorway have so far actually been completed.

There was a wine-growing area to the south of Gellért Hill as late as the end of the last century, in the suburb of Budafok. Hardly anything of the vineyards, though, has survived: the vines were all destroyed by phylloxera at the turn of the century. However, the large wine cellars from that time have survived, and are still used by the state-owned wine producers. One of them, the Budafok wine cellar, is in fact the biggest wine, champagne and brandy producer in Hungary.

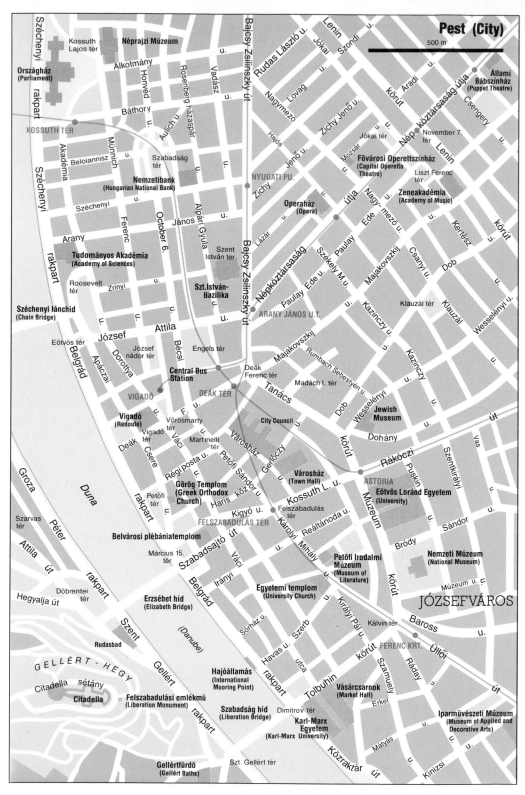

Pest (City)

500 m

Országház (Parliament)
Kossuth Lajos tér
Néprajzi Múzeum
Alkotmány
Honvéd
Vadász
Rosenberg házaspár
Báthory
Bajcsy Zsilinszky út
Rudas László u.
Lenin
Lovag
Lovag
Jókai
Szondi
Jókai
Aradi
Csengery
Állami Bábszínház (Puppet Theatre)
Akadémia
Beloiannisz
Münnich
Szabadság tér
Aulich
Hajós
Zichy Jenő u.
Jenő u.
Jókai tér
Mozsár
November 7. tér
Nép- köztársaság útja
Lenin
Kossuth tér
Nemzetibank (Hungarian National Bank)
Nyugati pu.
Fövárosi Operettszínház (Capital Operetta Theatre)
Liszt Ferenc tér
Széchenyi
Ferenc
October 6.
János
Alpári Gyula
Zichy
Operaház (Opera)
Nagy- mező u.
Ede
Zeneakadémia (Academy of Music)
Kertész
körút
Arany
Szent István tér
Lázár
Népköztársaság
Paulay
Paulay Ede u.
Székely M.u.
Majakovszkij
Csanyi u.
Dob
Tudományos Akadémia (Academy of Sciences)
Roosevelt tér
Zrínyi
Szt.István-Bazilika
Paulay Ede u.
Kazinczy u.
Klauzál tér
Klauzál
Wesselényi
Széchenyi lánchíd (Chain Bridge)
Eötvös tér
József
Attila
Engels tér
Arany János u.t.
Majakovszkij
Rumbach Sebestyén u.
Kazinczy
út
Vas
Belgrád
Apáczai
Dorottya
József nádor tér
Bécsi
Central Bus Station
Deák Ferenc tér
Madách I. tér
Tanács
Wesselényi
Dob
Jewish Museum
Szentkirályi
Vigadó
Szarvas tér
Duna
Deák
Csere
Vigadó (Redoute)
Vigadó tér
Vörösmarty tér
Martinelli tér
Váci
Petőfi Sándor u.
Városház
Geőczy
Deák tér
City Council
körút
Dohány
Rákóczi
Astoria
Puskin
Giroza
Péter
Régi posta u.
Görög Templom (Greek Orthodox Church)
Haris
köz
Kigyó u.
Városház (Town Hall)
Kossuth L. u.
Felszabadulás tér
Eötvös Loránd Egyetem (University)
Múzeum
Sándor
Attila út
Hegyalja út
Döbrentei tér
rakpart
Szarvas tér
Belvárosi plébániatemplom
Petőfi tér
Március 15. tér
Felszabadulás tér
Károlyi Mihály
Reáltánoda u.
Bródy
Nemzeti Múzeum (National Museum)
körút
Szent
Rudasbad
Erzsébet híd (Elizabeth Bridge)
Szabadsajtó
Irányi
Sörház u.
Egyetemi templom (University Church)
Petőfi Irodalmi Múzeum (Museum of Literature)
Múzeum u.
Józsefváros
Gellért-Hegy
Citadella sétány
Citadella
Belgrád
Váci
Havas u.
Szerb
Szerb u.
ufca
Kálvin tér
Királyi Pál u.
Baross
Ferenc krt.
Üllöi
Ráday
Felszabadulási emlékmü (Liberation Monument)
Hajóállamás (International Mooring Point)
Szabadság híd (Liberation Bridge)
Dimitrov tér
Karl-Marx Egyetem (Karl-Marx University)
Tolbuhin
Vásárcsarnok (Market Hall)
Erkel
Szamuely
Mátyás
Iparmüvészeti Múzeum (Museum of Applied and Decorative Arts)
Kinizsi
Gellértfürdö (Gellért Baths)
Szt. Gellért tér
Köztraktár út

152

PEST

Preceding pages: from Gellért's point of view; Parliament building; Chain Bridge. **Below,** nymph on Margithíd (Margaret Bridge).

There are probably three significant dates marking the rise of Pest to the big city which it has since become the unification of the three ancient cities of Pest, Buda and Óbuda to form the capital in 1872. First of all, there was the catastrophic flood of 1838, when nine-tenths of the houses (mostly shabby) were destroyed, which also led to the first permanent bridge between the two "unequal" towns being built during the aftermath. A marble tablet in the so-called **Százéves vendéglö** (Hundred-Year Inn) in Pesti Barnabás utca (one of the few surviving secular Baroque buildings in Pest) shows the high water level at the time. The second signifcant date was the combination of the three ancient cities to form a single capital in 1872. The third and final important date was the year of 1896, with its millennial celebrations of the rather arbitrary date of the "Taking of the Land" in AD 896 by the Hungarian tribes, which was to be the definitive important milestone in the rise of the city. Whole rows of streets rose out of the marshy ground. It is well worth for visitors to take a look behind the facades of these apparently very smart apartment blocks. Appearances were all-important – for a long time the sanitary systems of these primitive houses were maintained as they had been in 1900.

To give a clear picture of the way in which the town of Pest was laid out, indeed practically squeezed in, within the Greater and Lesser Ring (both starting at the Danube), it should be mentioned that both the City Park (with its zoo, its amusement park, its circus, the Széchenyi spa, the Gundel restaurant and the Agricultural Museum in the Vajdahunyad Palace) and Margaret Island, were still outside the city boundary at the turn of the century!

Margitsziget (Margaret Island): Today **Margitsziget** (Margaret Island) marks the meeting place of the two historic parts of the city. This became possible when, half a century after its completion, the Chain Bridge received an ornate rival in the form of the **Margithíd** (Margaret Bridge). This allows you to make a diversion (not by car, though) to Margitsziget. The Margithíd is a curious construction. It is formed of two parts, which meet just before the southern end of the island at an angle of 150°, with a side bridge, 230 ft (70 m) long, which was added to the point of the angle in 1901, leading onto the island. On the island there is a broad, well-cared for park with rare trees and plants. There are also two large international spa hotels. The island is a major area for sports and leisure, and apart from an open-air theatre capable of seating several thousand spectators it has several playgrounds, an indoor swimming pool, and one of the biggest thermal open-air spas (**Palatinus**) in the country, with various hot pools and broad lawns where tens of thousands can lie

out in the sun. In addition to the city bus routes, which are the only motorised traffic allowed on the island, the transport on offer is increased by several horse-drawn traps and bicycle rickshaws (ideal for families). For the people of the capital, and for visitors to Budapest too, the island (1½ miles/2.5 km long and about 547 yards/500 m wide, once known as Hare Island) has ample leisure facilites and considerable attractions. The latter description does not however include the topless sun-worshippers under the pillars of the bridge.

The Dominican convent: This island in the Danube received its present name from the daughter of King Béla IV. According to legend, the King had vowed to place his daughter Margit in a convent if he survived the invasion of the Mongols. Once the mounted hordes from the Asian steppes had withdrawn, he founded a convent of Dominican nuns, where the princess, after a short life but "one pleasing to God, died in her 28th year". In 1944 – when many of the Jews of Budapest had already been deported to Auschwitz – Margaret or Margit was canonised. Very little remains of the convent, which was quite important for Hungary, culturally speaking, because of the copying and illumination of manuscripts undertaken by the nuns. The same is true of the originally Romanesque church. The ruins are to be found not far away from one of the two hotels.

The spa hotels: If you want to drive to the **Ramada** and **Thermal** hotels in your own car, you will have to use the Árpád Bridge at the north end of the island. If you do not hear the cheerful voices of young people from the sports fields and the swimming pools, you could consider Margisziget with its wealth of flowers an oasis of quiet in the midst of the busy city. The island tends to be used more by people from Pest, as the people of Buda mostly live away in the leafy suburbs. Here, as a visitor, you can take a rest and reflect on your previ-

Ruins of the Dominican convent on Margisziget .

ous stay on the Buda side, before preparing for a busy sightseeing programme on the Pest bank.

Only nine of the ten historic districts in Budapest (which within the country is abbreviated Bp) are really worth seeing. The districts are always referred to by Roman numerals, and are the Castle Quarter, the Water City and Óbuda on the right, Leopoldstown, Theresiatown, Elizabethtown, Josephstown and Francistown on the left (the names date from the time of the Habsburgs, commemorating various members of the imperial family, and are still current today). There is also the X district, the working class area of Köbanyá (Quarry). The suburbs forming the other 12 districts – they were independent towns until 1950 – have only a marginal role to play today, particularly as they have partially been able to keep their provincial character.

It is a good idea to keep this in mind if you are going on to see the city off **Margaret** your own bat. In a city filled with inter-
Bridge.

esting sights as in Budapest it is unavoidable that some little side roads will have to be part of the itinerary, even if they don't rate a separate mention in any guide book. There is a wealth of detail in the Hungarian capital, which is particularly useful for those interested in taking photographs. Improvisation should be the name of the game, apart from those routes which we recommend. This, of course, is what the individualist really wants.

At the eastern bridgehead of the **Margithíd** (Margaret Bridge), which we have already described in some detail, you now have to come to a decision. Should you carry on along the extension of this bridge, decorated with stone statues of nymphs, leading to the **Szent István körút** and the **Nagykörút** (Great Ring), which follows a big curve around the tightly packed city centre and leads back to the Danube at the Petöfi Bridge, or should you turn south here at once and go in the direction of the Parliament?

The Parliament building: Together with the castle, the Matthias Church and the Chain Bridge, the Neo-Gothic, in places almost Baroque **Parliament** (Orságház) is one of the symbols of Budapest. It was built from 1884 to 1902 according to plans by Imre Steindl; at a time, therefore, when the Hungarian half of the Danube monarchy still stretched from the Carpathians to the Adriatic and from Lake Fertöto Transylvania, and had a population of more than 20 million. After the collapse of the Habsburg empire Hungary, which as an ally of Germany was on the losing side in World War I, had to give up two thirds of its former territory – parts of Yugoslavia, Rumania and Slovakia – at the surrender in the Trianon. The population was reduced to 7½ million. Some people are still unable to forget this loss even to this day.

The Parliament, however, has remained in the heartland of Hungary. The building is 879 ft (268 m) long and up to 387 ft (118 m) broad. The dome is 315 ft (96 m) high. Inside the building there are hundreds of rooms, large and small, 27 staircases and 18 inner courtyards. On the side facing the Danube the front of the building is broken up by arcades, and there are little towers sticking up on the roof.

The domed hall: This is where the National Assembly meets, and this is where the offices of the President, i.e. the nominal head of State, and of the Chairman of the Council of Ministers, i.e. the head of government, are situated. The magnificent staircase leads to the polygonal 16-sided **domed hall**, which, 89 ft (27 m) up, has a ceiling decorated with stars. The pillars around it bear the statues of some of the Hungarian rulers (those of Hungarian descent – the Habsburgs are not represented). Most of the state receptions are held in this domed hall.

It is possible to visit the Parliament building at certain fixed times, but only as part of a group. However, if you are with a group tour, there are no prob-

Parliament in session – a rare sight prior to 1990.

lems. You can take unlimited photographs anywhere you like.

Lajos Kossuth Square: In generously proportioned Lajos Kossuth tér there are two monuments depicting political rebels. One is that of the imperial governor and minister of finance Lajos Kossuth, the leading light of the 1848/49 revolution, who then had to flee out of the country and never set foot again in his homeland as a living man. The equestrian statue of Ferenc Rákóczi II honours the Transylvanian (and Protestant) leader of the peasant armies of the "Wars of Liberation", fought by the so-called Kuruz rebels from 1703 to 1711 against the Catholic Habsburgs, who had clearly established themselves as kings of Hungary after defeating the Turks in 1687.

Néprajzi Múzeum (Ethnographic Museum): The square opposite the Parliament is dominated by the **Néprajzi Múzeum** (Ethnographic Museum), which is well worth a visit. Research into folk culture is well developed in

A facade in the so-called government quarter.

Hungary, and there is a corresponding wealth of material which has been collected for over a century from all over the world, and which is well displayed in the museum. Peasant furniture, household utensils, jewellery, traditional dress from all parts of the country ruled by the former monarchy not only give a comprehensive picture of Hungarian folk art, but just looking at them is also an aesthetic pleasure. Here visitors will be able to see some fine examples of folk art and crafts, among them re-creations of furniture, tablecloths, blankets, pots or carpets, made with materials and based on designs taken from old models.

Sacrifice in Liberation Square: The **Eternal Flame** in this rather smaller, triangular square, formed by three streets only a few blocks away from Parliament, is a reminder of another famous politician of 1848/49. The bronze oil lamp honours the memory of Count Lájos Batthyány from Bratislava, the first Prime Minister of a Hungarian National Goverment, who on 6 October 1849, together with a dozen other political and military figures who had also been involved in the revolt, was shot against the barracks wall in what is now Szadabság tér (Liberation Square).

Szabadság tér: Liberation Square is the centre of that part of Pest which dates from the turn of the century and can be recognised by its right-angled street pattern. There are several ministries in this square, and the National Bank, the Academy of Sciences, consulates and embassies, including that of the USA, state television and other important and official buildings also have their home here.

St Stephen's Basilica: Only a few steps away, in **Szent István tér**, is the spiritual centre of the city. The biggest church in Budapest – a *basilica minor* – is dedicated to St Stephen.

The building itself has a dramatic history. Its construction was begun in 1851, but not finished until 1905. Why?

First of all, the much honoured architect Joseph Hild, who had started on the building project, died. Shortly afterwards, in 1868, work was interrupted again because the first dome collapsed. The death of the famous architect Miklós Ybl, who continued the work, caused another hiatus. The basilica, in its present form, is undoubtedly an impressive building, and its 315-ft (96-m) high dome (incidentally, just as tall as that of its secular equivalent, the Parliament building), towers mightily over the rooftops of Pest. Inside, though, it has less atmosphere than many small parish churches. The atmosphere is simply lacking, even when local people come to see the most precious relic which the church possesses: it is said to be the gilded right hand of St Stephen, the first king of Hungary and probably dates from the 14th or even the 15th century.

The sacred right hand was nonetheless displayed for several days at a time, with great ecclesiastical ceremony, in a dozen of the largest towns in Hungary in 1988, the 950th anniversary of the death of the man who brought Christianity to Hungary.

The Imperial Governor's Square: If you want to go back to the Danube from the basilica, follow József Attila utca. It passes József nádor tér, where Classical houses give a faint impression of how Pest must have looked at the beginning of last century. Despite a few rather less successful modern buildings, the square still presents a fairly intact appearance, architecturally speaking. It was named after Archduke Joseph, a grandson of Maria Theresia, who was the representative of the imperial family for 51 years, from the end of the 18th to the middle of the 19th century. As Palatine or viceroy of Hungary, he did a great deal for the development of the cities of Pest and Buda. His memorial dominates the square, which has undergone some civic restructuring in recent years.

The Academy of Sciences: It is only a

Tympanum of the basilica.

few steps from this point to **Roosevelt tér**, which once bore the name of the emperor and king Franz Joseph, and to the tiny **Eötvös tér**, named in honour of the former Minister of Education József von Eötvös, who was also a poet. The Neo-Renaissance building on the north side of this square, which is named after the American president, is the **Magyar Tudományos Akadémia** (Hungarian Academy of Sciences), and which was built from 1862 to 1864 according to plans by the Berlin architect Friedrich August Stüler. The impetus for the building came from Count István Széchenyi, as did that for the building of the Chain Bridge. The Count's memorial is almost hidden away in a small park not far from the opulent facade of the academy.

Lánchíd (Chain Bridge): Between the two squares lies the Pest bridgehead of the of the **Lánchíd** (pronounced *lahntz-heed*) or Chain Bridge. This is the oldest of the eight bridges crossing the Danube, with the Kossuth Bridge having provided not much more than a provisional post-war measure. It was built from 1839 to 1849. The impetus came from Count Széchenyi, the plans were drawn up by the Englishman William Thierney Clark, the construction was supervised by Adam Clark.

The people of Budapest are much attached to their Chain Bridge. This may be because the bridge was not only the first over the Danube, but was for its time a very modern construction, technically speaking, as well as being aesthetically pleasing. With its stone lions at the bridgeheads and the Classical pillars which support the iron chains, it has been and still is a symbol of Budapest. Although it was bombed in the winter of 1944/45, it was opened to traffic once more as early as 1949, a hundred years from the day after its first official opening. Incidentally, if you cross any one of the four city bridges on foot, you will appreciate the quite delightful views on both banks of the Danube.

The Chain Bridge – as remarkable today as it was in 1849.

On the Pest shore, on this side of the Lánchíd, is the starting point of the **Corso Promenade**, so often mentioned in older novels, stories and picture books, and adorned with benches and little trees. It has not been possible, though, to quite revive its former flair, the atmosphere of the supposedly "good old days". The wonderful, wide-open view of the Buda shore remains unchanged and unique.

On the northern side of the Duna Intercontinental Hotel is **Vigadó tér**, named after a magnificent building by the architect Frigyes Feszl, in the Romantic style of the middle of the last century (1859-64). Concerts, balls, gatherings and exhibitions took place in the **Vigadó** (Ballroom). The Vigadó was burned down during the war and remained as an ugly ruin on the edge of the city centre for 30 years. In the 1970s the facade was rebuilt, including the busts of certain great Hungarians and the Muses set between the tall windows. The halls within were largely adapted to

modern architectural and technical requirements, so that small conferences can be held here. A cafe, a restaurant with good home cooking and a gallery complete what the building has to offer, and are partly reminiscent of earlier times.

The Belváros (Inner City) district: At Vigadó tér, the Deák Ferenc utca reaches the Danube and you have now come to the part of Pest known as the **Belváros district** which forms the historic city centre of Pest. The northern city wall of Pest once ran alongside this street.

The centre of the city is surrounded by the **Kiskörút** (Lesser Ring), which is formed of the Tanács körút, Múzeum körút, Kálvin tér and Tolbuhin körút. However, when people talk nowadays of the inner city of Pest, of something like a city centre, they are referring to a considerably larger area, which includes at least those districts ennclosed by the generously proportioned **Nagykörút** (Greater Ring).

However, let us remain for the moment in the historic centre of Pest. There is no single obvious central point from which you could set out to continue (or begin) your sightseeing, but there are several places of interest, between which visitors have to make their way on foot, constantly finding surprises en route. The Hungarian capital does not give up its secrets to visitors unless they are on foot. Tourists can be sure of finding plenty of interesting and photogenic sights. However, it must be stressed once again that visiting Budapest, mainly because of the language barrier, would mean concentrating on the city's architecture. Thousands of other foreign tourists, therefore, will be taking in the sights of the historic city centre with you. The people of Budapest will meanwhile carry on with their work or about their personal business.

Vörösmarty tér, the focal point: From our last stopping place at Vigadó tér it is only a few steps to **Vörösmarty ter**, one of the focal points of city life in

Budapest (by day). Several factors are responsible for the importance of this little square, which forms an irregular rectangle. Here, and in the streets leading from the square, there are several bookshops, a few record shops, a luxurious department store, and the offices of some airlines. This is the starting point of the **Váci utca**, and in fact, the Budapest metro, the oldest underground railway on the continent of Europe, also begins here.

A public spectacle: Today, Vörösmarty tér is a cheerful, officially tolerated street theatre zone. Whole rows of portrait painters with academy qualifications are permitted to offer their services, a few jugglers perform harmless tricks, youthful conjurers of secondary-school age demonstrate their skills in public, talented and not so talented musicians perform, singly or in orchestral numbers, and on the edge of the square some youthful cyclists and breakdancers perform their numbers at risk of life and limb, so that the atmos-

phere is relaxed and cheerful almost round the clock. Vörösmarty Square is, of course, no Montmartre, but there are always plenty of spectators.

The Gerbeaud patisserie: Finally, the most famous patisserie in Budapest is to be found in the square named after the lyric poet Mihály Vörösmarty. Up until World War II it was known by the name of Gerbeaud, and after the war it was given the name of the popular Hungarian poet and literary critic. The people of Budapest, though, hardly took any notice of the changeover. They continued to go to the "Gerbeaud" to drink their coffee and to eat sweet gateaux while seated at the old-fashioned marble tables. The stubbornness of the people of the capital finally won the day. In 1984, on the occasion of the 100th anniversary of the cafe, an agreement was reached with the Gerbeaud family, now living in the West, about partial compensation, and the Vörösmarty cafe and patisserie officially once again became the **Confisserie Gerbeaud** – named after the baker who took over the concern from Henrik Kugler, who had founded the business in 1858 and who, like Gerbeaud, originally came from Switzerland.

The Váci utca pedestrian precinct: If you want to go shopping, you will probably find most of the souvenirs and gifts you are looking for in **Váci utca** or in the surrounding streets, alleys and passages. Here, apart from bookshops, the evidently obligatory florists, cafes, boutiques, branches of German and Austrian chain stores, second-hand bookshops with their prices adjusted to Western clientele, jewellers, and antique, craft and souvenir shops, you will find shops catering for more select requirements, where you can from time to time find quite original items. You can even have fashionable shoes made for you here. In the mid-1980s several shopping centres opened and thereafter the pedestrian precinct definitely became the centre of the busy life of the capital. One of the quiet oases in the midst of all this is the **Hermes Fountain** with its statuette which was cast around the turn of the century and has been preserved through two world wars.

If you are looking for architectural excellence, take a stroll along the Petöfi utca and across Martinelli tér to Város-ház utca. In **Martinelli tér**, which has been completely ruined for years by a multi-storey car park, there are two prominent buildings: one sacred – the Baroque **Servite Church** built between 1725 and 1732 – and one profane – the **Glass Mosaic Apartment House**, built in 1906 in a Jugendstil style, with its allegorical depiction of scenes from Hungarian history.

The Városház (Town Hall): After a row of Classical houses and Jugendstil buildings, you finally come to Városház utca 9-11 and to the biggest Baroque building in Pest. Because of the built-up nature of its surroundings, its dimensions are not easily recognisable, but they are considerable. The facade is 620 ft (189 m) long, but only two of the four planned inner courtyards were ever built. The building was constructed during the first half of the 18th century – it was intended to become a home for invalids disabled by the Turkish wars. Today it is the seat of the **Capital City Council** (Fövárosi tanács); in practice, therefore, the town hall for the administration of the capital – an eminent and important office in the country, which answers directly to the national government. After all, every fifth citizen of the country lives in Budapest. The Classical building with the three atmospheric inner courtyards, separated from the Town Hall by a street and a square, is a century younger. It houses the offices of the administration of the Comitat of Pest.

The original planned layout of Pest can still be traced today. Nearly all the interesting sights of the capital can be seen within this same district. A sight-seeing tour in 1990 would – apart from advertising hoardings and the extreme

Entrance to the Town Hall.

air pollution caused by tens of thousands of cars – appear identical in many places to a sightseeing tour undertaken around 1890. A present-day visit to Budapest, therefore, is for the most part a trip back to the last years of the 19th century. Perhaps this could be the reason for the constant faint mood of nostalgia in the air?

The rapid pace of development in this city, from which the first railway left for Vác in 1846 and the first horse-drawn tram in the city area began operations in 1866, can be illustrated with a few statistics. In 1688, two years after the retreat of the Turks, Pest had no more than 300 inhabitants (Buda, on the other hand, had a population of around 1,000); in the year of the American Declaration of Independence (1776), Pest had a population of 13,500 (Buda 21,665); at the beginning of the last century, in 1810, the figure was 35,348 (as against only 24,910 for Buda), only one generation later the population had doubled – there were 73,302 people living in Pest, and noticeably a smaller 38,974 lived in the sister city of Buda. The two cities, inhabited by many national groups (the German element was dominant for a long time), did not become predominantly Hungarian cities – i.e. with a mainly Magyar population – until the middle of the last century. The following figures were the result of a census in 1890: 399,772 inhabitants on the Pest bank, 92,465 on the Buda side of the river. The nationality statistics showed that every fourth inhabitant of the city area belonged to the German-speaking group. Every fifth inhabitant of the capital, which was not declared a royal residence by Vienna until 1893, was at that time of Jewish origin. In general, the various national groups got along well together.

The Inner City Parish Church: The **Belvárosi plébánia templom** (Inner City Parish Church) is to be found where the Váci utca, in its extension of the **Erzsébet híd** (Elizabeth Bridge), is interrupted by the Szabadsajtó út, by

Jugendstil apartment block in Martinelli tér, with motifs in the Hungarian national style.

Március 15 tér and by Petöfi tér. The lengthy walk once more brings the visitor to a historically very interesting part of the city centre of Pest. The church, with its twin-towered Baroque facade facing the Danube, is probably the most remarkable sacred building on the left bank of the river. Nearly every architectural style from the 12th to the 18th centuries has left its mark here. Only a little has survived of the Romanesque church which stood here in the 12th century, but the early and late Gothic elements, which date from the 12th to the 14th centuries, can easily be recognised. This is particularly true of the choir and its cruciform ribbed vaulting, of the windows and for parts of the side entrances, although some of these have been walled up, and for the seat recesses on both sides of the apse. The two niches for the sacraments in the side chapels on the north and south sides have survived from Renaissance times. Even a prayer niche or *mihrab* facing Mecca, dating from the century and a half when the church served the Turks as a mosque, has survived the passage of time.

Március 15 tér is a reminder of the outbreak of the revolution of 1848, as it was not far from here, in the **Cafe Pilvax** in Pilvax köz, that the youth of Budapest proclaimed their revolutionary programme on the morning of the 15 March and Petöfi read his poem "Arise! Our homeland calls, Magyars!" for the first time. Today most people come because of the church, which is well worth seeing, because of the beautiful view of the Castle Hill and because of the remains of the military base which the Romans once held on the left bank of the Danube. This point – today the site of the Elizabeth Bridge – is the narrowest point of the Danube as it flows through the area of the city of Budapest. Here it is only 935 ft (285 m) wide. The remains of the former fort can still be seen in the ruins which lie on a somewhat lower level.

Separated only by the shore road, Március 15 tér joins **Petöfi tér**, with its statue of the poet of liberty, who died very young in the battles of the 1848-49 revolution. The historical importance of this square is of a more recent date. On the afternoon of 23 October 1956 hundreds of students gathered at the feet of the statue of Petöfi, reciting his poem "Magyars arise!", demanding the removal of the hated Party leader Rákosi and the introduction of nationalist Hungarian policies. Afterwards, as the crowd made its way peacefully to the radio station, shots were fired. The Hungarian revolution, which had made the world hold its breath for weeks, had claimed its first dead. There is (as yet) no indication in Petöfi Square that these more recent events took place.

To the left of Petöfi's monument is the church of the Hungarian Orthodox community, built from 1791 to 1794. The iconostasis was carved 3 years later. Services according to the Orthodox rite are held here in the Hungarian language.

Street musician.

The University: In this district there are also famous public institutions such as the **Loránd Eötvös University**, named after a famous physicist, in Egytem tér 1-3, or the **Petöfi Literary Museum** in the Károlyi Palais in the street named after the country's first prime minister, Károlyi Mihály utca 16. This urban palace, a Classical building dating from the first half of the 19th century, keeps alive the memory of the famous left-wing liberal politician who, after the dissolution of the monarchy in 1919, had to make way for the Communist dictatorship of Béla Kun.

In this rather unattractive quarter there are also some churches which are well worth seeing. There is, for example, the **University Church**, a double-towered, opulent Baroque building dating from the first half of the 18th century. Inside the single nave church there are some precious wooden carvings: the figures on the high altar, the choir, the prelate's throne and the confessionals. These are the work of

Pauline monks, as the church was built for this order, which incidentally is the only one ever to have been founded in Hungary.

The **Serbian Orthodox Church** is to be found in a garden, almost lost among tall city buildings, in **Szerb utca**. This church, too, is a Baroque building, and dates roughly from the same time as the University Church. Its symbol is the tall slender tower, which art historians believe to be the work of the architect Andreas Mayerhoffer.

The Market Hall: If you are looking for some everyday life, go to the **Központi Vásácsarnok** (Central Market Hall). It is to be found on the corner of Tolbuhin körút and Dimitrov tér. The market hall is a steel framed brick building dating from the end of last century. It should really have upgraded long ago, but nonetheless the place is still very popular the way it is. The fruit and vegetable displays are famous, and meat and dairy products are also on sale.

Only a few steps away from the mar-

ket hall, in the former customs house on the banks of the Danube, is the renovated **Karl Marx University** of economic sciences.

The Applied and Decorative Arts Museum: It has been mentioned before that Budapest is a city of monuments. It could just as well be described as a city of museums. If you have a particular interest in Hungarian glass, porcelain and ceramics, furniture, textiles and pictures, you should not miss out on a visit to the **Iparmüvészeti múzeum** (Applied and Decorative Arts Museum) designed by Ödön Lechner. It is to be found in **Üllöi út**, only a few blocks away from Kálvin tér. Apart from the exhibits mentioned above, the work of goldsmiths and silversmiths is particularly prized by the experts. Such work can be seen on display together with old and new jewellery. There are temporary exhibitions, drawn from the museum's considerable stocks, and they provide useful information about particular artistic periods.

The Hungarian National Museum: If you carry on following the **Lesser Ring**, you will find that **Tanács körút** runs into **Múzeum körút** and you will soon come to the **Magyar Nemzeti Múzeum** (Hungarian National Museum), which is well worth a visit for the so-called St Stephen's Crown, the coronation mantle and the other coronation regalia alone.

St Stephen's Crown, the coronation mantle, the royal sceptre, the orb and the sword can be seen – under strict guard – in the great hall of the museum, where taking photographs is absolutely forbidden. Ever since 6 January 1978, when the former US Secretary of State Cyrus Vance, on behalf of his government, returned the Coronation Regalia to the Hungarian people in a solemn ceremony held in the Parliament, this hall has become a place of national pilgrimage. St Stephen's Crown is still the symbol of Hungarian national sovereignty, even though the country was only a kingdom *de jure* after World War

The Secessionist-style dome of the Museum for Applied and Decorative Arts.

I and was formally declared a republic in 1946.

There is a proposal to include the crown once more in the national coat of arms on the Hungarian flag. This is not to be seen as a monarchist act, but rather as a recognition of the founding of the nation in 1001, when the prince's son Vajk took the Christian name of Stephen and laid the foundations of his state, today one of the oldest nation states in the world. His canonisation is supposed to have followed, also in the 11th century.

It is absolutely certain, although by no means expressively mentioned in every brochure or catalogue, that the Crown with its lop-sided cross could not possibly be the same crown that – again according to the story – was sent by Pope Sylvester II to the successor of the Árpád princes and with which Stephen was crowned as the first king of Hungary. It consists of two separate sections, of which the lower may have come from Byzantium, probably from the second half of the 12th century. The cross hoops, though, with their figures of the apostles on enamel plaques, could well date from around the time of St Stephen. However, experts do not believe that they ever formed part of the earlier St Stephen's Crown. They probably formed part of a book cover or a reliquary. The question of when both parts, the "Greek" and the "Latin" sections, were welded together and the crown took on its present form, remains completely unresolved.

The history of the decorative coronation mantle is somewhat better defined. It was originally a sacred vestment, which, so it is claimed, King Stephen and his Bavarian wife Gisela presented to the coronation church in Székesfehérvár in 1031. Going by the Latin inscription on the garment, Hungarian researchers believe it was intended as a coronation robe.

The sceptre is probably older. It is a silver-plated shaft with a knob of rock crystal, which has three lions cut into it,

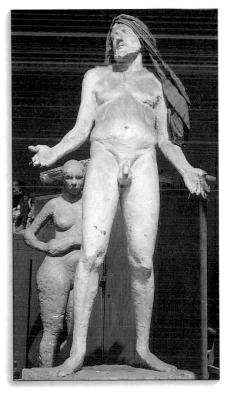

framed by a rosette of gold plate. Sceptres of this sort are unusual among Western coronation regalia, but more common among the peoples of western Asia. There is, therefore, a theory that the princes of the Árpád house could have brought the sceptre with them from their home in southern Russia to central Europe. On the other hand, in the opinion of Hungarian experts, the knob of rock crystal dates from the second half of the 10th century, so that the sceptre could have come to Hungary as a gift.

The orb and the sword remain to be considered. The former definitely dates from the 14th century, as it bears the lily coat of arms of the Angevin kings. The sword is even younger; it probably dates from the beginning of the 16th century and may have been a sort of "substitute" sword, as that sword which can be seen on some later miniatures is to be found in the treasury of St Vitus' Cathedral in the Hradcany Castle in Prague, where it is believed to have been taken in about 1270.

Whatever the objective or historical facts about St Stephen's Crown and the other individual items of the coronation regalia, their symbolical value still occupies a very firm position in the Hungary's view of history. Today, in a time of re-awakening nationalism, which often shows traces of chauvinism, their place is probably more secure than ever.

The museum, built from 1837 to 1847, is a Classical building of very harmonious appearance, designed by Mihály Pollack. A broad open-air staircase leads up to the portico, which has eight Corinthian pillars supporting a mighty triangular gable. This triangle is adorned with a tympanum, in the centre of which the allegorical figure of Pannonia can be seen with the Hungarian coat of arms, flanked by allegories depicting the arts and sciences. Even the exterior of the National Museum makes it clear that this is a building with which the nation can identify.

Fun in winter.

It is also worth visiting the National Museum to see other items from Hungary's history. For visitors with historical interests, the grave goods from the period of the Great Migration will be of importance. These date from the time between the end of Roman rule in Pannonia and the conquest by the Hungarian tribes at the end of the 9th century, the time when many peoples (including Germanic and Slavonic tribes and the nomadic Avars) settled for long or short periods in what was later to be known as the Pannonian or Hungarian Great Plain. On the first floor, where the rooms are devoted to the history of the country from the Magyar conquest in 896 to 1849, you should pay particular attention to the goldsmiths' work in the treasury. There are many pieces on display collectively portraying the golden age of Hungary during the reign of the Renaissance King Matthias Corvinus, who was also King of Bohemia.

The struggle for liberation: The whole of Hall IV is reserved for the heroically depicted struggle for freedom under Ferenc Rákóczi during the early 18th century. In Hall VII there are many exhibits from the 1848/49 revolution, from clothes worn by the poet of liberation, Sándor Petöfi, to the Debrecen Declaration of Independence, which unilaterally banned the house of Habsburg from the Hungarian throne. There are a number of curious objects in the collection, among them the waistcoat of the prime minister Count Lajos Batthyány, with the holes left by the bullets of the imperial Habsburg firing squad.

The biggest synagogue in the world?: Leave the museum in the direction of Deák tér and Tanács körút, where you will find the main synagogue of Budapest in **Dohány utca** (Tobacco Street), near the birthplace of Theodor Herzl. It claims to be the biggest synagogue in the world. Whether this is actually so or not, the building can hold a maximum of 6,000 people. It was built

Five million people have visited the National Museum in the past 10 years.

from 1854 to 1859 according to plans by the Viennese architect Ludwig Förster in the so-called Moorish-Byzantine style a typical Hungarian architectural style of the period. At the time, a quarter of the population of Budapest was Jewish.

A few years ago, an excellent museum opened in a side wing of the synagogue. This is the **National Museum of the Jewish Faith and Jewish History**, which provides information on the fate of Jewish communities in Hungary from Roman times up until the present day. The oldest exhibit in the museum is a Jewish tombstone dating from the 3rd century BC. During the period spanning more than 2,000 years for which there is evidence of Jewish presence in Hungarian territory, this minority has flourished at times but it has also known periods of extreme danger. In 1944 there were still about 825,000 Jews in Hungary, but by the end of the war there were only 255,000 survivors. Today there are about 70,000 people of Jewish

Left, the synagogue in Dohány utca. **Below**, Memorial to James Watt at the Eastern Railway Station.

origin – believers and atheists – living in the capital.

The synagogue was still the focal point of the **ghetto** towards the end of World War II. Until 1945 the 100,000 people who had not yet been deported to Auschwitz were crammed together here in inhuman conditions. The fascist, anti-Semitic Arrow Cross movement wanted to blow up the ghetto shortly before the Soviet troops arrived, but was prevented from doing so by the German military command, of all people. Many lives were saved and in this way the synagogue, too, was preserved unharmed.

Back outside, you will find yourself in the midst of the bustle of the big city. Kossuth Lajos utca and Rákóczi út, two shopping streets, are among the busiest in the capital. Here you will find the big department stores, shops for technical equipment, but also cinemas, bookshops and self-service restaurants. Rákóczi út crosses the **Nagy körút** (Greater Ring) and ends at the **Keleti pályaudvar** (Eastern Railway Station), one of the three international railway junctions of Budapest. This station – built in 1884 – is one of the four main railway stations and the biggest railway terminal in the capital. To the left and right above the main entrance there are statues of George Stephenson and James Watt.

Behind the Eastern Railway Statin, you will come to the **Népstadion** (People's Stadium), the biggest sports ground in Hungary. It was built between 1948 and 1953 and nowadays can hold just about 100,000 spectators. During the legendary fame of the Hungarian national football team in the early 1950s, Ferenc Puskás famous eleven, this was a "place of pilgrimage" for many fans.

On the other side of Kerepesi út lies the **Kerepesi temetö** (Kerepesi Cemetery). The entrance is in Mezö Imre út, which branches off south from the Eastern Railway Station. Up until the 1960s the cemetery was open to all, but now

CEMETERY LIFE

Every capital city has an important cemetery, in which prominent people from political and cultural walks of life are buried. Munich has its Waldfriedhof, Paris has Père Lachaise, where the tombstones read like a volume of Who's Who, and London has Highgate Cemetery, where Karl Marx has to share accommodation with major capitalists. Apart from small cemeteries in Óbuda, Angyalföld and Raákospalota, Budapest has a huge central cemetery on the borders of Pestlörinc and Köbaánya, where ordinary mortals find their final rest under plain gravestones and colourful plastic flowers. The graves of two of Hungary's most famous sons lie in the Farkasréti cemetery in Németvölgyi utca. Zoltan Kodaly was buried here – as was Béla Bartók, although not until 1988, when his remains were transferred from New York, where he died in exile in 1945.

The most famous of all cemeteries in Budapest, though, is the Kerepesi cemetery. On no account should any visitor miss taking a walk in this quiet and peaceful cemetery.

There lie the tombs, nearly all of them just a bit too big, looking like stranded whales. In one of them lies the coffin of the grand old man of Hungary, Ferenc Deák, lawyer and leader of the liberal reformers of the last century, who was partly responsible for the Austro-Hungarian Ausgleich or Compromise of 1867. The mausoleum of Kossuth, whose remains were brought here from Turin in 1894, has its own warden, who can tell you all there is to know about the Kossuth mausoleum. Kossuth was the leader of the Hungarian independence movement, who reinforced the opposition to the government in Vienna to the point of an open break in 1848. The Kerepesi cemetery also has a magnificent funeral monument to the countless people who belonged to the Hungarian workers' movement.

Every visitor to Kerepesi can sense a faint whiff of the air of times past. Along the cemetery wall towering tombstones of decaying beauty rise out of the knee-high grass, spattered with green and white bird droppings. In a part of the cemetery favoured for their tombs by the wealthy middle classes of Budapest lies the family tomb of the Gerbeauds, one of whom founded the cafe of the same name in 1858. This establishment's elegant but opulent interior still attracts visitors today. The journalists and the bohème of the old Cafe New York – now the Hungaria – have moved their meeting place to Kerepesi, but one of their most prominent members, Ferenc Molnár, lies buried in New York. The author Móricz Zsigmond lies next door to the operetta composer Leo Weiner, and the actors Márton Rátkay and Artur Somlay died at almost the same time, as if they wanted to continue their never-ending debate underground. Among them lie great chess players such as Charousek, who beat the 16-year-old Bobby Fisher in Zurich in 1959, or Gedeon Barcza and Géza Maróczy, whose variation of the Sicilian Defence astonished the world of chess. The city of Budapest itself is a huge cemetery. Thousands upon thousands lie buried under its streets, with no memorial to remember them. In 1956, unknown revolutionaries were buried on the spot where they were found dead. The numbers of the dead who could not be buried in cemeteries were also high 12 years before, in the winter of 1944-45, when the German troops fought against the Red Army which was about to roll over them and the Nyilas were rampaging through the ghetto.

At the southern edge of Castle Hill there are a few Turkish tombs, among them that of Gül Baba, the "Father of Flowers", who died in Buda in 1541. Take a walk through Vérmezö and think of the meaning of its name: Field of Blood! This is where Ignác Martinovics, a former priest and later a convinced revolutionary, was executed together with his followers after his attempt to bring the French Revolution to feudal Hungary. Just imagine the *Place de la Concorde* in Paris being known as the *Place de la Guillotine*!

only the famous are buried here. Several prominent political figures of the last two centuries have had enormous mausoleums built here.

As late as 1989, this national cemetery was denied the body of Imre Nagy, executed in 1958. During his lifetime this popular prime minister broke away from Stalinism and proclaimed the neutrality of the country in the autumn of 1956. It was at grave plot no. 301 in the cemetery of Rákoskeresztúr, site of the solemn re-interment of Nagy, that Hungary underwent a kind of national renaissance. The occasion produced scenes and events which cannot adequately be described either in words or pictures. Four weeks after this ceremony, intended as a gesture of conciliation by the Hungarian Communist Party, the funeral took place of the former general secretary János Kádár, who in his last years became a controversial figure. This occasion demonstrated how deeply the nation is divided between the conservatives and those who want reforms. Kádár took his personal secrets with him to the grave. He refused to explain what part he had played in 1949 when his companion Rajk was arrested, or in 1956 during the occupation by the Soviet army, or, even worse, in 1958 at the time of the execution of Imre Nagy and other comrades. There is much tragedy in the air of this beautiful old cemetery. For the tourist, a visit is like a walk through more than a century and a half of Hungarian history, art and culture. A nation is represented in its tombs and memorials. It has to be said that in Hungary these represent the other side of the lives that are dedicated to the nation.

Cafe Hungaria: If you turn into Lenin körút from **Blaha Lujza tér** you will find, on the corner of the right side, a cafe and restaurant which became a legendary institution of literary and journalistic life in the early decades of this century – the **Hungaria**. During its heyday, though, it was known as the New York, after the insurance company

Preceding page, idyllic scene in the cemetery. **Below**, portraits to match at **Vörösmarty tér**.

178

which built it, in an extravagant Neo-Renaissance style, shortly before the turn of the century. All those who met here had a position or name in the literary world of Budapest at that time, or at any rate all those who believed that they had one or the other. Today it has lost this particular aura, but the somewhat old-fashioned looking cafe and the restaurant below are ideal as a meeting place for friends, due to both their fame and because of their easily accessible position.

The **Nemzeti Színház** (National Theatre) is in Hevesi Sándor tér. There is a special reason for such an impressive institution as a National Theatre being sited in this rather remote area. It has in fact already had to move site twice. From its founding in 1837 – up until that time all the so-called (German) theatres in Buda and in Pest had put on German language plays only – until the beginning of this century it stood opposite the present Hotel Astoria on the corner of Rákóczi út and Múzeum körút, but it

Heroes' Square – a national memorial.

had to move to make way for the extension of the Metro in 1966. Since then it has been housed in the modernised, but insufficient elderly theatre building in Sándor Hevesi Square, but it will probably not remain there much longer. The new National Theatre building should be ready anytime now. It is being built on the broad Dózsa György út by the City Park. Money has been contributed towards the new building by the people over the last few years, just as it had been for the first theatre a century and a half ago.

Népköztársaság útja: If you follow Lenin körút in a northerly direction, you will pass **Madách Színház**, one of the most famous theatres in the capital, and the Hotel Royal. Eventually, at November 7 tér, you will come to the showpiece among the streets of Budapest, **Népköztársaság útja**. You should make the effort to take at least one walk along the street, which is just over a 1½ miles (2.5 km) long and lined with tall trees. The avenue is well worth seeing if only because of the way it is laid out.

The attraction of this magnificent street lies mainly in the architecture, which stems from the same period. This is where the upper middle classes of the second half of the last century built their fine town houses, and even though the individual buildings differ from one another, they were all influenced by the Neo-Romantic and eclectic spirit of the times.

The name of the street, difficult for foreigners to pronounce, is only some 30 years old. It means "Street of the People's Republic." When the street was planned, between the years 1870 and 1885 (at the same time as the Ringstrasse in Vienna), it was simply called Sugarút (Radial Street). Then it was given the much more impressive name of Andrássy útja, after Count Gyula Andrássy, the first Austro-Hungarian foreign minister of the monarchy and also a confidant of Queen Elizabeth, who is much revered by the Magyars under the name Erzsébet Királyne. After World War II the street bore Stalin's name, but this was immediately removed during the 1956 revolution. Since new forms of government are at present being discussed in the country as part of the general programme of reforms, the rather dry and neutral present name will probably not last very long.

Népköztársaság útja starts at Deák Ferenc tér, where it crosses the shopping street of **Bajcsy Zsilinsky út**. One of the most important buildings in the first section is the **Állami Operaház** (State Opera House). This is generally considered to be the most successful creation of the famous Miklós Ybl, who has left several buildings in the Neo-Renaissance style in Budapest. Ybl certainly succeeded in giving the interior a festive character. The big staircase to the boxes and the assembly rooms has great charm, the auditorium has a very harmonious appearance and also possesses excellent accoustics. This is reason enough for the people of Budapest to be proud of their opera house, which has always occupied an important position in the musical life of the capital.

Apart from famous Hungarian conductors such as Ernst von Dohnányi or Jenö Hubay, Gustav Mahler and Otto Klemperer, among others, held key positions at the opera house for long periods.

In the area around the opera house there are other theatres, in Népköztársaság útja as well as in the side streets. Mention must also be made of **Liszt Ferenc Zeneakaadémia**, the music academy founded by the composer and piano virtuoso of genius. There is also the **Fövárosi Operattszínház** (Capital Operetta Theatre) in **Nagymezöutca**, which even today is mostly devoted to operettas of the "Silver Age" and their major composers Kálmán and Lehár. Only one block further, in **Jókai tér**, is the second theatre of the **Állami Bábszínház** (State Puppet Theatre), which has very high standards and de-

lights adults as well as children. The first theatre of this company lies in Népköztársaság útja between **November 7 tér** and **Kodály Körönd**, a circular compound named in honour of Adolf Hitler before the war.

From this point on it is the two squares that give the street its own special style. November 7 tér (still named after Mussolini in 1939) was renamed in memory of 7 November 1917, the date of the October Revolution in Russia. Its octagonal shape forms an elegant extension of the crossroads with Lenin körút. Kodály Körönd, on the other hand, elegantly solves the problem of a round space with the arcaded facades of four of the palais edifices and the four garden areas in front of them, where tall plane and chestnut trees provide shade. Four monuments to Hungarian freedom fighters complete the architectural appearance of this extension of the six-lane road, which from here as far as Heroes' Square takes on almost the character of a city promenade, especially as the former bridleways between the road and the pavements have become footpaths (of course there are some drivers who, against regulations, park their cars here).

Heroes' Square and the Millenial Monument: Népköztársaság útja runs into **Hösök tere** (Heroes' Square), in the middle of which is the **Millennial Monument**. It was created in 1896 by the architect Albert Schickedanz and the sculptor György Zala for the 1,000th anniversary of the so-called "Taking of the Land". In the middle of the monumental group is a pillar, 118-ft (36-m) high, crowned by the figure of the Archangel Gabriel. The pedestal is adorned by a bronze equestrian group with Prince Árpád and the six tribal leaders. Beyond, forming two semicircles, are colonnades and between their pillars are statues of several kings, rulers and princes of Transylvania of Hungarian descent. Not all the rulers of Hungary have been immortalised here: all the bearers of St Stephen's Crown who

Right, Heroes' Square as playground.

BUDAPEST BY NIGHT

The sun gradually disappears behind Castle Hill and the pale, scrubbed blue of the daytime sky slowly turns inky black. In the cafes and restaurants, in the bars and espresszós, nightlife begins. Around 32-esek Square heavily made-up women appear, wearing miniskirts and plunging decolletés, and in front of the Józsefváros church, Bishop Pázmány, who tried so hard to reconvert Hungary to Catholicism in the early 17th century, watches from his pedestal, powerless to prevent the indecent goings-on.

Traffic decreases, and the taxis now dominate the streets, driving up and down the boulevards, but the rattle of tram wheels becomes deafeningly loud. People taking a stroll linger in Vörösmarty tér, forming circles round fire-eaters and street mimes, or swinging their feet to the rhythm of a South American band.

Theatres, concert halls and bars with live music swallow up the pleasure seekers disembarking from the first of the night buses. The musical pub Mészöly Söröző (Beer Room) fills up with a mixed audience; a jazz band strikes up on the upper floor, while below, in the bar, people are whetting their whistles with beer or fröccs, so-called spritzer. Jazz fans meet regularly in Kati's Jazzbár, where by this time the audience is being brought to fever pitch.

While the theatre performances are gradually coming to a close, there are more and more tables free in the pubs, the smells from the kitchen are no longer overpowering, but the air in the pubs is now barely breathable. This is the moment when, in the nightclubs such as Moulin Rouge, Savoy, Lidó or Orpheum, the oily compéres come into their own, as do the go-go girls and the dancers. This is the time for champagne, fat Havanas and flirting glances.

The night makes its early start in Maxim's Varieté, and begins somewhat later in the Lidó. Here there is a little band tucked away in a dim niche, and then the master of ceremonies appears on stage with his assistant, a very young girl. The show in the Orpheum is less over the top, the volume of the music is softer. Vocal imitators, who can mimic just about any style of singing from Sinatra to Gilbert Bécaud, work together with the go-go girls to draw the audience's attention to the stage. The old Moulin Rouge attracts its guests by comparing itself to the Parisian place of entertainment. But even if Budapest is known as the Paris of the East, by midnight there is no comparison at all.

Lovers of the night throng the Trojka söröző in Népköztársság útja to watch videos, or they go for the strong coffee in Pierrot's at Fortuna utca in the Castle district, where a pianist is still playing. Malicious tongues may claim that there is no nightlife in Budapest, but this is simply not true. However, like all the beautiful things in Hungary, it flourishes in hiding.

Budapest's very own individual charm unfolds in the grey hours of morning when the first of the joggers bump into the last of the drunks, when the cleaning machines are sweeping the streets and pavements for the working day. You can go shopping in the night market at the 7 November Square or in Éjjel-nappal csemege, to buy fruit and vegetables for the day or just for the fun of shopping at an hour when sensible people are in bed.

When the night sky is reflected for the last time, grey-blue in the waters of the Danube and the waves reflect the first light, when the shadows of trees and buildings take shape, the blackbirds start their morning concert and the only people you meet are those like yourself. For some people, that is a happy moment in Budapest.

came from the house of Habsburg are missing, which means that 4 centuries of history have simply been ignored. The second half of the 19th century, after all, marked the peak of nationalism and chauvinism, especially in Central Europe.

Museum of Visual Arts: The Millenial Monument is flanked by two buildings dating from the end of the previous century. To the left of the memorial is the **Szépmüvésti Múzeum** (Museum of Visual Arts), designed in imitation of a Greek temple, to the right is the **Mücsarnok** (Art Gallery), in which special exhibitions are held.

The Budapest Museum of the Visual Arts has always been among the top rank of art collections in Europe and probably in the world. The **Graphic Collection** is most famous, ranging from drawings by Leonardo, Rembrandt, Dürer, Lucas Cranach and Rubens to works by Delacroix, Corot, Courbet, Cézanne, Monet, Manet, Renoir, Sisley, Picasso and Toulouse-Lautrec. There are believed to be about 10,000 sketches in the collection. In the **Prints Chamber**, too, all the famous names of this branch of the arts are represented.

Of no less importance is the **Gallery of Old Masters**. The core of its stock is formed by the former collection of the Esterházy princes, which was sold to the state in 1872. It comprised more than 600 paintings, about 3,600 drawings and around 50,000 prints. Among the paintings, apart from works by Titian, Tintoretto, Veronese, Murillo, El Greco, Ribera, Rubens and Brueghel, is Raffael's Madonna and Child with St John, the pride of the museum. The collection of works by Hungarian artists is housed in the National Gallery in the castle.

Városliget (City Park): Behind Heroes' Square lies the **Városliget** (City Park), the biggest park in the city. In it is a lake with an island on which a highly romanticised castle is to be found. It is not particularly old and also owes its existence to the Millenial celebrations. This is **Vajdahunyad-vára**, a copy of the former palace of János Hunyadi in Vajdahunyad, which today lies in Romania and is known as Hunedoara. In winter the castle serves as a romantic backdrop for hundreds of skaters on the artificial skating rink.

In the castle courtyard is an interesting monument to certain aspects of Hungarian history: the figure of *Anonymous* by Miklós Ligeti, portaying the nameless chronicler who is believed to have written the oldest chronicle of Hungarian history in the 12th and 13th centuries. The statue shows a figure in a monk's robe, the features of his face deliberately obscured by the shadow of his hood and barely recognisable.

Also within the bounds of the City Park are the Széchenyi Baths and Swimming Pool, the Gundel Restaurant, the zoo, the main circus of the capital and Vidám Park, which is an amusement park similar to the Prater in Vienna.

Left and **right**, City Park and Vidám Park – a children's playground.

EUROPE'S OLDEST UNDERGROUND RAILWAY

Budapest can boast the oldest underground railway on the continent of Europe. It began operations in 1896, at the time of the "Millennium", the 1,000th anniversary of the settlement of the Hungarians in the Danube valley. The metro in Paris followed in 1898, in Berlin in 1902: the Stadtbahn of Vienna (which was actually a sunken tram system, not an underground railway) came into existence in 1898. The Hungarian capital's system is the third oldest in the world, preceded only by London and Glasgow: New York did not follow until 1904. This is reason enough for the people of Budapest to be proud of their "Ferencz József földaltti villamos vasút" (thus the official name).

Up until 1970 the original line was the only one in the capital. Since then, it has been joined by two new metro routes: the east-west connection and the north-south link. All three meet in the middle at – or rather underneath – Deák tér, the nodal point of the metropolis.

This is where the Underground Museum is to be found, housed in a disused section of tunnel of the first underground. Here the visitor can learn practically everything about this underground railway, which was well ahead of its time. In the museum you can see the old carriages of the railway. With their copper panels and lacquered wood they seem quite home-like.

Only one example of the "Royal" or "Court Coach" survives. The emperor Franz Joseph I took his place in this splendid carriage on 8 May 1896, when he visited Budapest for the millennial celebrations and also inspected the underground railway, opened only 6 days before. This carriage, in a rebuilt form, was still in circulation in 1955 – at any rate, that is what it says in the museum.

Here visitors also learn that this first underground railway in mainland Europe was not only built in a remarkably short time (within 20 months), but also had to start operations within the same time limit. The official departments made it a condition of allowing construction to go ahead that the railway had to be finished in time for the millennial celebrations. A copy of the document allowing construction to proceed can be seen in the museum. It is dated 9 August 1894. At the time, the electric underground railway was described as "one of the most notable developments in the capital". One prophecy was soon fulfilled: "This railway will shortly become one of the most essential means of mass transport."

The old underground line, drawn in yellow on the maps, originally ran from Vörösmarty tér to the City Park, following below ground the line of the smart street of Népköztársaság útja, where the opera and some theatres are to be found. The route was 4,034 yards (3,689 metres) long. After World War II it was extended as far as the new residential areas around Mexikói út.

The capital's metro network, which should be finished by the turn of the millennium, at present comprises the 6.3 mile (10.1 km) long east-west link, drawn in red on the maps, which runs from the Keleti pályaudvar (Eastern Railway Station) to the Déli pályaudvar (Southern).

As it passes through almost every important public transport junction in the city, it is one of the most frequented connections in the capital. The north-south link, drawn in blue, has not yet been completed. At present it runs from Élmunkás tér (around the level of Margaret Island and the Árpád Bridge) to the southeastern district of Kispest. When it is finally completed, the line will be 12.9 miles (20.7 km) long.

The trains run at very short intervals, so that it is possible to get from one end of Budapest to the other very quickly. During its first few years of operation no tickets were necessary for the metro; you simply threw a forint into the money box at the entrance to the platform. Nowadays, in times of economic reforms, you need a 5-forint ticket, which has to be inspected at the entrance.

Right, construction of the Budapest subway system (1890).

CHISELLED AND CAST

The 15th of March is the Hungarians' most solemn festival. It is not a church festival – the Magyars are not a particularly religious people – but a national one. On 15 March 1848, the revolution of the Hungarian people against the house of Habsburg began – with the declamation of his poem by a young poet. Sándor Petöfi, standing on the steps of what is now the National Museum, read out his incendiary poem:

"Arise, Hungarians, the time has come, it's now or never…to throw away our chains…we will no longer be slaves.

Arise, our homeland calls, Magyars!
Slaves we have been, traitors
To the spirit of our fathers,
Who have found no peace in the grave,
Since freedom has been shamed.
Let us swear by the God of our fore-fathers:
Never again
Will we bow to the tyrant!
Never again!"

For 15 months the Hungarians – not for the first time and not for the last time in their thousand years of history – fought in vain for liberty. Foreigners, too, fought beside them against Austrian and Russian troops. The Pole Józef Bem had the rank of general and commanded an army of revolutionaries before fleeing into exile and becoming a pasha in Turkey.

Sándor Petöfi is believed to have died in the last big battle in 1849. Today, cast in bronze, he stands on the Pest Danube embankment, with a determined look, his right hand pointing to the way forward. On 15 March the little square in front of the memorial is covered with flowers and red, white and green paper Hungarian flags. Here, in the neighbourhood of the university, it is traditional for groups of students to gather before marching in a wide arc over the

Statue at the Agricultural Museum in the castle of Vajdahunyad.

Margaret Bridge to the other side of the Danube and the memorial of the revolutionary general Józef Bem. The same statue, i.e. Bem's, was the goal of tens of thousands of people on 23 October 1956, who at the time wanted to show their support for the Polish struggle for freedom. It was, indirectly, the start of the revolt against the Soviet occupation, those 10 days which, if they didn't shake the world, certainly shook Central Europe.

The Hungarians love their monuments and they have many of them, not only for the purpose of holding demonstrations in front of them. One researcher of monuments – yes, even that profession exists in the Hungarian capital – counted around 10,000 statues, monuments and marble memorial plaques in Budapest alone. Next to the Budapest Parliament, the poet Attila József gazes thoughtfully at the Danube, while on the other side an old man, the "Red Count" Mihály Károlyi, every inch an aristocrat, leans on his stick. Károlyi took the helm of the newly founded republic in 1918, after the collapse of the monarchy. The square beyond the Parliament is dominated by the so-called Heroes of Liberation Ferenc Rákóczi (rebelled against the Hasburgs) and Lajos Kossuth.

However, the pantheon of Hungarian history is to be found in **Hösök tere**, in Heroes' Square. In 1896 the Hungarians celebrated the assumed 1,000th anniversary of the "Taking of the Land", the year in which the first Magyar tribes – who came from the other side of the Urals range – are believed to have moved from the region between the Carpathians and the fringes of the Alps to the Hungarian plain.

There they are, some of the rulers from Hungarian history, lined up in a semicircle. From King István (Stephen) I, who converted Hungary to Christianity, to Count Batthyány, whom the Austrians had executed in 1849, here is the line of Hungarian politics and history, which was not always as glorious

There are four lions altogether on the Chain Bridge, named after Count Széchenyi.

as the heroic, determined expressions on the faces of the princes, kings, bishops and politicians.

One of these men of bronze now no longer stands in the place where the self-confident people of Budapest had placed him before the turn of the century. Franz Joseph I, Emperor of Austria and King of Hungary, today turns his kindly but not too intelligent gaze on other members of the highest ruling house – in a former chicken coop in a suburb of Budapest. This is where the Budapest museums administration had hidden the great ones of the *ancien régime*, demoted after the Communist takeover in 1948. In the early 1960s this curious collection was expanded to take in a few Soviet soldiers, intimidating figures which had been set up in the face of the Budapest public, who were no longer all that friendly towards Communists. As often happened in their married life together, the statue of Franz Joseph's wife Elizabeth (known as "Sissi"), soon left the side of her

husband. Queen Elizabeth – Erzsébet Királyné in Hungarian – has, since 1986, been sitting once again next to the white Danube bridge named after her, though not on the Pest side, as in previous years, but in Buda – within sight of the former royal palace. The city administration of Budapest arranged for this re-instatement in honour of the special regard which the restless Bavarian princess and her Hungarian subjects felt for one another. Even today, occasionally, there are still flowers lying on the graceful statue of the former queen of Hungary, whose name has also been given to a long street and a hotel in the city centre.

Many statues of the Habsburgs were melted down in the early 1950s and turned into new monuments of the walrus-moustached dictator from Georgia (Joseph Stalin) or the Communist leader Mátyás Rákosi – "Stalin's best pupil" – who was hated throughout Hungary. "Habsburg blood flows in Stalin's veins" – the people of Budapest joked and laughed, fearfully and nervously. At the time, bands of Stalinists terrorised the whole country. The biggest of all the statues of Stalin in Budapest, the one near to Heroes' Square, fell in October 1956 amid the cheers of the truly revolutionary masses of the time. The hammer blows delivered to the Stalin monument were the first signals, heard far and wide, of de-Stalinisation, with which some East European countries are still struggling today.

On the site of the once god-like Stalin there now stands a big block of red marble, and in front of it, looking rather lost but still slightly bigger than life size, is Lenin. The father of the Soviet revolution still watches the 1 May parades from this spot, admittedly with a somewhat less self-confident air than in the previous decades, which were ruled by the Communist Independent Socialist Workers' Party.

The biggest statue, which dominates all of Budapest, is to be found on the

Left, the Kuruz leader György Dózsa. **Below**, a nation of heroes, even though they have never won a war?

Citadel on Gellért Hill. It is the statue of a young woman, obviously a goddess of victory, bearing a palm branch in her raised arms. She is flanked by two groups of statues depicting wildly battling heroes, and is intended to be a memorial to the Soviet liberation of April 1945.

This liberation – as a newspaper in Budapest has recently reminded its readers – is referred to (historically quite correctly) as an occupation in Soviet school and history books. Actually, this lady should have been holding an aeroplane. She was commissioned by the governor, Admiral Miklós Horthy, during World War II, in memory of his son István, who was shot down on the Russian front. The Soviet general who occupied Budapest liked this statue, commissioned by a Fascist dictator, so much that he had a palm branch stuck into her hands and let her be erected as planned. The sculptor who in 1947 carried out this alteration, requested by the new rulers, without protest was called Zsigmond Kisfaludi Strobl.

In Budapest the external symbols of Soviet might – the red stars, monuments, pictures and slogans – are more thinly spread than in any other capital of communist Eastern Europe, but nonetheless they are as well and as visibly placed as if a sort of monumental strategist had picked out the most important positions. The Liberation Monument on Gellért Hill is only one example. Two more are the **Ostjapenko Memorial** on the M1/ M7 motorway and the **Lenin statue** in front of the Csepel works.

Lieutenant Ostjapenko, a soldier of the Red Army, was sent in January 1945 with a white flag as an emissary to the German troops barricaded into Budapest. The young officer never returned and the Germans fought on. Today the little Soviet lieutenant stands beside the most important exit road to the west. The road goes on past Ostjapenko to Lake Balaton and to Vienna. The

Below left, a hussar – synonymous with Hungary. Below, sculpture by Margit Kovács.

Budapest police like to hide behind the big statue to catch and tame over-confident fast drivers from the West right at the entrance to the city. Ostjapenko is a meeting place for hitchhikers and an easily visible reference point for drivers who have lost their way.

Lenin, too, knows the right way to go. This is the other Lenin, erected in front of the Csepel steelworks, the red heart of the Budapest working class. Energetic, determined and self-confident, Lenin stretches out his hand. A few years ago this statue was the talk of all Hungary; not because of its artistry, however, as it is too reminiscent of the mass production of the workshops of Socialist Realism. On the contrary, the "Father of the Workers" had become the butt of the country's jokes. On the very night after an official announcement of drastic price rises an unknown worker, as a sign of protest, had placed something in the outstretched hand. It was a small thing, but well known to all Hungarians from their own kitchen

tables – a piece of bread and dripping.

Hardly anyone goes to Budapest to look at the Communist statues, to which even the people of Budapest hardly pay any attention, seeing them as familiar but by no means loved figures. Foreign visitors will probably prefer to walk up to the castle or stroll through the old town of Buda. There, they will pass by the statue of the general Andreas Hadik, who fought against the Turks. A travel guide may be there explaining to her group the traditions of the brave hussar and the story behind that statue. The ladies in the group shove their way to the front, to listen attentively. The gentlemen stand obligingly to one side and admire the equestrian statue from an unusual point of view – the rear. The memorial is covered in verdigris, but something glitters by the belly of the horse. Once a year, according to tradition, the students of Budapest set out to polish this something. These are the sexual organs of the fiery steed, and they gleam of brilliant gold...

THE BATHS
OF BUDAPEST

The figure is impressive. There are 123 hot springs in the Budapest area, which altogether serve 31 medicinal baths, lidos and swimming pools.

Does this mean that the Hungarian capital can also be described as a spa? To label it so would not be quite incorrect. Before World War I and in the years between the wars, before mass tourism existed, Budapest attracted visitors with its medicinal springs and its opportunities for cosmopolitan entertainment. One would come to Budapest to take the waters, spending the day in the baths appropriate to one's health condition. The evenings would be reserved wholly for entertainment. There were more than enough hotels, theatres, bars and other establishments to while away those hours.

The battles fought in the last months of World War II heavily damaged the baths, the hotels and also the entertainment establishments, and not all the damage has been repaired to this day. Over the last 15 years a series of hotels have been built, and old ones have been renovated and modernised, so that it would be possible once more to accommodate the guests who might come to take the waters in Budapest.

However, the extension and modernisation of the baths have unfortunately not kept pace with this process at all. All the baths which existed before the war have been resurrected to their former glory, but unfortunately, they no longer meet with modern demands and thus are not able to accommodate all those who want to take a plunge. Consequently, there is a mad rush for the Turkish baths as well as for both the open-air and indoor swimming pools, and this commotion apparently is not to everyone's liking.

Budapest as a city of baths is definitely a legacy of the Turks, although they were not the first to discover the hot springs at the feet of the Buda Hills and their therapeutic effects. The Romans, as excavations have proved, had bathing establishments in Aquincum. In the Middle Ages, too, travellers from the west described the baths below the castle. However, it was the Turks who, from the 16th century on, created a whole network of baths in Budapest.

Of those baths from that time which are still "functioning" today, visitors from the West, travelling to Budapest by car, will first come across the **Rudas Baths** at the western bridgehead of the Elizabeth Bridge. It can be recognised by its hemispherical dome which covers an octagonal pool. The gleaming green pillars around the pool support a barrel vault with eight gaps in it. For this reason, the Rudas Baths are also often known as the "baths with the green pillars".

The Rudas Baths, like the nearby **Ráczfürdö** (Serbian Baths, also known as Imrefürdö), date from the second half of the 16th century. These baths are fed by the various springs at the foot of Gellért Hill. The mineral composition of the waters and the uses to which it is put, whether as a drinking or a bathing cure, vary accordingly. The Serbian Baths, incidentally, derive their name from the Serbs who at that time had settled along the southern wing of the castle. However, their quarter of Tabán no longer exists today.

Upriver, on the right bank of the Danube, there are more baths dating from Turkish times. One such establishment is the **Király fürdo**, the King's Baths in Föutca, not far from Bem József tér. Its name is derived not from former royal patrons but from a Mr König (German for king), who bought the baths at the turn of the last century and extended them, later Magyarising his German name to Király. The baths originally date from the period between 1566 and 1570 and are considered by many patrons to be the most beautiful of the former Turkish baths of Budapest. The building is indeed very harmonious in style. Above the octagonal pool of the bathing hall are great dome arches, with little glass panes in different colours which permit the light to fall through into the hall in a subdued manner, creating an atmosphere of relaxation and well-being.

Further upriver, where Rose Hill slopes down towards the Danube, there is another Turkish bath. This establishment is the **Császárfürdö** (Emperor's Baths). These must be one of the first Turkish baths in Buda, for there is an inscription chiselled in the stone which states that they were renovated as early as 1570 by the governor Sokoli Mustafa Pasha.

The **Lukácsfürdö** (Lukas Medicinal and Swimming Baths) are linked to the Császárfürdö. The therapeutic parts of the baths can only be used on medical advice, but the three thermal swimming pools are open the year round and can be used by the general public.

Nearly all the baths dating from Turkish times have had extensions added, which contain swimming pools, tub baths, massage and other treatment rooms. Before visiting one of these baths you should find out about the composition of the springs concerned and also about the opening hours. For instance, the thermal bath of the Rudas Baths is open only to men, while the big pool of the Király Baths is open for men one day and for women the next.

Of the more modern baths on the right bank of the Danube, it is probably the **Gellért Baths** at the foot of the hill with the same name which are the most popular. These were opened immediately after World War II and are in a way a multi-function concern, comprising medicinal baths, pools for sport and amusement, and a first class hotel. The architectural framework, with its red marble, gilded pillars and turquoise coloured tiles, was intended to give a Middle Eastern flavour. Gellért offers an indoor swimming pool and, in the summer, a swimming pool with wave effects in the open-air.

For some, a diversion by the pool.

There are also therapeutic baths under medical supervision: carbonated, steam, mud and sulphur baths and anything else that can be extracted from the 22 springs which feed the baths. Apart from all these features, the Gellért Baths are a firmly established institution of social life for the people of Budapest, and not even World War II and socialist restructuring have been able to change that.

In Budapest the baths are not only situated on the right bank. There are some on Margaret Island and in Pest too. On the long, stretched-out Margaret Island the new five-star **Thermal Hotel** offers the most modern hydrotherapy and physiotherapy, with equipment to match. Next door is the **Grand Hotel**, which dates from before the war but which has since been renovated, and which also has baths. Its guests can make use of the facilities of the neighbouring Thermal Hotel.

Young people in particular like to go to the **Palatinus strandfürdö** (Palatinus open-air baths), which have several pools with water from thermal springs at differing temperatures. Its broad lawns can hold about 30,000 people. Sports swimmers train in **Hajós Alfréd Nemzeti Sportuszoda** (Alfréd Hajós National Sports Swimming Pool), which is named after the double-medal victor at the first Olympic games of the modern age, who designed the pool in his role as architect. International swimming competitions in the capital mostly take place on the island.

In Pest the **Szechényi Baths** in the City Park take pride of place. These are medicinal baths, but they also have three large open-air swimming pools which are open all the year round.

The appropriate hydrotherapy is available for a number of different conditions, but in general it could be said that the hot springs of Budapest are recommended for the treatment of degenerative ailments of the joints and of the spine, meniscus problems and neuralgia, gout and rheumatism.

Sensuality in the Széchenyi Baths.

THE OTHER
BUDAPEST

A typical potential visitor would have the desire to describe the city of Budapest in a different way from that used by other people.

Again and again one finds the same mixture: every travel writer mentions the Turkish and the modernised baths, the Classical cafés and those done up in the "old style", the traces of the monarchy and the villas of the nouveaux riches, the now rather expensive "in" bars and the "really good" pubs which the local people jealously guard as their own private secrets (but then apparently go and tell everyone about them anyway). The visitor can enjoy this version of Budapest, there's no doubt about it. But the Budapest that doesn't get into Baedeker – the special city – is the one that in fact doesn't get served up to tourists on a plate.

As we all know, the showpiece of the city is the much-described Danube embankment, where the *korzó* (Corso) runs between the promenade cafés and the "reborn" luxury hotels. It caters for all the tourists from the West, for the well-off of Budapest and for "black market" dealers experienced in the handling of currencies.

Also named after the Danube embankment is one of the most interesting and controversial institutions of unofficial Budapest: the so-called Rakpart (Embankment) Club, where all sorts of subjects are discussed, including those which are – even after the policy of "opening up" – considered taboo by the government. This popular debating club makes no distinctions between Party and opposition members, between young and old, and between individualists and conformists.

In the beginning meetings of the Embankment Club would be held in private homes or cellar bars. More recently, the favoured location is the Jurten Theatre in the **Népliget**. This place

is now bursting at the seams. It is also a meeting place for many other "grassroots" movements which apparently have mushroomed overnight. The Rakpart Club is also where the nationalist-dominated populist Democratic Forum meets, as do the many of the small urban, intellectual groups which are members of the "Federation of Free Democrats."

During the evenings discussion among friends. You do not have to know the language of the country in order to pick up the fearless rebelliousness, the grand gesture, the fiery pathos and the general atmosphere of starting afresh which characterises the youth of Budapest today.

If you want to visit the theatre, don't miss out on a walk through the **Népliget** (People's Park). In contrast to the much more famous **Városliget** (City Park) behind Hösök tere (Heroes' Square), nowadays a definite feature of every tour of Budapest. Once the territory of the upper classes, the Népliget belongs,

Left, quality control in one of the salami factories of Szeged. Right, farmer's wife.

as is obvious from the name alone, to the "people", that conglomerate of workers and intellectuals. These are the same people who, in the neighbouring football stadium of the traditional club Ferencváros, frequently engage in heated discussions of academic-like depth and detail about the flight path of a precise flanking kick.

Various publications like to mention that strolling and relaxating on Margaret Island is characteristic of the people of Budapest. It may also be among the middle-class virtues to order *fekete* (black) coffee with cake (coffee with milk in it is only drunk as a light beige breakfast drink); to go to the Grand Hotel, now restored to its former glory; never to set foot in the Thermal Hotel, which is "black listed" among connoisseurs not just because of the strong smell of sulphur, but because of its modern atmosphere.

But, to be honest, it would surely be more pleasant to wander down the long Csepel Island, much of which has been left to Nature, to observe the anglers at their easygoing activities and, if you're lucky, to be able to grill over an open fire a fish from the Danube that you have caught yourself…

If, when on Csepel Island, you do want to do something for your knowledge of culture, you can visit the Baroque **Palace of Ráckeve**, the first building constructed for Prince Eugene of Savoy by Lukas von Hildebrandt, the architect of the Belvedere in Vienna. Or you can go and see a Serbian Orthodox church in the middle of town dating from 1487.

To the south of the capital, the romantic landscape of the Danube awaits you; to the north, loud screeches of enjoyment on Óbuda Island. The attractions in the 9 May Park are a bit more modest than those in the more central **Vidám Park**, the funfair at the edge of the City Park, but the amusement it provides is by no means less.

If you happen to be in the area, there is the district of **Óbuda** itself with its hid-

Critical young FIDESZ communists.

den treasures. It is well worthwhile and most pleasant to stroll through the few remaining old alleys with their marvellously restored houses and glimpses of secluded backyards. Then you come to the other side of the coin: the gloomy rows of modern apartment blocks, which form the most unsuitable background imaginable for the excavations of the Roman city of Aquincum; nightmarish dormitory hives, destined to be the slums of tomorrow. Let's get out of here and move on...

Nearby is one of the tourists' favourite spots: the **Rómaipart** (Roman Bank) bathing beach along the Danube. What a contrast to the famous baths of Budapest! Here in the natural surroundings along the Danube, people are much less inhibited than in the elegant and formal atmosphere of the Széchenyi, Lukács or Gellért Baths. To make use of an analogy from the world of operetta, this is a scene more for commoners, not the aristocrats. In surroundings like these, differences of opinion can lead to violent intervention. These differences are very rarely about politics. Whichever country they belong to, people are brought to emotional boiling point by sport.

Budapest also moves with the times. For years, football had its undisputed position as the top popular sport. It is now on the verge of losing its dominant role. The new delight of the masses is Formula One motor racing. To the east of Budapest the **Hungaroring**, the first such racetrack in a Socialist country, has been created from the rolling ground of the puszta. You can experience the roar of the engines, the wild and exciting attraction of speed, the atmosphere of the wide world when the Formula One circus with all its camp followers arrives in the country once every year.

In order to be part of this cosmopolitan scene, many people in Budapest are prepared to sacrifice a couple of weeks' wages. This way, they keep a tiny door at home open to the world.

Sport for the masses: Formula One at the Hungaroring.

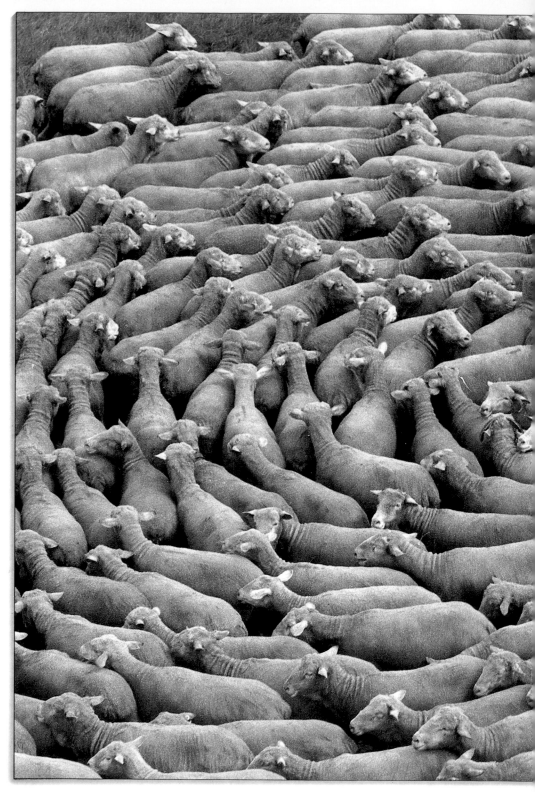

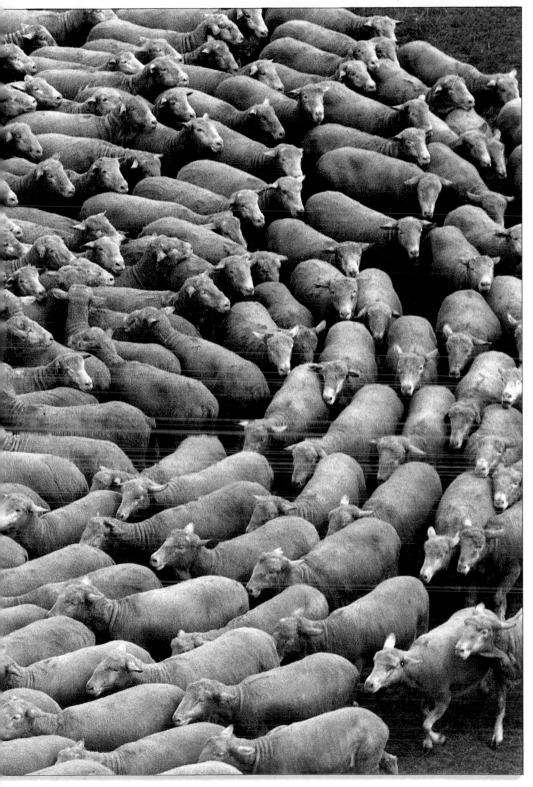

EXCURSIONS

Budapest is the starting point for a number of worthwhile excursions. First of all, there is the Danube Bend, to the north of the capital, where the river suddenly leaves its west-to-east flow and takes a sharp bend to the south. On the right bank of the Danube, in the midst of quite delightful scenery, lie **Szentendre, Visegrád** and **Esztergom**, towns with a rich and often dramatic history. **Vác**, the Baroque town on the left bank of the Danube, is another place which ought to be seen.

If you love still waters, you need go no further than **Lake Velenceitó**, a paradise for birds of almost dreamy tranquility. If you prefer historic places, you can take a look around **Székesfehérvár**, which is near the lake.

If you're in Hungary, you will probably want to get to know the proverbial puszta. The best opportunity is provided by a visit to the national park of the **Bugac Puszta**, near **Kecskemét**, an hour's drive to the south of Budapest.

These three trips will give you some indication of the variety of landscapes in Hungary. If you have any time left over, you will certainly not regret taking a trip westwards, to **Tata** and to **Zsámbék**.

The Danube Bend: Szentendre is only 12 miles (19 km) upriver from Budapest and is probably the most picturesque place you could imagine. It can easily be reached by the rapid railway system (HÉV) from Batthyány tér, by bus, by car along trunk road no. 11 and by boat during the summer. The city is interesting from three points of view: as the spiritual and cultural centre of the Orthodox Serbs in Hungary; as a former important and busy centre of trade serving the southeast region of Europe; and nowadays as an artists' colony and tourist attraction.

Its skyline is dominated by the towers of seven churches: four Serbian Orthodox, two Catholic and one Reformed. In earlier years there used to be six Orthodox church with Serbian names; names such as Ciprovacka, Preobrazenska, Blagovestenska. They all date from the 18th century and were built by those Serbs who had settled in the town since the end of the 17th century after fleeing from the Turks.

The Serbs, however, were not the only people to turn Szentendre into a trading centre of the first rank. In the 18th century, Greek and Dalmatian families settled in St Andrea. They also had trading links stretching out to all points of the compass. Their houses around **Marx tér** still bear witness to their wealth. In the middle of the square is the Greek Orthodox **Merchant's Cross**, erected in 1763 by the "Privileged Serbian Trading Company".

The wealth of Szentendre depended in large part on the trading privileges which the Austrian emperors had bestowed on the citizens of the town.

A centre of the Orthodox Church: In Marx tér is the **Blagosvestenska Church**. As a museum, it is the only Orthodox Church easily accessible to a broad spectrum of the public. It has a fine Baroque portal. Inside the building, the great iconostasis, carved of lime wood, is fascinating.

The **Belgrad Cathedral** on the Castle Hill, near the medieval, originally Gothic Catholic church, is the Serbian Orthodox episcopal church. It is surrounded by tall trees and a wall with gates that are locked most of the time. If you want to see the church, you may probably find someone in the adjacent building who will kindly unlock it for you. This is where the bishop once used to take his seat, but the administration was moved to Buda quite some time ago. The main entrance to the church, with the Rococo carving on the massive oak door, is remarkable. Inside, two pillars of red marble support the gallery, below which the women took their places, while the somewhat lower central section of the church was reserved for men. The chancel and the iconostasis are remarkable for their ornate carving.

The collection of **Orthodox church art** in Engels utca is impressive. The icons, the goldsmiths' work, the paintings and the sacred vestments, dating from the 16th to the 19th century, on exhibition here help you to recognise the important position which the Serbian Orthodox church once had in Hungary. It is also a pleasure to see how the influence of Central European Rococo had a soothing effect on the conforming styles of Byzantine art.

Only a few Serbian families still live in Szentendre today. There is an atmosphere of mortality and decay around the churches and in the nearby cemetery. Otherwise, Szentendre is a very lively place.

A colony of artists: Artists began to settle here as early as the turn of the century, by which time the town had lost its importance as a trading centre. They set up their studios, founded galleries, arranged exhibitions, and in time Szentendre developed into an artists' colony. It still is one today. This is proved by the museums with their permanent exhibitions of works by painters such as Károly Ferenczi and his children, also famous as artists, by Béla Czóbel, Jenö Barcsay or Lajos Vajda, as well as by the works by contemporary painters, graphic artists and sculptors which are on show in the galleries. The permanent exhibition of ceramics by Margit Kovács, housed in the vaults of one of the old merchant's houses, should not be ignored. Margit Kovács, influenced by folk art and the way it was used for everyday objects, created her own highly individual world of jugs and plates, figures and reliefs.

In recent years tourism has taken over the town, and a trip to Szentendre is on the programme of almost every tour of Budapest. Antique and souvenir shops have opened along the Danube and in the narrow streets of the town centre. In the main season it does get quite

Szentendre is the centre of the Serbian Orthodox Church in Hungary.

crowded. In the evenings, though, when the streets are empty and most of the tourists have left, the town's charm returns once more.

Visegrád: If you drive further up the Danube on highway no. 11, after 14 miles (22 km) you will come to **Visegrád**, historically speaking the most important town of the Danube Bend. First and foremost, Visegrád is a reminder of Hungary's greatest Renaissance king, Matthias Corvinus. Here, in the second half of the 15th century, was where he had his residence. Over the last few decades, its remains have been carefully excavated from the heaps of rubble over the centuries.

Visegrád is also in an extraordinarily attractive part of the Danube valley. The ranges of the Börzsöny Hills on the left and the Pilis Hills on the right have narrowed it, and the scenery is reminiscent of the Rhine or the Moselle, except that there is far less traffic on the river and along the banks.

The royal castle: If you really want to experience Visegrád, you will have to drive up to the castle, which rises steeply from the river. From the bastions and terraces you will have an astonishing view down into the valley and further out across the landscape of the hills of northeast Hungary. There are two good roads leading up to the castle and to the nearby Hotel Silvanus. The hotel's situation makes it one of the most scenically attractive in the whole of Hungary.

The best preserved part of the castle is the pentagonal gate tower, through which you enter the castle site. From the ruins of the inner part of the castle you can still see today how far the site originally extended and how its separate elements were linked together via the various inner courtyards, all of which lie at different levels.

Visegrád was, after all, not just any old castle. For years St Stephen's Crown and the other coronation insignia were kept here. However, it was also from this place that they were

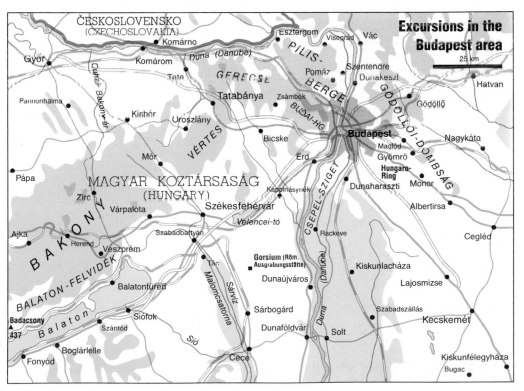

removed, for the first time in their complex history.

The royal residence was at the foot of the castle hill, near the Danube. It was a generously laid out complex of buildings, where the kings of the houses of Anjou and Luxembourg had already had their palaces. King Zsigmond of the house of Luxembourg extended the palace at the foot of the castle. However, the palace achieved its full splendour under Matthias Hunyadi, known as Corvinus. Matthias (Mátyás in Hungarian) was the younger son of János Hunyadi, general and regent for King Lasdislas V. Matthias was brought out of imprisonment in Prague and crowned king in 1458. He was considered a true Renaissance prince: an excellent soldier, administrator and linguist, and a patron of learning and the arts. His collections of manuscripts, statues, paintings and jewels were famous all over Europe.

The 350 rooms and halls that are supposed to have existed here lay on

three different levels. There was a series of courtyards, with fountains of red marble to cool the air. The courtyards and terraces were linked by broad stone staircases, with balustrades constructed by the most skilful stonemason. Not all parts of the palace have yet been brought to the light of day. The most important of the sections still underground is the wing in which the king's third wife, Beatrix of Aragon, gathered musicians and artists from all over Europe around her.

The sections of the palace which have already been excavated can be found in the museum of Visegrád. These are the remains of fountains, stair rails, pillars and other structural and decorative elements. The museum is to be found in the hexagonal **Solomon Tower**, 102 ft (31 m) high, on the eastern edge of the castle. Among the exhibits are parts of the late Gothic **Lion Fountain**. The fountain which now stands on the original site in front of the wall of the uppermost courtyard is only a replica. However, the three side walls of the Renaissance fountain in the ceremonial courtyard are original. In the Solomon Tower museum you can also see a reconstruction of another palace fountain, the late Gothic **Anjou Fountain** from the older part of the palace.

The massive Solomon Tower with its five stories was part of the lower castle. From here traffic on the Danube and on the Danube bank could be easily controlled. No-one knows why the tower bears this name, for when the Hungarian king Solomon (1063-74) was imprisoned in Visegrád after his fall this particular tower had not yet existed. It was not to be built for another two centuries. The tower is linked to the upper castle by a partly-ruined wall. It is possible to follow this wall on foot and climb up to the castle, but it is more comfortable to drive up one of the two roads.

Esztergom: If you are going to the Danube Bend, then you simply must visit Esztergom, 12 miles (20 km) to the

Baroque palaces on the streets of Esztergom.

west of Visegrád (the distance from Budapest to Visegrád via Dorog is 30 miles/48 km). This is where the scenery along the Danube, described over the centuries with such enthusiasm by travellers (among them Hans Christian Andersen and the Austrian Franz Grillparzer), really begins.

The town of Esztergom has roots that go far back into history. It was the first residence of the rulers of the Árpád dynasty. It was here that King Stephen was christened, and it was here that he was crowned in the year 1000, or probably a year later, with the crown that legend claims Pope Sylvester sent him from Rome, which as St Stephen's Crown became the symbol of the Hungarian nation, even though it dates from the 12th century.

The spiritual centre of Hungary: Esztergom is the oldest diocese in Hungary. Its bishops have borne and still bear the title Primate of Hungary. Nowadays the bishop of Esztergom, as chairman of the Bishop's Conference, is the spiritual head of the Catholic church in Hungary.

The symbol of historic and spiritual significance of the town is the **Várhegy** (Castle Hill), crowned by the Classical **Basilica** of outstanding proportions, which dates from the first half of last century. It is the biggest and most massive church in Hungary, with a west facade having a total length of 387 ft (118 m) and a width of 131 ft (40 m). Twenty four pillars support a huge dome, claimed to be the fifth largest in the world. Six massive Corinthian pillars support the roof of the porch. The basilica was consecrated on 31 August 1856, with Franz Liszt conducting his *Esztergom Mass*, composed specially for the occasion.

However, the artistically most precious part of the basilica dates from the beginning of the 16th century. This is the southern side chapel, the **Bakócz Kápolna**, named after Tamás Bakócz, one of the most important of the bishops of Esztergom. Its walls are faced with red marble, and the altar, the work of the

Florentine sculptor Andrea Ferucci, is of gleaming white marble. The chapel is the survivor of the earlier episcopal church, which was destroyed by the imperial armies in 1683, while they were taking Esztergom from the Turks, who had turned Castle Hill into a strong fortress. The church bore the name of Adalbert, first bishop of Prague, who converted Prince Géza of the Árpád dynasty and also his son István or Stephen, the first King of Hungary. When the new Basilica was being built, the chapel was taken apart and rebuilt as part of the new construction.

The **castle museum** now surrounds whatever remains of the former royal palace, which was later used by the archbishops, and whatever that was excavated or reconstructed. Particularly worth seeing is the castle chapel with its Romanesque entrance and the early Gothic rose window above, probably the work of French masters of the 12th century, who could also have been responsible for the vaulting of the

The biggest church in the country: the Basilica in Esztergom.

choir and the capitals of the pillars. In the so-called **Lapidarium** parts of the Porta speciosa can be seen, the western entrance of the old St Adalbert's Cathedral. Above lie the royal chambers and the reception halls with their remains of former glories. At the Basilica, the visitor should make it a point to visit the **treasury**. It holds a rich collection of sacred objects going back nearly a millennium. A crystal cross dating from Carolingian times is believed to be the oldest piece. Golden cups and crosses studded with jewels, among them the cross of the royal oath-taking dating from the 13th century, form the pride of the collection.

Today the archbishops of Esztergom no longer reside on Castle Hill but in a palace which was built in the quarter below the hill at the end of last century. This building also houses the **Museum of Christian Art**, the most famous collection of art in the country apart from the National Gallery. If you want to get some idea of religious art of the

15th and 16th centuries, you should not pass this collection by. It contains works of art not just from present-day Hungary but also from the great era of Hungarian cultural influence, parts of which now belong to Czechoslovakia, Romania and Yugoslavia. For instance, there is in this collection a fanciful wood carving on wheels, which was drawn through the streets during Easter Week, the "Holy Tomb of Garamszentbenedek." Also there for you to admire are the works of Austrian and Bavarian panel painters of the end of the Middle Ages.

In Esztergom it is worthwhile strolling through the streets and taking a look at the little Baroque palais and the houses in mid-18th century style in **Széchenyi tér** and the surrounding streets.

Hills and Forests: The Pilis Hills are popular for excursions in the vicinity of the town. They form a wooded landscape with steep hills and valleys that have only a few villages. In the old days they serve as a royal hunting preserve, and today the stags, deer and wild boar here are hunted as game for well-heeled foreigners. The highest peak is **Dobogókö** (2,526 ft/770 m), where there is also a hotel which is very popular with those who come for the hunting. From the peaks in the vicinity you can get marvellous views down into the Danube valley.

Vác: The left bank of the Danube also has its attractions, but they are more obscured than those on the right bank between Esztergom and Szentendre. The first major town upriver, going from Budapest, is Vác, 20 miles (32 km) to the north of the Hungarian capital. It is an ancient town, founded as early as the 11th century, when King Stephen (the saint) created a bishop's seat here, together with a cathedral, which has however not survived the stormy events of the past.

The churches of Vác: Present-day Vác is characterised by the Classical **Cathedral** in Konstantin tér, lined by tall

A woman from the Slovak minority in Vác.

trees. It does not dominate its surroundings as much as the Basilica of Esztergom, but it does add the definitive touch to the appearance of the town, even if the building dating from the second half of the 18th century does look a little unharmonious. After all, three architects had worked on it, at times spurred on and at times hindered by the self-willed Bishop Migazzi, who had commissioned the building and who later rose to be the Archbishop of Vienna and a cardinal.

Apart from the Cathedral, Vác's churches and secular buildings make it a Baroque town. The **Bishop's Palace** opposite the Cathedral and most of the churches of the town are Baroque creations. There is the **Franciscan church** in Géza Király tér, built from the stones of the medieval cathedral, which was destroyed in the battles with the Turks. Further north is the **Piarist church** with its two slender towers, and in Március 15 tér there is the **Upper City Parish Church** which boasts its beautiful Rococo facade.

The bourgeois town: This is where the town of the merchants and middle classes begins. Around the square (underneath which lie a number of branching and interconnecting wine cellars) is a row of pretty houses in the Baroque and mid-18th century styles, starting with the beautiful town hall with its Baroque gate and the elegant balcony above. All over the country, the square is considered to be the most beautiful architectural ensemble in the Baroque style.

One peculiarity of Vác is the **triumphal arch** which Bishop Migazzi had bult in 1764 on the occasion of a visit by the Empress Maria Theresia. Surrounded by low, rustic houses on the northern edge of the town, about on the same level as that of the local jail, it looks strangely lost nowadays.

Velenceitó: This lake, 12 miles (20 km) to the southwest of Budapest, has only been discovered by the tourist and recreation industries in the last few decades. It covers 10 sq miles (26 sq km) and is very shallow (the average depth is only 5.3 ft/1.6 m). Half of it is covered with dense growth of reeds, mainly along the northern shore. This is where countless water birds build their nests, among which are some rare species such as the white heron. The lake is also the El Dorado of anglers, who are not at all delighted by the increase in tourism.

The towns visited by tourists, **Agárd, Gárdony** and **Velencefürdö**, lie on the south shore. At the moment there are only a few hotels, restaurants and Csárdas inns here, so that the tourist crowds are perforce limited. However, the many new weekend cottages and the expanding camping sites are proof that Velenceitó has become fashionable for holiday seekers.

A trip here is easily combined with a visit to Gorsium and the old Hungarian royal cities of Székesfehérvár and Veszprém. In Érd, there is a minaret dating from the Turkish period.

The Catholic church declares its loyalty to the state in every service.

The coronation city: Székesfehérvár, the former coronation city, is only 37 miles (60 km) away from Budapest and can be reached quickly via the M7 motorway. You should not miss making a trip to this town, as this will put you in touch with an important place in the history of Hungary. After all, Székesfehérvár was, for 500 years, the city where kings were crowned and buried, and where the coronation regalia were also safely kept.

Very few historical monuments from the past glory of this city have survived into our times. There is the so-called **Romkert** (Garden of Ruins) in the centre of the town behind the Bishop's Palace, but only the foundations remain of the basilica, where 38 kings received St Stephen's Crown and 18 of them found their final resting place. The royal tombs have been plundered, and what remains of the funeral chapels can be found in the gallery which surrounds the Garden of Ruins, a kind of open-air museum.

Also in the gallery is the sarcophagus which for a long time was held to be the coffin of St Stephen. It presumably dates from the 11th century: that is, around that time a master mason may have adapted a Roman sarcophagus from the nearby Roman site of Gorsium, though whether the body of the first Christian king of the Árpád house really ever rested in this coffin is not proven.

The atmosphere of present-day Székesfehérvár in the heart of the town is determined by its Baroque and its mid-18th century style. On the gentle hill upon which the Árpád princes built their first castle in the 11th century (at the time, it stood in the middle of a marshy area), the **Cathedral**, which dates from the mid-18th century, stands today.

Right next door to it is the most beautiful building in the town. It has survived from the Gothic period. This is **St Anne's Chapel**, with a doorway surrounded by stone staff work. In the little

Left, one in four Hungarians is below the age of 18. **Right,** the Rococo Hiemer house in Székesfehérvár.

streets around the Cathedral you can find a number of pretty though modest burgesses' houses dating from the 18th and 19th century. Their stucco facades exude an atmosphere of peace and calm.

In the main square of Szabadság tér it is the town hall and the bishop's palace which attract attention. The former consists of two buildings linked by a covered walkway at first floor level, one of which was built in 1690, immediately after the departure of the Turks. The other building is 100 years younger and was once the palais of Count Zichy. The ostentatious **Bishop's Palace** (unfortunately closed to the public) diagonally opposite also dates from the same period. Art historians view it as a masterpiece of the transitional mid-18th century style, with the playful decoration of Rococo and the lushness of Baroque already crossing over to the strict lines of Classicism.

In the pedestrian precinct of Március 15 útca is the Pharmaceutical Museum (which used to be the Black Eagle Phar-

macy), well worth seeing for its Rococo interior. A similar masterpiece of wood carving can be admired in the sacristy of the **Cistercian church** opposite. Here there is a complete church interior in miniature, with tabernacle, side altars, benches and confessionals — all carved of dark oak wood. Both works are the product of the Jesuit's carpentry workshops, which was carried on after the dissolution of the order in 1776 by the Pauline monks.

In the last months of World War II, Székesfehérvár suffered much in the battles to the north of Lake Balaton. Today most of the damage has been repaired, and industrial districts have developed around the old core of the town, especialy businesses dealing with electronics and computers, as well as aluminium works.

Zsámbék: Twenty five miles (40 km) to the west of Budapest, in the direction of Vienna and a mere 6 miles (10 km) away from the M1 motorway, is the town of Zsámbék, which is well worth

Street in Székes-fehérvár.

visiting for its Romanesque church ruins. This ruins has an important place among the clerical buildings of Hungary. Like Ják near Szombathely and Lébény to the west of Györ, it belongs to the so-called family churches. For each of these churches, building began in the 13th century, sponsored by an aristocratic family, but the church was later given to a religious order.

These family churches all date from the transitional period between the Romanesque and Gothic styles. Their construction was obviously interrupted time and again, and thus took very long to complete. As a result, the churches feature a mix of various styles, which only adds to their charm.

The church at Zsámbék lies above the town, and its two towers are a symbol of the area. Strangely enough, the troubles of the past left it untouched, but the earthquake of 1763 was to be its downfall. The fact that it was not restored again afterwards is due to the different tastes of the Baroque age.

It must have been an impressive church. It had three aisles, the central aisle towering high above the other two. The northern aisle no longer exists, and only the pointed arched arcades and the pillars separating the central and side aisles remain of the southern.

It was the two towers with their Romanesque windows that best resisted the earthquake, and the gallery between them is also still in existence, but the Gothic rose window above the doors, which once must have been very beautiful, has suffered much. As the church has no roof, wind and weather can continue their damage. They cannot take away, however, the magnificence of this building.

Tata: In Tata, 44 miles (70 km) to the west of Budapest and also reached by the M1 motorway, there is a museum housed in an old mill. Under the name of the "Great Swabian Trail", it is devoted to the history of the Germans in Hungary. It gives information not just about the settlements near Budapest and to the

Romanesque family church in Zsámbék.

west of Székesfehérvár, but also about the villages near Pécs and Baja in the south of the country.

The **Swabian Trail Museum** is in the Miklós Mill, which was built by Jakob Fellner, a master of the mid-18th century style. It gives an excellent visual representation of the great colonisation programme, under the auspices of the Imperial Court in Vienna, which caused depopulated regions during Turkish rule to be resettled and put back under the plough. Incidentally, only the first few settlers came from the German region of Swabia, while the others came from the Rhineland Palatinate, from the Moselle, and from Bavaria or Upper Austria.

However, this historical exhibition is not the only attraction of the town, which lies between two lakes. The castle, on the rocky plateau above the Öregtó, the Old Lake which covers 568.1 acres (230 hectares), is very picturesque. Its bastions reach out into the lake and give the castle a defiant, war-like look. The castle of Tata, marked on old prints and maps as Totis or Dotis, was after all one of the hard-fought border fortresses between Habsburg and Turkish rule in Hungary.

Lovers of faience will find themselves rewarded in the **Domonkos Kuny Museum** housed in the castle. It was named after the Frenchman Dominque Cuny who founded a faience factory in Tata in the 18th century. Its products, with their blue-green decoration on a white background, were very popular and even influenced the rural ceramics of Hungary.

Architecturally, Tata's appearance is determined by the mid-18th century transitional style of Jakob Fellner. The town owes its parish church of the Holy Cross, situated on a hill above the lake, to this architect, who came from Moravia. Above the entrance is the Esterházy coat of arms. Fellner was also responsible for the Esterházy palace project.

The Bugac Puszta: During the Cold

Puszta farmer.

War, the Iron Curtain forced film directors who wanted a totally flat landscape with draw wells and shepherds in shaggy sheepskins to make do with the landscape in a corner of the lakes of the Austrian district of Burgenland. This led some audiences to imagine that the true puszta (pronounced *pussta*, never *pushta*) began immediately beyond the Austro-Hungarian border. This is not the case at all. If you want to get to know the real puszta, you will have to travel a good deal further than Budapest.

The **Bugac Puszta**, today part of the Kiskunság National Park, begins some 78 miles (125 km) to the south of the capital.

The park covers an area of 30,000 hectares and is divided into six separate regions, of which five are to be found west of the E5, roughly speaking between Kecskemét and the Danube. The landscape of this region has many different aspects, and it is this diversity that gives it its charm. There are the pastures and the steppe around Bugac; further to the west and also to the north there are marshes, marshy forests and alkaloid lakes, wandering sand dunes and vast areas of woodland, the trees of which were not planted until this century, in order to protect the ground from wind erosion.

The puszta praised by Hungary's national poet Sándor Petőfi, who was born in nearby Kiskörös, in the words "my eyes glide over the plain into the immeasurable," no longer exists. However, visitors can get an impression here of what the puszta once was like.

This typical impression, though, is not really provided by the "programme" offered to the coachloads of tourists. Riders perform tricks, there are races of six-horse wagons, comfortable coach rides on the sandy paths and visits to the puszta museum. The true impression of the puszta is given away by the atmosphere which captivates you when the tourist hordes have not yet arrived or have already gone again.

You can enjoy this atmosphere be-

Magnificent example of Hungarian Jugendstil – the Cifra palais in Kecskemét.

cause nowadays you no longer have to spend the night in a hotel in Kecskemét or one on the E5. You can also stay in one of the bungalows in Bugac itself or, if you like, in one of the farms which are still in cultivation along the edge of the natural park, or which have already been turned into guesthouses. Those who like riding will also find stables in the vicinity where they can hire horses for rides. This individual form of puszta tourism has been much encouraged in the last few years, as there are of course certain limits imposed on mass tourism in a nature reserve.

In **Kecskemét**, the centre of the region between the Danube and the Tisza, there is the "Puszta-Tourist" tourist office, run by the Bács-Kiskun comitat, which gives information on "puszta tourism," and also in its individualistic forms.

However, Kecskemét should not be seen just as the gateway to the Bugacs Puszta. The town, with its population of 105,000, is well worth a visit for its own

Piroshka today – she's often blond.

sake. For one thing, it is the main producer of Barack-Pálinka (pronouced *borattzk-pahlinnka*), apricot brandy, which is to the Hungarians what *slivovitz* is to the Yugoslavs: a national drink. The raw materials are provided by the hundreds of thousands of apricot and peach trees in the vicinity.

It is worth taking a look around Kecskemét even without *barack*. The town centre consists of four interconnecting squares with some really quite interesting buildings. There is, for instance, the Cifra palais (*Cifra palota*), a highly individualistic variation on the Viennese Secessionist style. Its facade, adorned with coloured majolica tiles, the colourful wavy line of the pediment, and the whole ornamentation of the building, all combine to give a cheerful impression.

Famous for drama and music: In Kecskemét you will come across several reminders that two great Hungarians were born in the town. József Katona, the classic playwright of Hungarian historical drama, was born here. His work *Bánk Bán*, written in 1830, is still firmly part of the repertoire of the theatres in Budapest. The theatre in Kecskemet, of course, bears his name, as does a park and one of the four squares mentioned above.

There is also a Katona museum. The second famous son of the town is Zoltán Kodály, whose *Psalmus Hungaricus* is world famous and who, like Béla Bartók, was influenced by Hungarian folk music.

The "Institute of Music Teaching", housed in one of the decorative Baroque buildings and with students from many nations, was named after him. As a school for young musicians, it has a high reputation throughout the world. If you add the annual festival of folk music, where ensembles from many countries regularly take part, Kecskemét is much more than a flat market town surrounded by orchards, as it was once described by the vain Budapest literati.

TRAVEL TIPS

GETTING THERE

BY AIR

Budapest is served by several European and a few non-European airlines. There are regular scheduled flights several times a day to and from the Hungarian capital and most European cities on the Hungarian airline Malév as well as on major European airlines.

Normal scheduled air fares are subject to a variety of discounts (APEX, etc). Your travel agent will have the details, or you can contact the airlines directly. There are charter flights in the main summer season.

There are two airports in Budapest: Ferihegy I and II. Foreign airlines land in Ferihegy I (some 12 miles/20 km away from the city centre). The new airport, Ferihegy II (about 16 miles/25 km away) is reserved exclusively for the national airline Malév.

Malév overseas branch offices:
Britain: 10 Vigo Street, London W1.
USA: 630 Fifth Avenue, New York, NY 10111

Malév offices in Budapest:
Malév Central Office
Hotel Atrium Hyatt
Budapest V, Roosevelt tér 2
Tel: 1172-911, 1183-033.
Bookings and reservations
Budapest V, Dorottya utca 2,
Tel: 1184-333.
Airport, tel: 1579-123.

Information by phone on flights
Central Flight Information: 1579-133
Malév (arrivals): 1587-406
Malév (departures): 1578-768, 1577-831
Foreign airlines: 1572-122

BY SEA

From early April till the end of October, it is possible to reach Budapest from Vienna by the river route, using the Hungarian jetfoils or Austrian hovercrafts. In either case you will need to reserve a seat.

JETFOILS

1 April-1 October, daily, leaving at 8 a.m., in either direction. During the main season (up until mid-September), a second boat leaves in each direction in the early afternoon (1.30 p.m. and 2.30 p.m. respectively); from 1 May on in Vienna, from 1 June in Budapest. Journey time: 4 hours downriver from Vienna, 5 hours upriver from Budapest. Reservations can be made at IBUSZ offices abroad and at the main MAHART office in Vienna: Karlsplatz 2/8, A-1010 Vienna, tel: (0222) 5 05 56 44.

Reservations can be made in Budapest at the central MAHART office of the Hungarian Danube shipping company, International Mooring Point, Budapest V, Belgrád rakpart, tel: 1181-953; information, tel: 1387-186.

HOVERCRAFT

Daily (except Wednesdays) from the end of April to the end of September, in either direction; leaving Vienna 8.10 a.m., leaving Budapest 2.10 p.m.

Three times a week throughout October; leaving Vienna Mondays, Wednesdays, Saturdays; leaving Budapest Tuesdays, Thursdays, Sundays. Journey time: 4 and 5 hours respectively. Reservations: Erste Donau-Dampfschiffahrts-Gesellschaft (DDSG), Handelskai 265, A-1020 Vienna; travel service, tel: 2 18 59 19; time-table information, tel: 15 37.

BY RAIL

Rail travellers to Budapest usually have to change trains at the West Station in Vienna (the journey continues from the South Station, Wien-Süd). Arrival is at the Keleti pályaudvar (Eastern Railway Station) in Budapest. Some long-distance international trains have coaches going directly to Budapest: the Oostende-Vienna Express (Cologne-Frankfurt-Nürnberg-Passau-Linz); the Orient Express (Paris-Kehl-Stuttgart-Munich-Salzburg); the Wiener Waltzer (Basle-Zurich-Innsbruck-Salzburg).

In general, reservations are required for long-distance international trains. Note the deadlines for the purchase of seat, sleeping car or couchette reservations. You can interrupt your journey as often as you wish.

You can also make your reservations for the return journey before leaving home. This could save you queuing for several hours at the ticket offices of the Budapest railway stations (another possible way out of this is to make use of the customer service office of MAV – Hungarian State Railways).

MAV Customer Services
Budapest VI, Népköztársaság útja 35
Tel: 1228-049, 1228-056
Open Mon-Fri 9 a.m.-6 p.m., Sat 9 a.m.-1 p.m.

There are two direct trains to Budapest from Vienna:

Lehár (with first class coach from May to October) departs Wien-Süd 7.45 a.m.; departs Budapest 6.20 p.m.; arrives Budapest Southern Railway Station 10.45 a.m.; arrives Wien-Süd 9.20 p.m.

Arrabona departs Wien-Süd 6.05 p.m.; departs Budapest 7 a.m.; arrives Budapest Eastern Railway Station 9.40 p.m.; arrives Wien Süd 10.40 a.m.

Please note: for train journeys, too, it is essential to obtain a visa for Hungary before travelling.

RAILWAY STATIONS

Of the four railway stations in Budapest, two serve Western Europe:
Keleti pályaudvar
(Eastern Railway Station)
Budapest VIII, Baross tér
Tel: 1224-352.

Déli pályaudvar
(Southern Railway Station)
Budapest I, Alkotás utca
Tel: 1315-512.

CONNECTIONS

The railway stations of Budapest have good connections to the rest of the public transport system (Metro, buses, trams).

There is a direct Metro link between the Southern and Eastern railway stations.

If you prefer to travel to your hotel by taxi (which could take much longer than going by Metro), you can order a taxi at the border at Hegyeshalom by approaching an official who goes through the train. This will save you a tiresome wait on your arrival.

There are various reduced fares for young people under the age of 26, e.g. the Interrail card, which are also valid in Hungary.

BY ROAD

There are regular long-distance coach connections between southern Germany and Austria and Budapest. Contact:
Central long-distance coach station
Budapest V, Engels tér.
Information and bookings, tel: 1172-511, 1172-369.

Volánbusz
Budapest V, Engels tér
Tel: 1172-562.

Note: when travelling in scheduled coaches, it is essential to obtain a visa for Hungary before starting your journey.

BY CAR

Travel Documents: For travellers from Western Europe, a driving licence, a nationality sticker on the car and entry papers are sufficient. A green card is not actually essential but motoring associations do recommend that you take one, and also take out an insurance policy which in the event of an emergency will guarantee the return of the damaged vehicle. Information is available from the AA and RAC.

Crossing The Border: The most direct route is the trans-European route E5 from Vienna via Hegyeshalom to Budapest. Work on extending the motorway is being carried out on both sides of the border, with somewhat more vigour on the Hungarian than on the Austrian side.

The border crossing station is Nickelsdorf/Hegyeshalom. In general, traffic moves smoothly. Visas are available on the spot. Other crossing points from Austria to Hungary are, from north to south:

Klingenbach/Sopron
Deutschkreuz/Kópháza*
Rattersdorf/Köszeg*
Schachendorf/Bucsu*
Heiligenkreuz/Rábafüzes
(* denotes of local importance only.)

Car drivers can apply for visas at the road border crossings. The length of time you have to wait depends upon the volume of traffic. During the main season it is advisable to get your visa before you leave. There are photo booths available.

Traffic Regulations: The Hungarian road network – especially the trunk roads – is well developed and, generally speaking, in satisfactory condition.

The highway code and the road signs follow international usage. Seat belts are obligatory.

Beware! There is a total drink-and-drive ban in Hungary. The legal limit is **0.0 milligrams!** There are strict rules and harsh penalties if you are over the limit. Up to 0.8 milligrams, there is a maximum fine of 10,000 forint (Ft); over 0.8 milligrams, prison sentences can be given (foreigners are not exempted).

Maximum speed limits: Take care – these are lower than those in Western Europe. Breaking the speed limit is not tolerated, even if the drivers are foreigners.

Built-up areas	60 km/h (37 mph)
Country roads	80 km/h (49 mph)
Trunk roads	100 km/h (62 mph)
Motorways	120 km/h (74 mph)

TRAVEL ESSENTIALS

VISAS

To enter Hungary you will need a passport which is still valid for at least another 9 months. You will also need a visa. This can be obtained from Hungarian embassies abroad or at the borders. Application forms can be obtained from embassies, Malév offices and at travel agencies abroad.

Visas are also issued at the road border crossings, at the international airport Budapest-Ferihegy and at the international shipping office in Budapest, but not on scheduled bus journeys or in trains.

A warning: To avoid the long wait when you apply for a visa at the border crossings, it is a good idea to obtain your visa before starting your journey.

Embassy of the People's Republic of Hungary
35B Eaton Place, London W1
Tel: 01 235 7091.

EMBASSIES IN HUNGARY

British Embassy
1054 Budapest V, Harmincad utca 6
Tel: 182 888.

USA Embassy
1054 Budapest V, Szabadsag tér 12
Tel: 126 450/328 933.

VISA EXTENSION

Your visa is valid for 30 days from the date of entering the country (a transit visa is valid for 48 hours). You can apply for an extension 48 hours before your visa expires.
KEOKH
(Aliens' Registration Department)
Budapest VI, Népköztársaság útja 12
Tel: 1115-889, 1180-800.

REGISTRATION

You must register with the police within 48 hours of entering Hungary. If you are staying in a hotel, the hotel will take care of this for you. If you are staying in private accommodation, it is your own responsibility. The necessary form can be obtained at post offices and tobacconists'. In Budapest you register with the appropriate district police station.

MONEY MATTERS

The Hungarian unit of currency is the forint (Ft). 1 forint = 100 fillér. There are bank notes to the value of 50, 100, 500, 1,000 forint, as well as coins to the value of 1, 2, 5, 10 forint and 10, 20, 50 fillér.

The exchange rate is set weekly by the Hungarian National Bank. At time of press, the rates were 1 = about 90 Ft.

There is no obligatory amount which must be exchanged. Foreigners are not allowed to import or export more than 100 Ft. Exchangeable currencies can be imported in any quantity. Certain services (such as rent-a-car) must be paid for in foreign currency. You can exchange currency on the train and at the border crossings, as well as in any bank, hotel (at official rates) or travel agency office.

In Hungary there is a flourishing black market in Western currencies (with rates that are noticeably more advantageous than the official ones). The temptations are great, but so are the risks. You could be cheated or you could be caught. If arrested, you will have to pay a high penalty (fine) for currency offences.

It is definitely worthwhile bringing Euro-cheques (with cheque card – limit 9,000 Ft) and credit cards with you. They are accepted in the larger hotels, restaurants and shops. Most importantly, they are essential for the tourist when shopping in the foreign currency shops.

HEALTH

The standards of hygiene and of public health precautions in Hungary are not always up to Western European norms. The state of some public toilets leaves much to be desired.

WHAT TO WEAR

The climate in Budapest is temperate continental. In the summer it can become quite hot during the day, and light summer clothing would be suitable. In the evenings, however, you would be comfortable with a sweater or cardigan in the open air. You should expect some rain the year round, so bring along suitable protection against it.

The elegance of the people of Budapest (especially of its female population) was once proverbial, but it has not survived the years of socialism undamaged. The old-fashioned conventions of dress have disappeared. Young people are enthusiastic about jeans and the leisure look – the more casual, the better (as it's more "Western"). However, this is no excuse for the visitor to treat the centre of Budapest as if it were the beach at Benidorm, promenading up and down the pedestrian precinct in shorts, sleeveless T-shirts or even vests (which can frequently be seen). As a tourist, you don't have to be conspicuous at all costs.

ANIMAL QUARANTINE

Dogs and cats need an official veterinary certificate detailing their inoculations before entering the country. Dogs need an additional inoculation against rabies and distemper.

Veterinary Hospital and Clinic
Budapest XIII, Lehel utca 43-47
Tel: 1409-717.

CUSTOMS

Entering the country: In some respects, Hungarian customs regulations are weighed down by bureaucracy, but in others they are surprisingly liberal for an Eastern Bloc country. Articles for personal use can be imported free of duty, as can food supplies for 3 days, 250 cigarettes (or 50 cigars, 250 gm of tobacco), 2 litres of wine, 1 litre of spirits, and once-a-year gifts to the value of 6,000 Ft. Pornographic material, horror films and printed matter which is against the Hungarian nation and its political system are prohibited. A special licence is necessary for hunting weapons.

Video recorders can be imported if a deposit is paid.

It is advisable to declare video cameras when entering the country.

Car telephones must be registered (the customs office will provide you with the conditions of use).

Leaving the country: The export of a whole range of articles – from sausage (the legendary salami!), baby and children's clothing, to works of art (only permitted with a special licence) – is prohibited. However, if you buy these things in a foreign currency shop, you are allowed to take them with you. Keep the receipts!

Gifts to the value of 300 Ft (about £100) can taken out of the country duty-free.

Getting Acquainted

GOVERNMENT & ECONOMY

As capital of the Hungarian People's Republic and a member of the Warsaw Pact, Budapest today is the centre of a fascinating experiment. A country of the socialist bloc is breaking out of the ideological barriers imposed on it by the "system" and, inspired by Gorbachev's reforms in the Soviet Union, is searching for new political and economic goals, even if these can only be met by dialogue with the West.

This new development is expressed in many different ways; in grassroots democratic groups which are subverting the Communist Party's monopoly of power (the words "multi-party state" have already been mentioned); in the tireless attempts of official departments to attract Western capital into the country to link up with Western Europe, or at least to reduce the gap, through joint ventures; in the relaxation of currency restrictions and a certain opening up of the borders for the country's citizens. Budapest today is a city on the verge of far-reaching changes. People are betting on the future.

However, the relaxation of traditional structures does not mean that they have been eliminated. Hungary still has a constitution based on the Soviet model, and the primacy of the Communist Party MSZMP remains relatively untouched, if no longer indisputable. The means of production are still largely in state hands. Whether the expansion of private economic interests and activity, tolerated and encouraged by the state, will ever develop into a broadly based privatisation depends not only on a favourable political atmosphere, but also on the necessary (and at the moment still non-existent) capital cover.

According to the constitution, the National Assembly, whose members are elected every 5 years, is the highest political authority in the country. The collective head of state is the Praesidial Council with its 21 members. Its chairperson takes on the function of state president. According to proposals by the Praesidial Council, the National Assembly elects the Ministerial Council, which is headed by the Prime Minister. Political power is held by the Hungarian Socialist Workers' Party MSZMP (the official name of the Communist Party of Hungary), which was for a long time the only tolerated political organisation in the country. The leadership of the Party is in the hands of the 130 members of the Central Committee, which meets four times a year. The executive body of the Party is the Politburo, which has 11 members, under the leadership of the General Secretary. The Central Committee decides on the course of the ministries and the state departments. Since 1988, the offices of the General Secretary of the Party and of the Prime Minister have been separated.

Administratively speaking, Hungary is divided into 19 comitats, 5 urban districts and the capital Budapest.

The administration of the capital, structurally speaking, follows that of the nation. Budapest comprises 22 districts. The 2,045 members of the district councils elect the Capital Council (201 members), from whose numbers an executive committee of 17 members is chosen, which forms the actual governing body of the city. At its head is the chairperson of the Capital Council, equivalent to a city mayor in the West, who is aided by six deputies ("city councillors") with responsibility for their own portfolios.

Budapest is the most important economic and industrial centre in Hungary. Twenty-six percent of Hungarian industry and just under 23 percent of the workforce have settled in the capital (many people living in the towns and villages work in Budapest).

GEOGRAPHY & POPULATION

Budapest is the political, administrative, economic and cultural centre of Hungary. There is hardly another country in which the whole spectrum of life is as dominated by one single city as it is here. All roads, all rail routes lead into and out of the capital. The major part of the creative potential of the country is gathered in Budapest, as if concentrated by a lens.

With its population of 2.1 million, Budapest has for some time been the largest city in the Danube valley, leaving Vienna far behind. Twenty percent of the population of the country is concentrated in this busy city. The most recent incorporation of outlying communities into the city increased the number of districts to 22, and the Roman numerals in each address give the appropriate district. The area of the city has now grown to 203 sq miles (525 sq km) – compare 160 sq miles (410 sq km) for Vienna. Of the total area, 67 sq miles (173 sq km) lie on the Buda side (the right bank of the Danube), 136 sq miles (352 sq km) are on the opposite Pest bank.

Population density varies considerably (overall average: 4,000 per sq km; VII district: 38,000 per sq km; XXII district: 1,640 per sq km). The city stretches for some 16 miles (25 km) north to south, and for just under 19 miles (30 km) east to west.

The left, or Pest, bank of the Danube is level ground, while the right or Buda side is hilly. The Danube runs north to south for 17 miles (28 km) through the city; on average, the river is 10-13 ft (3-4 m) deep and 1,300-2,600 ft (400-800 m) wide. Within the city area the river is crossed by eight bridges: Árpád Bridge, Margaret Bridge (Margithíd), Chain Bridge (Lánchíd), Elizabeth Bridge (Erzsébethíd), Liberation Bridge (Szabadsághíd), Petöfi Bridge, and also by the northern and southern railway bridges.

The city centre lies at latitude 47°28'56"N (about the same latitude as Orléans and Basle) and longitude 19°08'10"E (about the same as Stockholm and Gdansk). The lowest point in the city is the level of the Danube – 317 ft (96.5 m) above sea level. The highest point is the Jánoshegy (St John's Hill) at 1,735 ft (529 m).

TIME ZONES

Hungary is in the Central European Time Zone. Summer time, as elsewhere in mainland Europe, runs from April to September, and the clocks are moved forward by one hour.

CLIMATE

The climate of Budapest is one of the most pleasant in Europe. It is temperate with a slight continental influence. The winters are rather cold and relatively dry and the summers are warm, at times hot.

There is relatively little rainfall, which is evenly spread throughout the year (short thunderstorms are common in early summer). The amount of sunshine is remarkable (on average 7 to 10 hours a day from April to September). Winds from the northwest provide fresh air in summer. Fog and damp, cold weather are quite rare. Air pollution is considered to be above normal levels.

LONG-TERM CLIMATIC STATISTICS

Temperature (annual average): 10.8°C
Coldest month: January 1.2°C
Warmest month: July 22.4°C
Number of days in the year with average daily temperature above 30°C: 20
Number of days in the year with an average daily temperature below 0°C: 30
Sunshine hours per year: 2,055
Daily average: 5 hours
From May-September: 1,330 hours
Daily average: 8 hours
Annual rainfall: 23 inches (600 mm)
Wettest month: June (3 inches/74 mm)
Driest month: February (1.5 inches/38 mm)

BEST TIME TO TRAVEL

We recommend spring in particular and autumn as the best times to travel. In the winter the weather is relatively harsh; in the summer it can get very hot at times. Also, the city is hopelessly overcrowded in the main season. Many visitors to Budapest swear by the spring: from April onwards, the sun shines, Nature does its "spring cleaning", the air is mild, clear and pure – just right for walks and strolling around the city. Almost equally pleasant is September, still flooded with sunshine, when the bustle and the heat of the summer days are replaced by a relaxed and almost contemplative mood.

WEATHER FORECASTS

Telephone forecasts: Budapest, 1353-500; the provinces, 1171-833

Radio forecasts: Every hour after the news, alternately on the Kossuth and Petöfi channels, but in Hungarian only.

TV forecasts: After the evening news (Tue-Sat about 8 p.m., Sun about 8.30 p.m.; no news on Mon).

WEIGHTS & MEASURES

The metric system is valid in Hungary. In the shops, weights are measured in kilogrammes (kg) and decakilos (dkg, deka). It is therefore not the usual practice in the captial city to weigh in Imperial pounds or ounces. 100 gm= 1 decakilo.

Electricity voltage used is 220 v.

BUSINESS HOURS

The opening hours in Budapest vary considerably. Food can be bought from 7 a.m. onwards, but if you have forgotten your shaving cream you will have to wait until 10 a.m. – the shops, in central Budapest, do not open until then (department stores open at 9 a.m.). Hairdressers are particularly hardworking; they open from 7 a.m.-9 p.m., Mondays as well. All shops are open all day, and there is no lunch break.

Shops usually shut at 6 p.m., 1 p.m. on Saturdays. Thursday is "late shopping day", shops are open up until 7 p.m. or 8 p.m. Some supermarkets are open on Sunday mornings (8 a.m.-1 p.m.), as are tobacconists, florists and sweet shops. In some restaurants you can buy milk, bread and other bakery products on Sundays.

Official departments and offices have varying opening hours on weekdays; usually 9 a.m.-1 p.m., but sometimes 8 a.m.-5 p.m.

Banks are open Mon-Fri 8 a.m.-1 p.m., OTP bureaux de change are open 8 a.m.-3 p.m. or 4 p.m. (closes at 7 p.m. on Mon, and 1 p.m. on Fri), post offices are usually open Mon-Fri 8 a.m.-7 p.m., AFOR petrol stations are usually open from 6 a.m.-8 p.m. (Shell stations are open 24 hours). Pharmacies are open Mon-Fri 8 a.m.-6 p.m. (there is an emergency cover system for weekends). Museums are open Tue-Sun 10 a.m.-6 p.m. and are closed on Mon.

Listed below are the opening hours of businesses and government departments. Only to be used as a guideline.

Shops: Mon-Fri 10 a.m.-6 p.m.; Sat 10 a.m.-1 p.m.; Sun closed, with the exception of some supermarkets (8 a.m.-1 p.m.)

Department stores: Mon-Fri 9 a.m.-6 p.m.; Sat 9 a.m.-1 p.m.; Sun closed.

Food shops: Mon-Fri 7 a.m.-7/8 p.m.; Sat 7 a.m.-4 p.m.; Sun closed, with the exception of some supermarkets (8 a.m.-1 p.m.)

Tobacconists: Mon-Fri 7 a.m.-8 p.m.; Sat 7 a.m.-4 p.m.; Sun closed.

Hairdressers: Mon-Fri 7 a.m.-9 p.m.; Sat 7 a.m.-4 p.m.; Sun closed.

Post offices: Mon-Fri 8 a.m.-7 p.m. except the main post office (9 a.m.-7 p.m.) and the post offices at the Western and Eastern Railway stations (Nyugati and Keleti Pályaudvar respectively) which are open 24 hours.

Banks: Mon-Fri 8 a.m.-1 p.m.

Bureaux de change: Mon-Fri 8 a.m.-3/4 p.m.; closes at 7 p.m. on Mon, and at 1 p.m. on Fri.

Petrol stations: Mon-Fri 6 a.m.-8 p.m.; Sat 6 a.m.-8 p.m.; Sun 6 a.m.-8 p.m. Shell stations open 24 hours.

Pharmacies: Mon-Fri 8 a.m.-6 p.m., with a weekend emergency cover service.

Museums: Tue-Fri 10 a.m.-6 p.m.; Sat 10 a.m.-6 p.m.; Sun 10 a.m.-6 p.m. Mon closed.

Government departments: Mon-Fri 9 a.m.-1 p.m.

The following shops are also open on Sun 8 a.m.-1 p.m.

Kispesti Centrum Aruház
Budapest XIX, Kossuth tér 4-5.

Aruház
Budapest VII, Klauzál tér 11.

Sugár shopping centre
Budapest XIV, Örs vezér tere.

ABC store
Budapest I, Batthyány tér.

ABC store (near Marx tér)
Budapest XII, Szt. István körút.

HOLIDAYS

There are few public holidays in Hungary.
1 January – New Year's Day
15 March – Day of National Uprising
(1848). This traditional national public
holiday, abolished in 1949, was re-intro-
duced in 1989. The date 7 November,
anniversary of the "Great Socialist October Revolution" in Russia, has been
dropped as a public holiday.
4 April – Liberation Day (1945)
Easter Monday
1 May – Labour Day
20 August – Constitution Day
25/26 December – Christmas

If the holiday falls on a Thursday or Tues-
day, the Friday or Monday will be taken off
as well and added to the weekend. The work
missed on this working day has to be made
up in advance or at a later date.

FESTIVALS

Despite being known as the "European
Capital of Culture", Budapest has not much
to offer in the way of festivals and similar
events. The biggest event is the Spring Festival in March, with its lesser counterpart in
the autumn, the Budapest Art Weeks (which
do last much longer than the spring festival
– 5 weeks).
March: Budapest Spring Festival: "10
days, 100 venues, 1,000 events" – such is the
self-confident claim of one of the promo-
tional slogans of this event. There are orchestral and soloist concerts by Hungarian
and foreign artists; productions of opera,
ballet and the theatre; folk music events;
film festival premieres; exhibitions.
1 May: "Labour Day Celebration" in
Tabán Park. Festival concert; bands; folk
music; puppet theatre.
July: Theatre and concert performances
in the open-air theatres on Margaret Island
and in Városmajor, in the Dominican Courtyard of the Hilton Hotel and in the so-called
Hild Court.

20 August: Constitution Day. Fly-past
and water parade on and above the Danube
at the level of the Parliament building. Music
and folk music programmes. Fireworks display in the evening.
September/October: Budapest Art
Weeks. Concerts and theatre performances
by local and visiting artists. "Contemporary
Music" series. Special exhibitions in the
theatres.
November: Vox Pacis choir festival with
international participation.
31 December: New Year's Eve with fireworks display.

RELIGIOUS SERVICES

Details of services held by the various
denominations can be obtained from the
notices put out by the various religious
communities. Early mass is said daily in all
Catholic churches.

SUNDAY SERVICES

High Mass (Catholic) in the Matthias
Church, with excellent musicians, every
Sunday at 10 a.m.

RELIGIOUS OFFICES

Roman Catholic Church
Archiepiscopal Office
Budapest V, Eötvös Loránd utca 7
Tel: 1174-752.

**Protestant Church/National Church
Office**
Budapest VII, Üllői út 24
Tel: 1130-886.

Reformed Church
Reformed Church Episcopal Office
Budapest IX, Ráday utca 28
Tel: 1180-753.

Jewish Community
Budapest VII, Síp utca 12
Tel: 1421-335.

COMMUNICATIONS

MEDIA

Newspapers & Magazines:
Neueste Nachrichten (Daily News): A bilingual newspaper published 5 days a week by the Hungarian news agency MTI.

A monthly brochure is published in English (and German) by the Hungarian Tourist Office which gives detailed information about all kinds of events and valuable information and tips. It is free in hotels, tourist information offices and travel agencies.

News from Abroad: Major western newspapers can be found – one or two days out of date – but at only a few newsstands, such as the one in Váci utca 10 and in the pedestrian underpass Ráckóczi út. Western periodicals and magazines can only be obtained at the newsstands in the major hotels.

Radio & Television:
Hungarian State Radio has three main channels – Budapest I (*Kossuth*) and Budapest II (*Petöfi*) on medium wave as well as *Rádió Bartók* on VHF.

Rádió Petöfi, Mon-Fri noon-12.05 p.m.: News in English, Russian and German.

Rádió Bartók has excellent, almost continuous music.

Hungary has two television channels and is, relatively speaking, at an early stage of development. Every Tue 8 p.m., a news programme in Russian, English and German is broadcast on Channel 2. Cable and satellite TV is still in its infancy in Hungary.

POSTAL SERVICES

In general, post offices are open from 9 a.m.-6 p.m. The following post offices have longer opening hours:
Main Post Office (8 a.m.-7 p.m.)
Budapest V, Városház utca 9-11
Tel: 1185-398.

Post Office 62 (24 hours)
Western Railway Station
Budapest VI, Lenin körút 105-107
Tel: 1120-436.

Post Office 72 (24 hours)
Eastern Railway Station
Budapest VII, Verseny utca 1
Tel: 1428-118.

Mail boxes are emptied once or twice a day. They are red and are either fixed to the walls of buildings or free-standing on wrought-iron stands at the roadside. Stamps can be bought at post offices or at the tobacconists. The address for poste restante is: 1364 Budapest 4, Petöfi Sándor utca 13-15.

POSTAL CHARGES

Letter: within Hungary, to socialist countries and Austria – 4 Ft; to other countries – 8 Ft.

Postcards: within Hungary, to socialist countries and Austria – 2 Ft; to other countries – 5 Ft.

Additional charges: Airmail to Europe – 1 ft; to other countries – 2 Ft.

Registered mail: to Europe – 6 Ft.

Express mail: to other countries – 10 Ft.

TELEPHONE & TELEX

Almost all of Hungary is linked to the STD network. You can dial calls abroad direct from the red public telephone boxes; the yellow and grey phone boxes are for local calls only. The usual surcharge is added to calls from hotels. For local calls, you will need 2-Ft coins, for long distance calls 5, 10 and 20-Ft coins are also used.

TELEPHONE CHARGES

	7 a.m.-6 p.m.	6 p.m.-7 a.m.
Local calls	2 Ft (3 mins)	(6 mins)
Trunk calls		
Inland (3 mins):		
– Zone I	10 Ft	6 Ft
– Zone II	18 Ft	12 Ft
– Zone III	24 Ft	18 Ft
International calls (3 mins):		
– Western Europe		67.50 Ft
– Austria		54 Ft
– GDR		50 Ft

HOW TO DIAL

Local calls: Lift the receiver; for coin-operated phones, insert 2 Ft; await dialling tone (burring sound); dial number.

Trunk and international calls: Lift receiver; for coin-operated phones, insert 5/10/20 Ft; await dialling tone; dial 06 (00 for international calls); await high-pitched beeping tone; dial STD code (for international calls, international code and STD code) followed by number.

Budapest telephone numbers have seven digits, those in the rest of Hungary have three to five digits.

At present, an international long-distance call is cheaper than sending a telegram abroad.

Code for dialling from abroad: Hungary – 01036; Budapest – 1

Trunk and international calls which cannot be connected under the STD system have to be made by dialling 01 (Hungary) or 06 (international calls). Calls made via the operator can be very time-consuming.

Telegram	02
Dial-a-Time	08
Early morning calls	1172-522

Foreign language directory enquiries (7 a.m.-8 p.m.):

Inland	1172-200
International	1186 977

TELEX

Most hotels in Budapest have a telex connection which can also be used by guests (in some places fax is also available).

EMERGENCIES

SECURITY & CRIME

As in all socialist countries, personal security for local people and for visitors is quite good. You can walk through the city quite late at night without any worries. Don't leave valuables in your car!

However, if something should happen to you and if physical harm or damage to your property should result, please contact the police at once:

KEOKH (Police/Aliens Office)
Budapest VI, Népköztársaság utja 12
Tel: 1118-667 (24 hours).
Mon, Tue, Wed and Fri 9 a.m.-noon; Mon also 2 p.m.-6 p.m.

Emergency phone numbers
Fire brigade   105
Police   107

LOST PROPERTY

Central Lost Property Office
Budapest V, Engels tér 5
Tel: 1174-961.
Mon-Thurs 8 a.m.-4.30 p.m. (Fri till 4 p.m.)

Lost Property Office of the City Public Transport Systems
BKV
Budapest VII, Akácfa utca 18
Tel: 1226-613.
Mon-Fri 7.30 a.m.-3.30 p.m. (Wed till 7 p.m.)

Taxi Central Lost Property Office
Budapest VII, Akácfa utca 20
Tel: 1344-787.
Mon-Thurs 8 a.m.-4 p.m., (Fri till 4 p.m.)

Volántaxi
Budapest XIV, Jerney utca 54-56
Tel: 1835-780.
Daily 6 a.m.-7 p.m.

If you lose your passport:
Contact KEOKH (Police headquarters, Aliens Department)
Budapest VI, Néköztársaság útja 12
Tel: 1118-667, 1118-668.

MEDICAL SERVICES

As a foreign visitor to Hungary, you are entitled to free first aid treatment in all hospitals and clinics. Ambulance, tel: 104

British subjects are entitled, on production of their passports, to free hospital treatment and to see a general practitioner. There is a nominal charge for prescriptions. Nonetheless, it is recommended that you take out an insurance policy against accident, illness and loss of luggage.

Premiums:

No. of days	charges (US$)
1-3	1
4-15	2
16-21	3
22-30	4

The insurance premiums of the state Hungarian insurance association
Allami Biztositó (AB)
Budapest VIII, Üllöi út 1
Tel: 1181-866.

Its branches cover medical costs of up to US$500 for outpatients, US$1,000 for in-patient treatment.

DENTISTS

One special feature of the medical scene in Budapest is the very cheap (for Western standards) dental treatment, which includes conservation, surgical and prosthetic treatment. The dental surgeries in the luxurious Hotel Thermál on Margaret Island and most recently in the not so luxurious Hotel Volga have been specially set up for tourists. Even including hotel costs, dental treatment in Budapest is still much cheaper than in some other Western cities.
Dental Emergency Service (day and night)
Budapest VIII, Mária utca 52
Tel: 1330-189.

PHARMACIES

Medicines and drugs can only be obtained in pharmacies. Most are available only on prescription, only a few can be sold freely.
Opening hours: Mon-Fri 8 a.m.-6 p.m.

There is a regular emergency cover service (for night-time and holidays). In every pharmacy there is a notice indicating the nearest pharmacy offering emergency cover.

GETTING AROUND

MAPS

Town plans to various scales can be bought from bookshops. Also very useful, is the practical *City Atlas* published by Cartographia of Budapest as it contains a brief guide to the city. Simplified maps which give a general view of the city and its sights can be obtained free in hotels and travel agencies.

FROM THE AIRPORT

Airport buses run to and from the International Coach Station to the Ferihegy I and II airports. The buses leave the airports every hour on the hour from 5 a.m.-11 p.m. Ferihegy I: journey time 30 minutes, 20 Ft. Ferihegy II: journey time 40 minutes, 30 Ft.

AIRPORT TAXIS

Taxi fares from the airport to the city centre range from 150-200 Ft. (Watch out for sharks demanding up to 50 dollars!).

Scheduled city buses also run to both airports from Kübánya (terminus of the Metro route 3): Black bus no. 93 to Ferihegy terminal I, Red bus no. 93 to Ferihegy II. Check in one hour before departure. Tel: 1579-123.

FLY & DRIVE

This practical arrangement is also possible in Budapest. Further information and prices are available from your airline or travel agent.

WATER TRANSPORT

There is a ferry service which runs from both banks of the Danube to Margaret Island. Of the 13 departure points (4 on the Buda bank, 7 on the Pest shore, 2 on Margaret Island), the ones for tourists are Buda: Batthyány tér – Gellért tér; Pest: Vigadó tér. For more information, contact
BKV (Budapest Public Transport Systems) Budapest XIII, Jászai Mari tér
Tel: 1295-844.

PUBLIC TRANSPORT

Public transport is good, rapid and cheap. A closely-knit network of trams and buses, the underground railway (Metro) and the suburban railway (HÉV) provide access to all parts of the city in any direction. In the Buda Hills there are also the rack railway, the Pioneers' Railway and the chair lift, the cable railway up Castle Hill and the minibus in the Castle Quarter. The motor boat ferries crossing the Danube also belong to the public transport system. The speed of travel is higher than in most big European cities. On average, some 1,600 million passengers are transported per year. There are ticket franking machines instead of conductors.

Tickets (best bought in bulk in advance) can be obtained from vending machines, at stations, at the tobacconists, at the Metro ticket offices and in travel agencies. There are two categories: blue, 6 Ft, for buses; yellow, 5 Ft, for the Metro, tram, trolley-bus and suburban railway (as far as the city limits). Each ticket is only valid for one journey. They are not valid for transfers. For a longer stay, we recommend that you obtain a monthly season ticket (valid until the 5th of the following month), which can be bought from the special season ticket sales points as well as from the ticket offices of the Metro and the suburban railway.

Beware! If you are caught fare-dodging, you will have to pay a heavy fine. There are no exemptions for tourists.

Operating Hours:
Metro, buses 4.30 a.m.-11 p.m.
Trams 4 a.m.-midnight
24-hour and night-time routes:
Trams: 6, 12, 28, 31, 49, 50
Buses: 3, 42, 78, 11, 144, 173, 179, 182, C.

TRAMS & BUSES

In Budapest there are about 40 tram and more than 208 bus routes. Express buses have red numbers and only stop at certain points. The 12 trolley-bus routes mostly link up with the Metro routes; route 73 is a direct link between the Western and Eastern Railway Stations.

METRO

The Metro system is the quickest way of getting around Budapest. There are three routes. The "little Metro" (1) links the city centre with Mexikói út. Route M2 runs from west to east, from the Southern Railway Station (Déli pu.) under the Danube to the other bank, passing the Eastern Railway Station (Keleti pu.) and on as far as Örs vezér tere. The M3 runs from north to south on the Pest bank from Árpád Bridge as far as Köbánya-Kispest. The M1 is signed in yellow, the M2 in red, the M3 in blue. The three routes cross at Deák tér. Total journey times: M1 11 mins, M2 18 mins, M3 26 mins.

SUBURBAN RAILWAY (HÉV)

The HÉV is a rapid link with the immediate surroundings of the capital. Within the city boundaries the yellow tickets are valid. For longer journeys tickets can be bought from the ticket offices of the individual stations. The suburban railway has four routes:

From Batthyány tér (M2 station) via Obuda (Acquincum) to Szentendre
Operating Hours: 3.50 a.m.-11.40 p.m.
Journey time 42 mins. From Örs vezér tere (MZ terminus) to Gödöllö
Operating Hours: 4.30 a.m.-11.20 p.m.
Journey time 49 mins. From Boráros tér to Csepel Island
Operating Hours: 4.30 a.m.-11.30 p.m.
Journey time 15 mins. From Vágóhíd to Ráckeve at the southern end of Csepel Island
Operating Hours: 3.20 a.m.-12.10 a.m.
Journey time 72 mins

TAXIS

For Western visitors taxi rides in Budapest are an affordable luxury. The basic fare is 8 Ft/km, the tariff is 7 Ft, and waiting is at 2 Ft per minute. Because of the constant traffic jams, it is not really advisable to take a taxi within the city centre (nor, of course, is it a good idea to take your own car).

Apart from the 4,000 taxis of the two state-owned taxi companies Fötaxi, Voläntaxi – there are at least 3,000 "private" taxis. Within the city there are at least 160 taxi ranks (not for the "private" taxis); you can stop an empty taxi (the roof light will be switched on), or you can book a radio cab by phone (the trip to the pick-up point is charged).

Taxi phone numbers:

Fötaxi	1222-222
(to pre-book a taxi: 1188-188)	
Volá+ntaxi	1666-666
Taxi-Unió	1555-000
City-Taxi	1228-855
Radio-Taxi	1271-271
Buda-Taxi	1294-000, 1568-569
Lux Taxi	1532-532
Ero-Taxi	1805-555
Hotel-Taxi	1389-704

Transporting goods by taxi:

Fösped	1330-330
Tefu-Taxi	1328-328
Boy-Szolgálat	1123-523

For rail and air travellers a taxi can be arranged to collect you at the station or airport. Airport taxi, tel: 1579-123.

OTHERS

Cable Railway: This runs from Clark Adam tér opposite the Chain Bridge up Castle Hill. The original wagons have recently been renovated. Every 3 minutes from 8.30 a.m. to 8 p.m. Single ticket: 10 Ft.

Rack Railway: From Városmajor up Széchenyi Hill. 4 a.m.-12.25 a.m., every 15 minutes. (Monthly season tickets are not valid!)

Pioneers' Railway: From Széchenyi Hill to Hüvösvölgy (Cold Valley) and over, 8 miles (12 km). Apart from the driver, the train is manned by children and young people. Fares vary according to length of journey. Tickets available at stations.

Chair Lift: From Zugligeti út up János Hill. Terminus near the viewing tower. 8 a.m.-4 p.m. (winter), 5 p.m. (summer).

Micorbus: Runs on Margaret Island. Tour guide (in Hungarian).

Horsedrawn Omnibus/Carriage: A horsedrawn omnibus dating from the turn of the century runs through Óbuda.

A special tourist attraction for those who like such things is a trip through the Castle Quarter in a carriage drawn by two horses. Journey time: around 30 mins. Fare: 250-300 Ft. Carriages available outside the Matthias Church.

PRIVATE TRANSPORT

Following international trends, Budapest now also has car hire organisations which collaborate with international companies. If you have booked your car before setting out on your journey, it will be waiting for you at the airport, station or hotel. On payment of a surcharge the car can also be delivered outside Budapest or even abroad and returned later.

The Budapest car hire companies offer Eastern Bloc cars and Western or Japanese models – the latter can only be hired with Western currency. Hirers must be at least 21 years old.

IBUSZ – Rent-a-car
Budapest V, Martinelli tér 8
Tel: 1184-158, 1184-240, 1186-222.

Fötaxi – Hertz Interrent
Budapest VII, Kertész utca 24
Tel: 1221-472, 1116-116;
Airport:1579-123
FÖTAXI also has a chauffeur-driven limousine service available.

Volá+ntourist – Europcar
Budapest IX, Vaskapu utca 16
Tel: 1334-783.

Cooptourist – Budget
Budapest V, Kossuth Lajos tér 13-15
Tel: 1118-803;
Budapest IX, Ferenc körút 43
Tel: 1131-466;
Airport: 1117-034.

Contrex
Budapest II, Alkotás utca 20-24
Tel: 1563-485;
Budapest VI, Nčszáros utca 56A
Tel: 1752-058.

The major hotels also offer a car hire service. Information about the public transport system can be obtained from:
Fövinform (day and night)
Tel: 1171-173.

SELF-DRIVE

The Hungarian Autoclub will provide information on all matters relevant to car drivers, including a legal aid service. The Autoclub also provides forms in case of accident. These forms should be carried with you as a precaution.
Magyar Autoclub
Budapest II, Rómer Flóris utca 4-6
Tel: 1152-040, 1152-212, 1152-886.

Service Centre
Budapest XI, Boldiszár utca 2
Tel: 1669-480, 1850-805, 1805-722, 1805-875;
Budapest II, Vörös Hadsereg útja 224
Tel: 1886-128.

USEFUL TIPS

Cars are not allowed in the Castle Quarter or on Margaret Island. Exceptions are made for guests of the Hilton Hotel. You can drive to the hotels on Margaret Island via the Árpád Bridge.
Traffic Reports: Budapest, tel: 1171-173; Provinces, tel: 1227-052, 1227-643.

FUEL

Apart from AFOR there are no self-service petrol stations. The attendant will be counting on a suitable tip (about 20 Ft).

Foreign currency is not accepted at petrol stations (not even at those run by "foreign" companies). Be sure to take enough forints with you!

Diesel is only available on production of coupons (these can be obtained at the border crossings and at IBUSZ offices) or the Euroshell credit card. There is no refund for unused coupons. More and more petrol sta-

tions are stocking lead-free petrol.
Petrol Stations: Apart from those run by the state-owned Hungarian AFOR company, there are Shell, BP and Agip petrol stations in Hungary. The petrol, however, all come out from the same tanks.

Openings hours: usually 6 a.m.-8 p.m.; Shell petrol stations open 24 hours.

Some **24 hour petrol stations**: Budapest V, Martinelli tér (multi-storey car park); Budapest XII, junction of Alkotás útja-Hegyalja út; Budapest II, Szilágyi Erzsébet fasor; Budapest XI, Müegytem rakpart.

PARKING

Opportunities for parking are very limited – yet another reason to leave your car in the hotel garage when strolling around the town. Incidentally, if you are planning to travel in your own car, make sure that your hotel has garaging or parking space available, otherwise you could have problems!

Multi-storey car parks: Budapest V, Martinelli tér 8; Budapest V, Arankéz utca; charges: 12 Ft/h; 100 Ft/day.

There are also supervised car parks with varying charges (Mon-Fri 8 a.m.-6 p.m., Sat 8 a.m.-2 p.m.) from 4 Ft/h to 20 Ft/h in the city centre.

You might have the good fortune to find a "free" parking meter which runs for 2 hours.

If you park in a prohibited area the police have the right to have your car removed. In such cases, apart from the imposed fine, you will also have to pay the service fee for towing the car away. You can enquire about cars which have been towed away by ringing 1572-811.

ACCIDENTS

If you are involved in a road accident, even if no-one is hurt, you must inform the police (tel: 107), who will prepare a report. You should get a statement of any damage to the car, which can be shown on leaving the country. The accident must be reported within 24 hours.
Hungária Insurance (Car damage claims)
Budapest XIV, Gvadányi utca 69
Tel: 1835-359
Mon-Thur 7.30 a.m.-7 p.m.; Fri till 3 p.m.; Sat 8 a.m.-noon.

BREAKDOWN & RECOVERY SERVICE

The "yellow angels" of the Hungarian Autoclub are on duty round the clock. Vehicle recovery service at reduced rates.

Magyar Autoclub
Breakdown Service (24 hours)
Tel: 1260-668;
Vehicle recovery service (24 hours)
Budapest XIV, Francia út 38B
Tel: 1691-831, 1693-714;
Information service
Tel: 1353-101.

Further vehicle recovery services, (6 a.m.-11 p.m.) Budapest XII, Petneházi utca 72; Tel: 1207-119, 1208-208

Volán (24 hours)
Budapest VI, Lenin kórüt 96
Tel: 1129-000;
Budapest XV, Ifjú Gárda útca (24 hours)
Tel: 1409-326;
Budapest IX, Vaskapu utca (7 a.m.-9 p.m.)
Tel: 1334-783; 1666-666 (after 9 p.m.)

AFIT
Budapest XIII, Váci út 82-84
Tel: 1499-170.

REPAIRS

Proper spare parts are hardly available at all in Hungary. The best places to find help are the following repair workshops which have specialised in Western models:

Audi, VW, Porsche
AFIT, Budapest III, Mozaik utca 1-3
Tel: 1805-322, 1803-739.

BMW
Budapest III, Bécsi út 277
Tel: 1882-346.

Fiat
AFIT, Budapest XI, Boldizsár utca
Tel: 1452-909.

Ford, Opel
Hungaroszerviz, Budapest XIV, Mexikói út 15-19
Tel: 1631-003, 1631-001, 1835-975.

Mercedes, Volvo
Budapest XIV, Miskolci út 157
Tel: 1831-120, 1833-210.

Peugeot, Renault:
AFIT, Budapest XI, Bicskei út 3-5
Tel: 1664-600.

THEFT/LOSS/INSURANCE

Notify the appropriate police station immediately if your car is stolen.

Police Headquarters
Budapest V, Deák tér 16-18
Tel: 1180-800, 1123-456.

To be on the safe side, it is worth enquiring at the car pound: Budapest X, Szalió utca 5, Tel: 1475-594.

If you lose your **car keys**: door opening service and manufacture of replacement keys by
Sándor Simon
Budapest VII, Kertész utca 48
Tel: 1421-034
Mon-Fri 8 a.m.-6 p.m.

Insurance claims made against Hungarian citizens must be made through the central office of the state insurance association:
Allami Biztosító
Budapest III, Üllöi út 1
Tel: 1181-866, 1180-352.

WHERE TO STAY

As far as accommodation is concerned, Budapest after 1945 had a great deal of catching up to do. Almost all the great hotels fell victim to the war, and for 30 years this big gap was not filled. Also, because of lack of funds rather than because of complacency, the hotels that had survived were not equipped to satisfy the demands of the travel community.

Thanks to efforts undertaken over the last few years, the Hungarian capital today once more has a series of splendid luxury and several excellent four-star hotels to offer, but most hotels are still struggling to catch up, although it must be said that many guests enjoy the "pre-war" atmosphere more than the technically better equipped but interchangeable tourist hotels of today.

Every year the Hungarian Tourist Office publishes a register of accommodation, the *Hotel, Camping* handbook which is available free in the Tourinform office.

Don't travel on spec! As Budapest becomes more popular with visitors and for holidays, it is becoming more and more difficult to find accommodation without pre-booking, especially during the fine weather season.

HOTELS

Hotel rooms in Budapest are no longer as ridiculously cheap as they once were, but measured by Western standards they are still modest, even in the luxury class. According to international usage, they are divided into five classes.

In the hotels of the top two classes (luxury and first class hotels), all rooms come with attached baths; for the three-star ("good quality") hotels, about 75 percent of the rooms have attached baths. Among the two-star ("plain") hotels, there are many which classified below their actual standard – old, traditional hotels with faded charm which more than compensate for any possible deficiency of modern sanitation. The one-star ("modest") establishments, however, can only be recommended with a clear conscience to real backpackers who are not interested in anything other than a roof over their heads.

The following price guidelines (dating from time of press) are per person in double rooms or suites. The rooms are with bath or shower, with a bathroom on the same floor in Class 4. Single room surcharge is about 40 percent. Breakfast is included in the room price. Prices in pounds sterling.

Class	Double (£)	Suite (£)
L (5-star)	45-60	65-110
1 (4-star)	25-65	30-90
2 (3-star)	15-30	25-40
3 (2-star)	12-20	—
4 (1-star)	10-15	—

The prices above are for the main season (April-October). In the early season and out of season there are considerable price reductions, in the so-called peak season (for instance the Grand Prix weekend) on the other hand there are surcharges (not in the luxury class). Reductions and surcharges are both around the 20 percent level.

Aero
Budapest IX, Ferde utca 1-3
Tel: 1274-690.
For those who prefer hotels near airports. Good restaurant. Class 2; 139 rooms.

Astoria
Budapest V, Kossuth Lajos utca 19
Tel: 1173-411.
One of the nostalgic Budapest hotels. One advantage is the Metro station just outside the door with direct connections to the Southern and Eastern Railway Stations. Class 2; 192 rooms.

Atrium-Hyatt
Budapest V, Roosevelt tér 2
Tel: 1383-000.
The most recent addition to the chain of luxury hotels on the Pest bank of the Danube, a typical Hyatt building with a winter garden-style courtyard. Rooms are relatively good value, the suites expensive. Class L; 353 rooms.

Béke
Budapest VI, Lenin körút 97
Tel: 1323-300.
Well established, recently renovated hotel in the Jugendstil style, not far from the Western Railway Station. Class 1; 238 rooms.

Buda-Penta
Budapest II, Krisztina körút 41-43
Tel: 1566-333.
Good quality hotel right next to the Southern Railway Station. Class 1.

Budapest
Budapest II, Szilágy Erzsébet fasor 47
Tel: 1153-230.
The hotel with the most extravagant shape – a cylindrical tower. Class 2; 280 rooms.

Duna Intercontinental
Budapest V, Apáczai Csere János utca 4
Tel: 1175-122.
In the centre of the newly restored Danube promenade, next to the boat departure point. Class L; 340 rooms.

Erszébet
Budapest V, Károlyi Mihály utca 11
Tel: 1382-111.
A popular modern city centre hotel. Class 2; 123 rooms.

Fórum
Budapest V, Apáczai Csere János utca 12-14
Tel: 1178-088.
According to general opinion, the best-managed of the three grand hotels on the Pest bank of the Danube, classified, strangely enough, as Class 1 – though the prices certainly fall into the luxury class. 400 rooms.

Gellért
Budapest XI, Gellért tér 1
Tel: 1852-200.
The most famous of all the Budapest hotels – because of the gorgeous Jugendstil baths. On the Buda bank of the Danube near Liberation Bridge. Class 1; 235 rooms.

Grand Hotel Hungária
Budapest VII, Rákóczi út 90
Tel: 1229-050.
The biggest tourist hotel in Budapest, it has almost 1,000 beds. Near the Eastern Railway Station. Class 2; 582 rooms.

Grand Hotel Ramada
Budapest XIII, Margitsziget
Tel: 1111-000.
This palace of a hotel, built in 1873 on Margaret Island, was thoroughly renovated in 1987. There is an underground subway to the Hotel Térmal. Class 1; 163 rooms

Hilton
Budapest I, Hess András tér 103
Tel: 1751-000.
A great architectural success – modern glass walls which reflect the ornate little towers of the Fishermen's Bastion and the Matthias Church, and into which the Gothic remains of the Dominican monastery have been integrated with the greatest care. A further attraction is the casino. Class L; 323 rooms.

Olimpia
Budapest XII, Eötvös út 40
Tel: 1568-011.
Situated in the Buda Hills, this has a fitness centre and tennis courts and is a real El Dorado for sports fans and recreation seekers. Class 1; 168 rooms.

Palace
Budapest VIII, Rákóczi út 43
Tel: 1136-000.
Old, but good. The Jugendstil decor of the restaurant, under a preservation order, is especially attractive. Class 2; 91 rooms.

Park
Budapest VIII, Baross tér 10
Tel: 1131-420.
Near the Eastern Railway Station. Inexpensive (however, two-thirds of the rooms have no bathrooms). Class 3; 173 rooms.

Royal
Budapest VII, Lenin körút 47-49
Tel: 1533-133.
Traditional grand hotel dating from the turn of the century, modernised with respect for style. Class 1; 366 rooms.

SZOT
Budapest VI, Benczúr utca 35
Tel: 1427-970.
A guest-house hotel. Class 2; 91 rooms.

Termál
Budapest XIII, Margitsziget
Tel: 1111-000.
A luxury hotel built in 1979 on Margaret
Island – with its own dental clinic. Class L;
206 rooms.

Wien
Budapest XI, Budaörsi út 88-90
Tel: 1665-400.
On the edge of the city near the motorway
exit. Ideal for those travelling by car. Inex-
pensive (rooms without baths available).
Class 3, 110 rooms.

GUEST-HOUSES

These offer more modest accommodation
and are ideal for families and small groups of
all kinds.

Korona
Budapest XI, Sasadi utca 127
Tel: 1175-392.

Trió
Budapest XI, Ördögorom utca 20.

PRIVATE ROOMS

Because of the hotel situation in Budapest,
which is still precarious today, rooms in
private houses (27,000 beds as against
18,000 in the hotel industry) continue to
make up an important part of the accommodation available in the Hungarian capital.
In Hungary, only private individuals who
have special permission can rent out private
rooms. Those looking for rooms to rent can
either hire direct or via a travel agency. The
prices for rooms can be set by the owner, so
room prices may vary.
Non-compulsory guidelines for double
rooms or apartments of the better class: 500-
2,000 Ft per day. Simple beds can be had for
as little as 150 Ft per day. A limited number
of private rooms can also be booked through
travel agencies abroad.

Register of private rooms available at:
Budapest Tourist
Budapest V, Roosevelt tér 5
Tel: 1173-555;
Budapest VII, Lenin körút 31
Tel: 1426-521.

IBUSZ
Budapest V, Petöfi tér 3
Tel: 1184-848 (24 hours).

Volántourist
Budapest V, Belgrád rakpart 6
Tel: 1182-133.

CAMP GROUNDS

Off-site camping is prohibited in Hun-
gary. Camp sites in Hungary are divided into
three categories. Space, overnight stay and
parking spot prices are reckoned separately.
Space hire (according to category) 40-150
Ft, overnight stay per person 10-50 Ft. Re-
ductions available outside the main season.
For more information, contact:
Hungarian Camping and Caravan Club
Budapest VIII, Múzeum utca 11
Tel: 1141-880.

In the peak holiday season of July and
August the Budapest Exhibition Area offers
a space of 36,000 sq yards (30,000 sq
metres) with all the usual services for cara-
vanners. For more information, contact:
EXPO Autocamping
Budapest X, Dobi István út 10, Gate 4.

YOUTH HOSTELS

Youth hostels in the accepted sense do not
exist in Hungary. In the holiday months
(July/August) student hostels are converted
into youth guest hostels. For more informa-
tion, contact:
**Express Youth and Student Travel
Agency**
Budapest V, Szabadság tér 16
Tel: 1317-777.
An IYHF (International Youth Hostel
Federation) pass or ISTC (International Stu-
dent Tourist Conference) card is essential.

Youth hostels in Budapest (open all the year
round):

Express
Budapest II, Beethoven utca 7-9
Tel: 1158-891.

Ifjuság (Class 3, 100 rooms)
Budapest II, Zivatar utca 1-3
Tel: 1353-331, 1154-260;

Budapest II, Keleti Károly utca 37
Tel: 1150-663;
Budapest VII, Hársfa utca 4
Tel: 1220-456;
Budapest XI, Bartók Béla út 17
Tel: 1851-444;
Budapest XIV, Mogyoródi út 19-21
Tel: 1636 028;
Overnight stay 50-100 Ft.

Lidó (Class 4, 79 rooms)
Budapest III, Nánási út 67
Tel: 1888-160.

TOURIST HOSTELS

This is where young people can find the most inexpensive accommodation with the most basic provisions (dormitories, in some places do not have hot water).
Csúcshegyi, Category B
Budapest III, Menedéház utca 122
Tel: 1686-015.

Strand
Budapest III,Pusztakúti út 3
Tel: 1887-167.

BACKPACKERS

Over the last few years free sleeping bag space with toilets and washing facilities in the vicinity has been made available to backpackers. The place is Budapest X, Tündérfürt utca, open from mid-June to early September, from 4 p.m.

FOOD DIGEST

WHEN TO EAT

Breakfast (7 a.m.-10 a.m.): Hungary has joined the international trend of a buffet-style breakfast, even though it has done so reluctantly. At present only the luxury hotels conform to international standards.

A warning for coffee drinkers: in complete contrast to their usual habits (where coffee cannot be too black or too strong), Hungarians (like Italians with their *caffe latte*) love to drink an indifferent light brownish brew at breakfast time. If you want stronger coffee, you would do well to switch to mocha (*dupla*) for breakfast.

Lunch (noon-2.30 p.m.): This is the main meal of the day and normally consists of three courses: soup, a meat dish with vegetables, dessert. After food a strong Espresso is served.

Supper (7 p.m.-10 p.m.): The same as lunch. In most pubs you can find a relatively inexpensive set menu at lunchtime and in the evenings.

WHAT TO EAT

Basically, Hungarian cuisine is uncomplicated country food; heavy, substantial and anything but calorie-conscious.

Pork dominates the menu. The national spice is paprika (whoever would guess that it was once imported from America?) Goulash, the Hungarian national dish, needs a little explanation. The dish known outside Hungary as goulash or gulyás is called *pörkölt* by the Magyars (and unusual in that it is made with beef or veal). In Hungary gulyás is much more of a soup. The Hungarian fish soup *halászlé* deserves its fame. Many paprika-seasoned dishes are also Hungarian specialties: apart from pörkölt and gulyás there is the so-called Szeged (the correct term is Székler) gulyás, paprika chicken and paprika potatoes. The famous stuffed paprika, like *letsho* (sautéed paprika pods with tomatoes and onions), is a Balkan import. Preserved and stuffed cabbage come from Transylvania.

As an accompaniment to the main dish, apart from boiled potatoes, a form of pasta (*tarhonya*) is popular.

Paprika is also partly responsible for the flavour of Liptauer, a spread made from sheep's cheese mixed with butter, paprika, mustard, caraway and chives.

Among the desserts, the pancakes should be mentioned in first place. They are mostly made with sweet fillings (preserves, jam) but also with meat (*Hortobágy* pancakes).

WHERE TO EAT

The generally low cost of living in Hungary is most pleasantly noticeable when visiting a restaurant. Unless you decide to eat at one of the luxury hotels or at "Gundel", which emphasises its importance with especially high prices, in Budapest you can pay about half the amount you would have to put on the table in a restaurant of equal status in the West ("of equal status" here refers to the general atmosphere and service and not necessarily to the quality of the food).

Per person, a meal of three courses without wine would cost (approximate price guidelines):

Luxury	400-600 Ft
Class 1	1,200-400 Ft
Class 2	2,150-250 Ft
(good home cooking)	
Set meals:	
Class 1	80-120 Ft
Class 2	70-100 Ft

Restaurants (*étterem*) and inns (*vendéglö*) are divided into 4 classes. Menus in other languages are generally only available in the Class 1 and 2 restaurants.

LUXURY CLASS

Gundel
Budapest XIV, Allatkerti út 2
Tel: 1221-002.
The traditional best address in town. This luxurious establishment in the City Park entered culinary history as the birthplace of the famous Gundel *palacsinta* or pancakes. The service is perfect, the decor magnifi-

cent, and there is a charming garden. Open daily noon-midnight.

Alabárdos
Budapest I, Országház utca 2
Tel: 1560-851.
An evening restaurant in a Renaissance house in the Castle Quarter. You eat by candlelight in front of the open fire, accompanied by lute music. The prices are correspondingly high. Open Mon-Sat 7 p.m.-midnight, closed Sun.

CLASS 1

Aranyhordó
Budapest I, Tárnok utaca 16
Tel: 1556-765.
Also in the Castle Quarter. Wine bar in the cellar, beer room on the ground floor, excellent restaurant on the first floor (with gypsy music). Open daily 10 a.m.-midnight.

Margitkert Etterem
Budapest II, Margit utca 15
Tel: 1354-791.
A traditional inn of the good old days. Specialties include old Hungarian dishes prepared over a charcoal fire. Gypsy music in the evening. Open daily noon-midnight.

Sípos Haláskert
Budapest III, Fö tér 6
Tel: 1888-754.
In Obuda; the most famous fish restaurant in the city. Open daily noon-midnight.

CLASS 2

Híd Vendéglö
Old wine inn with excellent home-made food. Live music/cabaret.

Kis Kakukk
Budapest XIII, Pozsonyi út 12
Tel: 1321-723.
The menu – more than 100 meat, fish and game dishes – makes this restaurant a contender for the *Guinness Book of Records*. Gypsy music in the evenings. 10 a.m.-11 p.m., closed Wed.

Instead of an appendix, we'd just like to point out that all the major hotels have excellent restaurants.

Hungary has good wines. Their undisputed king is Tokay, a heavy, sweet white wine which, it must be said, is not necessarily the fashion these days. However, there are a number of excellent light white wines, especially those from around Lake Balaton.

The most famous red wine is the legendary Bull's Blood, and among the spirits the apricot brandy barack is top of the list.

Cocktails are not really that widespread in Hungary. However, at the bars of the big hotels you can still be served with even the most extraordinary of drinks.

PUBS & BARS

The "pub scene" actually comes alive during the day. Most of the pubs are stuffed full of young people in the uniform jeans-look of today's generation. The atmosphere is loud and noisy, people meet their friends and chat, without necessarily straining their wallets too much.

Amigo Drink Bar
Budapest IX, Tolbuhin körút 7
Tel: 1180-293.
Not far from the university and the Central Market Hall.

Húszéves ("20 years old")
Budapest V, Múzeum körút 39
Tel: 1180-769.
Near the Lóránd Eötvös University.

Inteam Drink Bar
Budapest XII, Orbánhegy út 1
The "in-team" – are you a member or would you like to go there and be one?

Mini Sörözö
Budapest V, Váci utca 36
Tel: 1180-310.
As the name says – a mini-beer room.

Gösser Sörpatika
Budapest V, Régiposta utca 4.
Gösser is a type of beer. Patika is a colloquial word for pharmacy. For those in medicinal need of beer.

Krokodil Drink Bar
Budapest I, Orságház utca 10.

Not every pub in the Castle Quarter has high prices.

Pepita Oroszlán ("the chequered lion")
Budapest V, Váci utca 40.
Lots of young faces.

Monika
Budapest IV, Kálvin-téri alujáró
Tel: 1184-545.
In the underpass at Kálvin ter.

Nárcisz Drink Bar
Budapest V, Váci utca 32
Tel: 1174-802.
Rather higher prices.

CAFES & COFFEE HOUSES

Even though the legendary glories of the Budapest coffee houses may have faded, the Hungarian cafe trade still shows that it is something to be reckoned with. The names, such as for example Ruszwurm and Gerbeaud, still have the same resonance as they did for our grandparents, and the greatest care is taken to preserve the pre-war atmosphere in the furnishings and the decor. A visit to one of the great cafes of Budapest is something of a nostalgic trip into the past. Even among the clientele, you can discover relicts of the "good" old days: white-haired ladies with strings of pearls, distinguished elderly gentlemen whose tailor-made suits have bravely withstood the ravages of time. Not forgetting the waitresses, members of a profession which one might have believed – especially in these parts of the world – to have long been extinct.

Café Hungaria
Budapest VII, Lenin körút 9-11.
The former Café New York, the famous haunt of artists and authors around the turn of the century. Open Mon-Sat 9 a.m.-10 p.m.; closed Sun.

Különlegességi
Budapest VI, Népköztársaság útja 70
Tel: 1321-371.
On Budapest's magnificent showcase street with the unpronounceable name: nehp-koez-tahr-sho-shahg-uhttyo. Open daily 8 a.m.-9 p.m.

Gerbeaud
Budapest V, Vörösmarty tér
Tel: 1181-311.
Open daily 9 a.m.-9 p.m.

Ruszwurm
Budapest I, Szentháromsag utca 7
Tel: 1755-284.
Open daily 10 a.m.-8 p.m.

THINGS TO DO

TOURIST INFORMATION

Tourist information on Hungary is available from:
The Danube Travel Agency
6 Conduit Street, London W1
Tel: 01 493 0263.

IBUSZ
630 Fifth Avenue
New York, NY 101112.

Tourinform
Budapest V, Sütö utca 2
Tel: 1179-800
Open weekdays 7 a.m.-7 p.m., Sat 8 a.m.-8 p.m. and Sun 7 a.m.-1 p.m. Visitors can obtain information in Hungarian, Russian, German, English and French on anything to do with tourism such as travel information, opening hours, addresses, telephone numbers, programmes and news of forthcoming events.

LEAFLETS & BROCHURES

The Tourist Promotion Department (IPV) publishes a large number of carefully prepared brochures, maps and leaflets on Budapest for the Hungarian Tourist Office (OIH). These are available free from travel agents and tourist enterprises as well as in hotel receptions.

IPV
Budapest XIV, Angol utca 22
Tel: 1633-406.

The *Programmes*, 48 to 64 pages thick, appear monthly. They can be obtained free of charge in hotels and travel agencies and, apart from theatre programmes and listings of concerts, exhibitions and other events, they contain useful tips for tourists in German and in English.

TRAVEL AGENCIES

Budapest Tourist arranges special events for your stay in Budapest, sightseeing tours, excursions of one or several days to other parts of the country. The accommodation service will book you rooms in private houses in any district of the city. The branches of Budapest Tourist offer all the usual services of a travel agency.
Budapest V, Roosevelt tér
Tel: 173-555.

TOUR GUIDES

Tour guides with foreign language qualifications can be arranged via the travel agencies. Some of the private taxi drivers' associations offer a tour lasting several hours with a taped guide. Prices by negotiation.
City Taxi, tel: 1288-855.
Lux Taxi, tel: 1532-532.

EXCURSIONS

Excursion boats run from the city centre upriver to the Arpád Bridge and back again. May-October, journey time about 2 hours. Depart from the Vigadó tér mooring point (Pest bank); 15 minutes later from Bem tér (Buda bank).

Among the excursions offered are a morning trip with a walk on Margaret Island, an afternoon excursion (with a band on board) and the popular evening entertainment of the "Budapest Lights". Very popular among young people is the "dance boat", which offers modern dance music at reasonable prices thrice weekly. You can also hire boats privately (for 2 or 4 hours, half a day, the whole day). For information and bookings, contact:

MAHART
Hungarian Shipping Company
International Shipping Office
Budapest V, Belgrád rakpart
Tel: 1181-704;
Vigadó tér mooring point
Tel: 1181-223, 1354-907; and
travel agencies.

Excursions to the Danube Bend (Szentendre, Visegrád, Esztergom) are available by boat (May-October) or by jetfoil (all the year round). Depart from Vigadó tér. Also calls at Bem tér.

Jetfoil: Daily departures at 9 a.m. and 3 p.m. Journey time: Visegrád 50 minutes, Esztergom another 100 minutes. Half-day excursion.

Boat: Daily departure at 7.30 a.m. Journey time: Visegrád 3 hours, Esztergom 6 hours. Full day excursion.

For information and bookings, contact MAHART, and other travel agencies.

SHORT STAYS

If you only have a short time to spend seeing the city, you should limit yourself first of all to the essentials. Later you will certainly get another opportunity to increase your knowledge of Budapest

One day:
Morning: Castle Quarter, Castle Museum.
Afternoon: Pest (Inner City, Parliament).

Two days:
Day 1, morning: Gellért Hill, Pest (Inner City), Parliament and surroundings.
Day 1, afternoon: Castle Quarter, Castle Museum.
Day 2, morning: walk along Buda Danube bank, Rudas Baths, Király Baths, Obuda, Aquincum, Margaret Island.
Day 2, afternoon: Heroes' Square, Museum of Fine Arts, Városliget (City Park).

Three days:
Day 1, morning: Inner City, Parliament and surroundings.
Day 1, afternoon: Castle Quarter and Castle Museum.
Day 2, morning: Gellért Hill, walk along the Buda Danube bank, Water City, Aquincum.

Day 2, afternoon: St István körút, Basilica, Népköztársaság útja, Liberation Square, Museum of Fine Arts, City Park, zoo.
Day 3, morning: National Museum, Museum of Applied and Decorative Arts.
Day 3, afternoon: Margaret Island or trip to the Buda Hills; in summer, perhaps a boat trip on the Danube.

Four days:
The 3-day programme plus a fourth day: Whole day excursion (boat or bus) to the Danube Bend.

CITY TOURS

Guided tours of the city, in special coaches, are organised all year round by various travel agencies. There are several tours a day in the main season. The city tours (which in summer also take place in an open-topped bus) usually last 3-4 hours.

Special programmes: tours of Parliament, the Castle in Buda, various museums; baths tour; walk through the Inner City; "Budapest in Depth" etc.

Evening programmes: Budapest by Night (includes visit to a night club); folk music evening with wine tasting; "Goulash-Party" (with gypsy music and folk dancing ensembles) etc.

Detailed programmes are available from hotel receptions, travel agencies and the various organisers.

COUNTRYSIDE TRIPS

Budapest Tourist also organises regular excursions to the countryside around the city. The most popular excursions are those to the picturesque Danube Bend (Szentendre, Visegrád, Esztergom) and Lake Balaton. There are also trips to the Bugac Puszta (with equestrian displays and rides in horse-drawn coaches) and to Zsámbék. Information can be had from hotel receptions, travel agencies and the various organisers.

BATHS

Budapest has no equal as a spa among any of the great cities of the world. Every day within the city boundaries 50 million litres of water with a temperature ranging from 20-70°C issue from 32 springs. The healing powers of these thermal springs are made use of in a dozen baths and several sanatoria. The medicinal springs are rich in calcium, magnesium, carbonated salts, chlorides and sulphates; some also contain fluoride and radioactive salts. Their therapeutic effects are most noticeable in treating diseases of the motor system, the digestive tract and respiratory organs, as well as gynaecological complaints. The most important medicinal baths are:

Császar
Budapest II, Frankel Leó utca 31
Tel: 1159-850.
Thermal steam baths. For treating the motor system; water drinking cures for the digestive tract, gall bladder. Tue, Thur, Sat, men only; Mon, Wed, Fri, women only. Mon-Sat 6.30 a.m.-7 p.m., Sun 6.30 a.m.-noon.

Gellért
Budapest XI, Gellért tér
Tel: 1852-200.
Famous not only for its Jugendstil swimming pool. Attached to the hotel of the same name. Mon-Sat 6 a.m.-8 p.m., Sun 6 a.m.-7 p.m. For treating the motor system, peripheral circulation problems.

Király
Budapest II, Fö utca 82-86
Tel: 1153-000.
Built in 1565-70 by the Pasha of Buda, these baths are among the most important buildings remaining from Turkish times. Mon, Wed, Sun, men only; Tue, Thur, Sat, women only. Thermal steam baths. Mon-Sat 6.30 a.m.-6 p.m., Sun 6.30 a.m.-noon.

Lukács
Budapest II, Frankel Leó utca 25-29
Tel: 1758-373.
Together with the Imperial Baths (Császár fürdö), these belong to the National Institute for Rheumatology and Physiotherapy, ORFI.

Margaret Island Thermal Baths
Budapest XIII, Margitsziget
Tel: 1111-000.
A combination of a spa and a luxury hotel, in the peaceful surroundings of Margaret Island. For treating the motor system, gynaecological problems.

Rác
Budapest I, Hadnagy utca 8-10
Tel: 1352-708.
Situated in Tabán Park at the foot of Gellért Hill, these baths, which are under a preservation order, are perhaps the most atmospheric of all the baths of Budapest. Mon-Sat 6.30 a.m.-7 p.m.; closed Sun. Tue, Thur, Sat, men only; Mon, Wed, Fri, women only.

Rudas
Budapest I, Döbrentei tér 9
Also situated in Tabán Park, these baths were well known as early as the 15th century. Some parts of the baths which were rebuilt in Turkish times (1566) have survived. Mon-Sat 6 a.m.-6 p.m., Sun 6 a.m.-4 p.m. For treating motor system; water drinking cures for digestive tract, gall bladder, respiratory system.

Széchenyi
Budapest XIV, Allatkerti körút 11
Tel: 1210-310.
These turn-of-the-century medicinal baths in the City Park have two open-air pools (open all the year round) with warm and somewhat cooler water. Mon-Sat 7 a.m.-7 p.m. (men and women). For treating the motor system, gynaecological problems. Water drinking cures for stomach and gall bladder.

Last admissions are always one hour before the times listed above.

CULTURE PLUS

Budapest has a relatively rich cultural life. Up-to-date details of events can be obtained free from all hotel receptions and travel agencies, and a monthly programme of events is available in English.

MUSEUMS

Budapest has a wealth of museums – there are three dozen of them altogether. The most important of them are listed below. A complete list can be found in the monthly programmes. Opening hours: 10 a.m.-6 p.m., Sun 9 a.m.-1 p.m., closed Mon.

Agricultural Museum
(Mezögazdasági Múzeum)
Városliget, Budapest XIV, Széchenyi sziget
Tel: 1423-198.
This collection of agricultural implements and products were displayed in the fairy-tale castle of Vajdahunyad in 1896. At the time, it was the first such museum in the world.

Aquincum
Excavated site of Aquincum and museum
Budapest III, Szentendrei út 139
Tel: 1804-650.
On a site 1,300 by 2,000 ft (440 by 600 m) you can see the excavated foundations of part of the Roman city. In the museum building there is a lapidarium and a display of commonly-used articles. The pride of the collection is the only surviving water organ.

Civilian Town Amphitheatre next to the excavations
Military Town Amphitheatre
Budapest III, Nagyszombat, corner of Korvin Ottó utca.

Ethnographical Museum
Budapest V, Kossuth Lajos tér 12
Tel: 1326-340.

In the building which formerly housed the Supreme Court. The collections concentrate on Hungarian folk history; there are also anthropological exhibitions from all the continents, mainly from Oceania.

Ferenc Hopp East Asian Museum
(Keletázsiai Múzeum)
Budapest VI, Népköztársaság útja 103
Tel: 1228-476.
In the former magnificent house of the the founder, Ferenc Hopp – a collection comprising 20,000 objects connected with Asia.

Fine Arts Museum
(Szépmüvészeti Múzeum)
Budapest XIV
(Hösök tere) Dósza György út 41
Tel: 1429-759.
The most important collection of paintings in Hungary; Egyptian department; Graeco-Roman department; Old masters. Apart from the Prado, this museum has the most extensive collection of Spanish masters in the world (El Greco, Velasquez, Murillo, Ribera, Zurbarán). Excellent graphics collection. The museum made the headlines in 1983, when seven masterpieces were stolen (and recovered three months later).

Historical Museum/Castle Museum
(Történeti Múzeum)
Várpalota, Szent György tér 2
Tel: 1757-533.
In wing E of the castle of Buda. Here you can see the building remains and the sculptures of the medieval castle, which came to light during restoration work after 1945.

Military History Museum
(Hadtörténeti Múzeum)
Várpalota, Budapest I, Tóth Arpád sétány 40
Tel: 1160-184.
In a former barracks in the Castle Quarter of Buda. The museum concentrates on the revolution years of 1848-49. In front of the building there are Turkish cannons dating from the 17th-18th century.

Military Town Museum
(Táborvárosi Múzeum)
Budapest III, Korvin Ottó utca 64
Tel: 1804-650.

Mosaic floor of a Roman villa
Budapest II, Vihar utca 31.

Museum of Applied and Decorative Arts
(Iparmüvészeti Múzeum)
Budapest XI, Üllöi út 31-37
Tel: 1175-222.
This museum, founded in 1872, was the third of its kind after the Victoria and Albert Museum in London and the Museum of Applied Arts in Vienna. If you are pressed for time, you should at least take a look at the building from the outside. Built from 1893-96, it is probably the most impressive work by the great Hungarian Jugendstil architect Ödön Lechner.

National Gallery
(Magyar Nemzeti Galéria)
Vápalota, Budapest I, Dísz tér 17
Tel: 1757-733.
In what were once the royal reception halls of the castle of Buda (wings B, C, D).

Medieval lapidarium. Gothic wooden sculpture and panel paintings of the 14th and 15th centuries; late Gothic altar panels; art of the late Renaissance and Baroque, 1500-1800; painting and sculpture of 19th century Hungary; Hungarian art of the 20th century.

National Museum
(Magyar Nemzeti Múzeum)
Budapest VII, Múzeum körút 14-16
Tel: 1134-400.
The most beautiful Classical building by Mihály Pollack, built 1837-47. The collection goes back to a donation by Count Ferenc Széchenyi, father of the reformer István, dating from 1802.

History of the peoples of Hungary up to the "Taking of the Land" (896); Hungarian history up to 1849; the Hungarian coronation regalia, including St Stephen's Crown. The Natural History Museum is housed on the second floor.

Remains of Roman baths
Budapest III, Flórián tér 3.

ART GALLERIES

Art Gallery (Mücsarnok)
Budapest XIV
(Hösök tere) Dósza György út 37
Tel: 1227-405.

This Neo-Classical Grecian temple in Heroes' Square is the biggest exhibition hall in the capital.

Óbuda Gallery
Budapest III, Fö tér 1
Tel: 1803-340.
In the former Zichy palais in Óbuda. Attached to a museum with works by Lajos Kassák and Victor Vasarely.

Studio Gallery
Budapest V, Bajcsy-Zsilinsky út 52
Tel: 1119-882.

Vigadó Galéria
Budapest V, Vigadó tér 2
Tel: 1176-222.
The Vigadó, that restored, impressive building of the Hungarian Historicist period (1859-64), is the splendid setting for a variety of exhibitions. Two exhibitions can be displayed at any one time on the two floors of the building.

This is where periodic exhibitions of the works of Hungarian and foreign artists are held. A list of the most important exhibition halls is available from: Budapest V, Dorottya utca 8, tel: 1183-899.

Budapest Galéria
Budapest V, Szabadsajtó út
Tel: 1171-001.

Duna Galéria
Budapest XIII, Rajk Lászlo utca 95
Tel: 1409-186.

Ernszt Museum
Budapest VI, Nagymezö utca 8
Tel: 1414-356.
Not a museum, but an exhibition hall – the biggest in the city apart from the Art Gallery.

Helikon Galéria
Budapest V, Eötvös utca 8
Tel: 1174-765.

There is no free art market in Hungary. The works on exhibition and also for sale in the various galleries have been put "up for sale" by a jury, which also sets the prices. Interested parties from abroad are welcome to pay in Western currency. Opening hours are Mon-Fri 10 a.m.-6 p.m., Sat 9 a.m.-1 p.m.

Art Galéria
Budapest I, Táncsics Mihály utca 5

Castle Gallery
Budapest I, Táncsics Mihály utca 17
Tel: 1569-239.

Csók Istvan Galéria
Budapest V, Váci utca 25
Tel: 1182-592.

Csontváry Terem
Budapest V, Vörösmarty tér 1
Tel: 1184-594.

Fotogaléria (Artistic photographs)
Budapest V, Váci utca 7
Tel: 1183-005.

Modern graphics
Budapest V, Váci utca 16
(In the Aranypók department store)
Tel: 1382-119

Pór Bertalan Terem
Budapest VII, József körút
Tel: 1140-225.

CONCERTS

The centre of the busy concert life of Budapest is the Music Academy, named after Franz Liszt, with its two halls. In the Ballroom (Vigadó) in Pest performances are mainly by soloists and chamber orchestras.

There are concerts all the year round, too, in the Buda Ballroom and in the Budapest Conference Centre. Occasional concerts are held in the Erkel Theatre, the second opera house of the Hungarian capital. In fine weather, especially during the months of July and August, there are regular open-air concerts in various places. Several churches also hold organ and choral concerts. There are choral concerts, often of old music, every Sun at 11 a.m. in the Castle. Concerts generally begin at 7 p.m., 7.30 p.m. at the latest. For information and bookings, contact:

Filharmonia
Budapest V, Vörösmarty tér 1
Tel: 1176-222.

Music Academy (Zenemüvészeti Föiskola)
Budapest VI, Liszt Ferenc tér 30
Tel: 1420-179.

Pest Ballroom (Pesti Vigadó)
Budapest V, Vigadó tér
Tel: 1176-222.

Buda Ballroom (Budai Vigadó)
Budapest I, Corvin tér 8
Tel: 1159-657.

Budapest Conference Centre
Budapest XII, Jagelló út
Tel: 1968-588;
Box office, tel: 1252-869.

Reformed Church
Budapest IX, Kálvin tér.

Lutheran Church
Budapest V, Deák tér 4-5.

Matthias Church
Budapest I, Szentháromság tér.

OUTDOOR VENUES

Buda Park Theatre
Budapest XI, Kosztolányi Dezsö tér
Tel: 1669-849.

Open-air stage in Városmajor Park
Budapest I, Városmajori park
Tel: 1353-178.

Dominican Court in the Hilton Hotel
Budapest I, Hess András tér 1
Tel: 1853-500.

Open-air stage of the Opera House on Margaret Island
Budapest XIII, Margitsziget
Tel: 1112-463.

Musical Court
Budapest II, Marcibányi tér 5A
Tel: 1353-786, 355-759.

Zichy Palace
Budapest III, Fö tér 1
Tel: 1686-020.

Information
Budapest Vi, Jókai utca 24

Tel: 1321-721;
Advance booking
Budapest XIII, Fürst Sándor utca 10
Tel: 1114-283.

OPERA & BALLET

Opera has a long and honourable tradition in Budapest. After all, Gustav Mahler was, before he went to the Hofoper in Vienna, in charge of opera in Budapest. The capital allows itself the luxury of two opera houses – the State Opera and the Erkel Theatre – which have a wide-reaching repertoire. For lighter music, there is the **Operetta Theatre**, which honours the memory of Franz Lehár and Imre Kálmán. The ballet company of the Hungarian State Opera is famous far and wide outside the country.

Ticket prices, compared to those in the West, are moderate indeed. Travel agencies abroad will accept up to 400 Ft worth of ticket bookings. Performances begin at 7 p.m. Ticket bookings at box offices: Thur, Fri, Sat 3 p.m.-5.30 p.m.
Central Booking Offices
Budapest VI, Népköztársaság útja 18
Tel: 1120-000;
Budapest VI, Lenin körút 108
Tel: 1120-430; and also
Budapest II, Moszkva tér 3
Tel: 1359-136.

State Opera House
(Magyar Allami Operaház)
Budapest VI, Népköztársaság útja 22
Tel: 1312-550.

Erkel Theatre
Budapest VIII, Köztársaság tér 30
Tel: 1330-108, 1330-540.

Capital Operetta Theatre
(Fövárosi Operettszinház)
Budapest VI, Nagymezö utca 17-19
Tel: 1126-470.

THEATRE

For those who cannot speak Hungarian it is of course difficult to take part in the rich theatrical life of Budapest. However, a visit to the theatre can have its positive side, even if you do not understand the Hungarian language (this is assuming that you know the play: you can then enjoy the acting in pure form, without being distracted by the content of the play). Even more concentrated "pure" acting can be experienced in the two puppet theatres and the mime theatre.

Castle Theatre
Budapest I, Színház utca 1-3
Tel: 1758-001.

Katona Theatre
Budapest V, Petöfi Sándor utca 6
Tel: 1186-599.

Children's Theatre/Arany János Theatre
Budapest VI, Paulay Ede utca 35
Tel: 1226-059.

Madách Theatre
Budapest VII, Lenin körút 29-33
Tel: 1220-677.

Chamber Theatre
Budapest VII, Madách tér 6
Tel: 1226-422.

National Theatre
Budapest VII, Hevesi Sándor tér 2
Tel: 1413-849.

Puppet Theatre (Allami Bábszínház)
Budapest VI, Népköztársaság útja 69
Tel: 1422-702.

Chamber Theatre
Budapest VI, Jókai tér 10
Tel: 1120-622.

People's Theatre (summer only)
Színház utca 2-4
Tel: 1360-390.

Centimetre Theatre (mime, summer only)
Budapest IX, Üllöi út 45
Tel: 1135-020.

MUSICALS

Without making a great fuss about it, Budapest has risen to be one of the world centres of the musical. In the spring of 1989 there were no fewer than nine productions being performed simultaneously, five of them the work of Hungarian composers and librettists. For years Andrew Lloyd

Webber's *Cats* has been running in the old and respected Madách Theatre, it runs on and on and on. Incidentally, the Budapest performance of the hit musical of the 1980s was the first to take place abroad after the London premiere.

These musicals, unlike in the West, are not performed in a continuous series. Repertory theatre is still valued in Budapest – this is a matter of principle, and not even the greatest financial success of a single play can change it. Take a look at the monthly programme, then, if you want to go to a musical.

CINEMA

Cinema lovers from abroad have a hard time in Hungary, as foreign films here are dubbed, almost without exception.

The major hotels have their own cable TV service offering (for a fee) films in other languages, including English. Classics of the cinema (these too are dubbed!) can be enjoyed in the Film Museum.

Filmmúzeum
Budapest VII, Tanács körút
Tel: 1220-3302.

ARCHITECTURE

Basilica, see St Stephen's Church.

Castle and palace
Várpalota, Budapest I
Szent György tér.

The medieval royal castle was extended in Renaissance times (King Matthias Corvinus) and completely destroyed in 1686. Not until 1749 did Empress Maria Theresia authorise the building of a new palace (completed in 1770). In 1890 the Baroque building was extended to twice its size in the Historicist style and given an enormous dome. The palace, completely destroyed in 1945 during the battle for Budapest, was rebuilt after 1950.

Castle Quarter
During the restoration work on Castle Hill the historic houses of the quarter were thoroughly renovated as well. During this work many old building elements were discovered behind the Baroque facades and can now be seen, e.g. the characteristic Baroque

seat niches. Today the quarter, restored in exemplary fashion, has attracted a number of boutiques, galleries, bars and restaurants and is one of the centres of the Budapest tourist industry.

Chain Bridge (Lánchíd)
This suspension bridge, the first permanent link between Pest and Buda, was built between 1839 and 1849. The initiative came from Count István Széchenyi, the plans were drawn up by the Englishman William Tierney Clark and the building was supervised by his countryman Adam Clark. With its pillars shaped like Roman triumphal arches it has become one of the symbols of the city. It was blown up, like all the city's bridges, in 1945 during the battle for Budapest. It was rebuilt exactly as before, except that the roadway was widened, and re-opened to traffic during the centenary celebrations in 1949.

Fishermen's Bastion (Halászbástya)
This construction in blinding white stone is of course not a bastion in the sense of a defensive fortification. It was built around the turn of the century in a Neo-Romanesque style. The view down onto the river and over the city is enough to make you forget the rather over-ornate architecture of the generously sized building. Its tower-crowned viewing terraces and steps are situated above the steep drop of Castle Hill right behind the Matthias Church.

Heroes' Square (Hösök tere)
This impressive square at the entrance to the City Park was laid out in 1896 for the Millennial Celebrations, the 1,000th anniversary of the Magyar conquest of Hungary. Its dominant central feature is the Millennium monument (1896-1929) and a column, 118 ft (36 m) high, surrounded by a group of statues portraying prominent historical figures and flanked by a colonnade forming a semicircle 279 ft (85 m) broad and 82 ft (25 m) deep.

Inner City Parish Church
(Belvárosi Plébánia templom)
Budapest V, Március 15 tér.
Situated at the Pest end of Elizabeth Bridge. Gothic choir with ribbed cruciform vaulting (14th/15th century), Baroque nave

with barrel vaulting (18th century), Baroque double tower facade (1795). A relict of Turkish times, when the church served as a mosque, is the prayer niche (*mihrab*).

Matthias Church (Mátyas templom)
Little remains of the church built in the 13th century for the German population of the Castle Quarter. The present-day building with its slender, 263-ft (80-m) high tower is essentially the work of the architect Frigyes Schulek, who had a gift for re-interpreting a medieval church in the Historicist style (1874-96).

Parliament
Budapest V, Kossuth Lajos tér 1-3.
Indubitably the most impressive building on the Danube bank, this is a huge Neo-Gothic complex dominated by its dome, and together with the Chain Bridge it has become a symbol of the city. The 880-ft (268-m) long, 387-ft (118-m) broad and 315-ft (96-m) tall building was constructed from 1884-1902 as a rival to the Houses of Parliament in London.

St Stephen's Parish Church (Basilica)
Budapest V, Szent István tér.
The biggest church in Budapest, this building is the product of Historicism. It was begun in 1851 in the Neo-Classical style by József Hild. Work continued in a Neo-Renaissance style under Miklós Ybl and the church was completed in 1905.

Synagogue
Budapest VI, Dohány utca 2-8.
This mighty Byzantine-Moorish building, a three-nave hall temple with a pair of onion-domed towers (1854-59), is the work of the Viennese architect responsible for the Ringstrasse, Ludwig Förster.

Vajdahunyad
Budapest XIV, Városliget
Széchenyi-sziget.
This building was erected in the City Park on Széchenyi Island for the Millennial Celebrations in 1896. It is supposed to represent the the various building styles of Hungarian history. It unites the details – precisely copied or freely interpreted – of Hungarian buildings from the Romanesque to the Baroque periods. The dominating Gothic wing of the building is a copy of the Rákóczi castle of Vajdahunyad in Transylvania – hence the name.

Western Railway Station
(Nyugati pályaudvar)
Budapest VI, Lenin körút 109-111
This wrought iron construction, built between 1874 and 1877 and restored to its original appearance in 1976, has a glass-roofed station hall which covers 270,000 square feet (25,000 sq metres) and is a masterpiece of the engineering of those times. It was built by the Parisian engineering company of Gustave Eiffel.

NIGHTLIFE

Focal points of night life in Budapest are the Castle Quarter and the Inner City of Pest. There is no lack of night bars and night clubs; all the big hotels have them. Those with a revue and floorshow are listed separately. One peculiarity of nightlife in the Hungarian capital is that many nightspots have the motto "Never on Sunday."

CABARET

For nightbirds, there is a lively cabaret scene in Budapest.

Vidám Színpad (The Merry Stage)
Budapest VI, Révay utca 18
Tel: 1328-916.

Kamara Varieté
Budapest VII, Lenin körút 106
Tel: 1120-430.

Mikroszkóp Színpad
Budapest VI, Nagymezö utca 11
(In the Thalia Theatre building)
Tel: 325-322.

DISCOS

Every evening young people rush to the discos, even though the entrance prices are quite high (up to 80 Ft).

Audio disco Bar
Budapest XIV, Erzsébet királyné útja 118 (In the Zuglói Restaurant)
Tel: 663-013.
Laser show, special events, open daily 8 p.m.-4 a.m.

Fekete Macska
Budapest IX, Knézich utca 1
Tel: 170-469.
A popular meeting place, open Thur-Tue 7 p.m.-3 a.m., closed Wed.

Fekete Lyuk
Budapest XIV, Városliget.
A newcomer to City Park open 8 p.m.-4 a.m.

Fortuna
Budapest I, Hess András tér 4
Tel: 756-857.
Roofed by Gothic vaults, open daily 9 p.m.-3 a.m.

Galaxis Disco
Budapest III, Szépvólgyi út 15
Tel: 1805-262.
In the Ujlaki Restaurant, open daily 9 p.m.-4 a.m.

Magistral
Budapest V, Gerlóczy utca 13
Tel: 1175-803.
The new in-place, open daily 8 p.m.-3 a.m.

Margithíd
Budapest V, Szent István körút 1
Tel: 1124-215.
One of the biggest discos, open daily 9 p.m.-4 a.m.

Old Firenze
Budapest I, Táncsics Mihály utca 25
Tel: 1160-686.
A high standard of entertainment at a high price, open daily 7 p.m.-3 a.m.

Randevú
Budapest XII, Lékai János tér 9
Tel: 1850-968.

As the name says – this is where everybody meets, open daily 8 p.m.-4 a.m.

Tó
Budapest III, Rozgonyi Piroska utca 3
Tel: 1689-529.
Near the Danube, on the Rómaipart, open daily 10 p.m.-4 a.m.

NIGHTCLUBS & BARS

Nightlife in Budapest is rather provincial in nature. Though the bands and the music they play, are very much with the times. Most places are open from 10 p.m. to 4 a.m.

Apollo
Budapest XI, Tass Vezéti utca
Tel: 1260-600.
Mon-Sat 10 p.m.-4 a.m., closed Sun.

Budapest
In the hotel of the same name
Budapest II, Szilágyi Erszébet fasor 47
Tel: 1153-230.
Mon-Sat 10 p.m.-4 a.m., closed Sun.

Casanova
Budapest I, Batthyány tér 4
Tel: 1351-113.
Open daily 10 p.m.-3 a.m.

Etoile
Budapest XIII, Pozsonyi út 4
Tel: 1122-242.
Bar with live piano music, part of an exclusive French-style restaurant, open daily 10 p.m.-3 a.m.

Gellért
Budapest XI, Gellért tér 1
Tel: 1852-200.
Equally famous as the hotel to which it belongs, Mon-Sat 10 p.m.-4 a.m., closed Sun.

Halászbástya
Budapest I, Halászbástya
Tel: 1561-446.
The elegant bar, with dancing, of the Hilton Hotel, open daily 10 p.m.-4 a.m.

Non-Stop-Bar
Budapest IX, Dimitrov tér.
Open 9 p.m.-3 a.m.

Pierrot
Budapest I, Fortuna utca 14
Tel: 1229-050.
Bar with live piano music in the Castle
Quarter, open daily 10 p.m.-4 a.m.

Pipacs
Budapest V, Aranykéz utca 4
Tel: 1185-505.
Established bar, open daily 10 p.m.-5 a.m.

FLOORSHOWS

The exotic, the erotic and lots of bare skin,
presented with more or less style and skill.
Unless stated otherwise, the programme
begins at 11 p.m.

Astoria
Budapest V, Kossuth Lajos utca 19
Tel: 1186-351.
The cheeky floorshow is at odds with the
comfortable, somewhat old-fashioned sur-
roundings. Tue-Sun 9 p.m.-3 a.m., closed
Mon.

Fortuna
Budapest I, Hess András tér 4
Tel: 1756-857.
Roofed by Gothic vaults: jazz and a mid-
night revue, daily 9 p.m.-4 a.m., programme
begins at 11.30 p.m.

Havanna Club
Budapest XIII, Margitsziget
Tel: 1321-100.
Mon-Sat 10 p.m.-4 a.m., disco on Sun only

Lidó
Budapest V, Szabadsajtó út 5
Tel: 1182-404.
A famous cafe up until 1945; now has an
"international revue programme", revue
daily 11 p.m.-4 a.m.; gypsy music 7 p.m.-11
p.m.

Hotel Emke
Budapest VII, Akácfa utca 3
Tel: 1420-145.
Mon-Sat 8 p.m.-4 a.m., closed Sun; revue
starts 8.15 p.m., 11.30 p.m., 1 a.m.

Moulin Rouge
Budapest VI, Nagymezö utca 17
Tel: 1124-492.

Decor reminiscent of the Belle Epoque.
Spectacular revue numbers. Open daily 10
p.m.-4 a.m.

Nirvána Bar
Budapest V, Szent István körút 13
Tel: 1118-894.
In the basement of the Berlin Restaurant. An
ambitious revue prgramme. Wed-Mon 10
p.m.-4 a.m., closed Tue.

Orfeum
Budapest VI, Lenin körút 97
Tel: 1323-300.
In the Jugendstil atmosphere of the Béke
hotel, Mon-Sat 9 p.m.-4 a.m., closed Sun.
Revue begins 10.45 p.m.

Savoy
Budapest VI, Népköztársaság útja 48
Tel: 1531-258.
In the theatre district, next to the Opera, daily
10 p.m.-5 a.m., revue begins 10.30 p.m.

CASINOS

On the top floor of the Hilton Hotel, the
Austrian Casino Company opened the first
casino behind the Iron Curtain, which by
now has more than a few holes in it. Bets are
placed in Deutschmarks – other Western
currencies are accepted. You can get rid of
your money – or make your fortune – playing roulette, baccarat, blackjack or the 40
"one-armed bandits".
Winnings are tax free and are paid in
Deutschmarks, so they can be exported
without difficulties.

Casino Budapest
(In the Hilton Hotel, Budapest)
Budapest I, Hess András tér 1-4
Tel: 1751-000.
Open daily from 5 p.m., entrance fee 5DM
(can be redeemed in chips).

A branch of the casino has been opened on
a boat with a restaurant in front of the Hotel
Fórum by the Chain Bridge. Money sources
are more or less the same as in the Hilton;
Hungarian nationals are not allowed to play.

SHOPPING

WHAT TO BUY

Budapest is a relatively good spot for shoppers. Hardly any visitor leave the city empty-handed. Empty wallets are rather more common.

What is it that makes shopping in Budapest so attractive to spoiled Western visitors? The enormous price gap definitely plays a part. Nearly all articles of everyday use are a good two-thirds cheaper than they are at home. This makes bringing some of it back with you an attractive proposition (it must be said here that the two leading products of the Hungarian food industry, goose liver pate and salami, are by now almost exclusively available only in foreign currency shops).

Among finished products pieces of craft work, especially those of folk art, are extremely popular. Visitors respect the fact that most of these handicrafts – from ceramics, leather and textile articles to lace and embroidery – are still genuinely handcrafted and not mass produced.

The cobblers and tailors of the Hungarian capital once had a legendary reputation. The "Budapest", a prototype of many men's shoe styles, has entered fashion history. These traditions are still kept up today, though in a more modest way. All the same, if you are patient (waiting lists of several months are the rule) and if necessary don't mind making a second visit for trying the items on, you can have your measurements taken from head to foot for an entire wardrobe (there are even shirt tailors) – and at prices that are about the same as those for medium-range off the peg clothes. If you want to be on the safe side, you can bring your own material.

The once generous supply of old books seems to have dried up (or maybe it has simply adapted to the rise in demand and "consolidated" itself), but connoisseurs still like to browse through the (state-owned) BAV antique shops. Here you repeatedly get the opportunity to find fine pieces which have come from private ownership. However, they may only date back to the times of our grandparents – all pieces over 100 years old are considered of "national value" and may not be taken out of the country.

Another source of shopping pleasure are the foreign currency shops. Here, for hard currency, you can buy just about everything your heart desires – from salami to the exquisite Herend porcelain and to stereo systems. At times, though, you have to remind yourself that you are in a land of planned economy; if you can't find an article on the shelf in one of the shops, you won't find it anywhere else either.

ARTS & CRAFTS

In Hungary, where its traditions are still kept alive, folk art has considerable status. There are thousands of craftsmen working in cottage industries all over the land, commissioned by the council which runs the craft shops in Budapest. These shops sell folk arts and crafts based on authentic patterns. Here you can buy hand-woven textiles, embroidery, little lace cloths, braid, beautiful ceramics, plates and jugs, earthenware, leather and textile goods, carpets, wood carvings and other items.

Budapest I, Szilágyi Dezsö tér 6
Budapest I, Országház utca 16
Budapest II, Mártrok útja 34
Budapest V, Kossuth Lajos utca 2
Budapest V, Régiposta utca 12
Budapest V, Váci utca 14 (also open Sat, Sun)
Budapest V, Kálvin tér 5
Budapest VII, Lenin körút 5
Budapest VII, Rákóczi út 32
Budapest XI, Bartók Béla út 50
Budapest XIII, Szent István körút 26

There are of course many other shops devoted to folk art. A few addresses:
Budapest VI Bajcsy-Zsilinsky út 56
Budapest V, Régi posta utca 4
Budapest V, Régi posta utca 7-9
Budapest I, Tárnok utca 10
Budapest I, Uri utca 26-28

Items of folk art and craft are available in

the gift shops:
Budapest V, Petöfi Sándor utca 8

Modern crafts, goldsmith's work and textiles:
Budapest V Kossuth Lajos utca 14 and 17
Budapest V, Haris köz 6
Budapest V, Kecskeméti utca 4

The foreign currency shops are also well supplied with folk art.

ANTIQUES

The antiques trade is in the hands of the state-owned organisation BAV, which works closely together with the foreign currency shops. In these goods are only sold for foreign currency. You can pay in forint in the following shops:
Budapest V Felszabadulás tér 3
Budapest V, Kossuth Lajos utca 1-3
Budapest V, Szent István körút 3

The best address for antiques is the Konsumtourist shop opposite the opera house: for paintings, miniatures, engravings, small sculptures, glass, small items of furniture, and coins.
Budapest V, Népköztársasag útja 27

Period furnishings and other interior decor items, as well as the greatest selection of paintings, can be found at the BAV shop in Szent István körút 3. If you are lucky, you may find the odd antique item in the flea-market in Nagykörösi út.

Excellent, rather expensive reproductions (not "genuine" antiques) of craft items on exhibition in museums (ceramics, boxes, etc.) can be bought in museum gift shops.
Múzeumi Souvenirbolt
Budapest V, József nádor tér 7
Tel: 1184-343.

AUCTIONED ITEMS

There are very few auctions in Budapest. Auctions take place two or three times a year and are always limited to a particular area. Viewing takes place a week beforehand.
 Auction dates:
Jewellery: March, November
Paintings: May, September, December
Books, prints: spring, autumn

SOUVENIRS

For some people a holiday is only complete when the souvenirs have been bought. In Budapest, you can find such things at:
Kalocsa
Budapest V, Felszabadulás tér 5;
Budapest V, Szent István körút 19.

Iparmüvészeti Vállalat Ajándékok
Budapest I, Uri utca 26-28.

Lady D.I.
Budapest V, Haris köz 3.

Satöbbi
Budapest V, Hajós utca 7.

A popular souvenir or gift is Herend porcelain. It can be bought in the foreign currency shops or directly from the producer:
Herend Porcelain
Budapest V, Kígyó utca 4
Tel: 1183-712.

LADIES' WEAR

The top address in Budapest is the salon that keeps alive the traditions of the famous Budapest couturière Klára Rotschild. Garments can be made to measure, from material brought with you if you prefer.
Clara Szalon
Budapest V, Váci utca 12
Tel: 1184-090.

Kék Duna
Budapest V, Kristóf tér 6
Tel: 1172-326.

Sikk
Budapest V, Haris köz 2
Tel: 1183-313.

Ferencné Eri
Budapest V, Haris köz 3
Tel: 1374-422.

Imréné Kárpáti
Budapest V, Régi posta utca 7-9
Tel: 1376-385.

MEN'S WEAR

The old traditions of Budapest tailoring are kept alive, among others, by:
Elegancia
Budapest V, Petöfi Sándor utca 7
Tel: 1185-086.
(Made to measure clothes for ladies too.)

Ekisz
Budapest V, József Attila utca 18
Tel: 1172-907.

Fövárosi Ruházati Vállalat
Budapest V, Váci utca 2
Tel: 1183-275.

András Kecskés
Budapest V, Váci utca 4
Tel: 1185-810.

Imre Móczár
Budapest V, Harmincad utca 4
Tel: 1172-544.

SHOES

The world-famous Budapest cobblers have a problem – there are not enough young people taking up the trade for the masters, all well advanced in years, to pass on their skills. There are hopes that the situation will improve the more the country opens up towards the West. In the meantime, you will just have to be patient: it takes months before a genuine pair of "Budapests" is ready. Take care when measurements are taken: the Hungarians prefer the tightest possible fit.

The retail shoe chain **Cipöbolt** also takes on made-to-measure shoes for ladies and gentlemen.
Budapest V, Felszabadulás tér 5
Tel: 1183-261;
Budapest V, Petöfi Sándor utca 14
Tel: 1183-375;
Budapest V, Váci utca 8
Tel: 1184-783.

Janovszky cipö szalon
Budapest V, Haris köz 1
Tel: 1183-365.

László Vass
Budapest V, Haris köz 2
Tel: 1182-375;

Budapest V, Kossuth Lajos utca 15;
Budapest VI, Lenin körút 120
Tel: 1317-700.

SHOPPING AREAS

Food – and certain household and general goods – can best be bought in the ABC stores, which are distributed throughout the city.

DEPARTMENT STORES

The range of goods on offer in the big department stores (áruház) does not quite measure up to Western standards either in quantity or in quality. It must be said that things are cheap. The question is whether they are value for money.
Corvin
Budapest VIII, Blaha Lujza tér 1-2
Tel: 1334-160.

Csillag
Budapest VII, Rákóczi út 20-22
Tel: 1316-000.

Luxus
Budapest V, Vörösmarty tér 3
Tel: 1182-277.

Skála Budapest
Budapest XI, Schönherz Zoltán utca 6-10
Tel: 1852-222.

Skála Metro
Budapest VI, Marx tér.

Verseny
Budapest VII, Ráckóczi út 12.

FOREIGN CURRENCY SHOPS

There is a fleet of these mini-department stores, with different names – Intertourist, Utastourist, Konsumtourist – but all under the same flag, taking hard currency (Eurocheques and credit cards are also accepted) and providing competition for the duty free shops in the airports. Apart from the usual everyday articles such as cosmetics, spirits and tobacco (here you can get genuine Havana cigars from Cuba), there are gift items such as the sought-after Herend porcelain (the prices tend to be too high) and crafts, but also the absolute latest thing in electronic entertainment.

By now every major hotel has its own foreign currency shop, which is generally open on weekends and holidays as well.

Intertourist Central Office
Budapest V, Kígyó utca 5
Tel: 1183-439.

Dukat
Budapest V, Galamb utca 6
Tel: 1183-673;
Budapest IX, Üllöi út 69
Tel: 1343-125.

MARKETS

You should not miss out on a visit to the Central Market Hall, which is indeed quite centrally situated – near the Danube bank by the Liberation Bridge (Szabadsághíd). The architecture alone of this massive building (490 ft/150 m long, total area nearly 110,000 sq ft/more than 10,000 sq m) with its iron construction and Historicist brick facade is impressive. Inside, the quantity and the colour of the produce on offer is overwhelming: fruit and vegetables predominate, but meat, fish and dairy produce are also sold. In the innermost part of this huge area the (state-owned) farming co-operatives offer their produce for sale, the private producers' stalls are further out. Prices are for the most part freely set, and differences are relatively minor.

Central Market Hall
Budapest IX, Tolbuhin körút 1-3.

The other weekly markets of Budapest are certainly not as spectacular as the Central Market Hall, but more "authentic" and earthy. Here, the individual stall owners still run things – or the farmers' wives who come in from the country with their fruit and vegetables as they did in their grandfathers' days.
Budapest II, Fény utca
Budapest V, Rosenberg Házaspár utca
Budapest XIV, Bosnyák tér

Also open on Sundays (6 a.m.-1 p.m.)
Budapest XI, Fehérvári út 14
Budapest XIII, Élmunkás tér

FLEAMARKETS

Just as in any big city, there is a fleamarket in Budapest, in the suburb of Kispest. And although – just like every other fleamarket in the world – it has long been in the hands of professional dealers, it is still well worth a visit to observe the colourful life of the market and – just perhaps – to discover the odd hidden treasure. Open Mon-Fri 8 a.m.-4 p.m., Sat 8 a.m.-3 p.m.
Budapest XIX, Nagykörösi út 156

SPORTS

PARTICIPANT SPORTS

It may seem a paradox when you consider the many gold medals that Hungarian sportsmen and women bring back from world championships and the Olympics, but the Hungarians haven't much interest in sport – that is, sport for all. If you don't want to let your muscles get rusty during your holiday, you won't find many opportunities for activity in Budapest. Golfers had to miss out anyway until very recently; now at last there is a golf course, but to get there requires a long-distance journey. If you don't count such "sports" as minigolf and bowling, the only sporting activity left is swimming (summer and winter) and in fine weather a little water sports by the Danube, hiking in the Buda Hills, fishing on Csepel island, and riding, as well as ice skating in winter. Eccentrics can, in the case of good snow conditions (rather rare) glide over the gentle slopes around the one ski lift in the vicinity of Budapest – we recommend that you make vigorous use of your sticks in order to move it along. One bright spot – in the indoor swimming pools of the hotels there are gyms, some with sauna, on Western lines.

SPORTS FIELDS

Entry to sports fields and running tracks is generally free. If you bring your running shoes with you, you can run round the track for free and do something to improve your fitness.
Budapest IX, Vágihíd utca 7
Mon-Sat 8 a.m.-1 p.m.

Budapest I, Csakó utca 2-4
April-October, Sat only 8 a.m.-4 p.m.

Nemzeti Sports Hall
Budapest XIV, Istvánmezei út 1-3
Tel: 1636-430.

Margaret Island sports complex
Budapest XIII, Margitsziget.

FISHING

Pollution has not yet been able seriously to affect the wealth of fish in the Danube. On Csepel Island, in particular, there are excellent opportunities for angling. You need an angling permit (daily tickets).
Hungarian Anglers' Association
Budapest V, Október 6 utca 20
Tel: 1325-315
Mon-Thur 8 a.m.-5 p.m., Fri till 4 p.m.

SWIMMING

Budapest has more swimming pools than any other big city – not surprisingly, when you consider the great number of medicinal springs in the city. Most of the swimming pools – indoor and outdoor – are supplied from medicinal springs. Some open-air pools can be used in the winter, as they are supplied with water from hot springs. Pools are usually open from 7 a.m.-7 p.m. Last admission one hour before closing time.
Sports pools
Nemzeti Sports Pool

Alfréd Hajós Indoor Sports Pool
Budapest XIII, Margitsziget
Tel: 1114-046.

Komjádi Sports Pool
Budapest II, Komjádi Béla utca 2-4
Tel: 1355-175.
The roof is opened in fine weather.

SPAS WITH SWIMMING POOLS

Entrance fee: 25-60 Ft.

Gellért Baths
Budapest XI, Kelenhegyi út 4
Tel: 1852-200.

Lukács Baths
Budapest II, Frankel Leó út 25-29
Tel: 1758-373.

Rudas Baths
Budapest I, Döbrentei tér 9
Tel: 1754-449.

Szabadság-fürdö
Budapest XIII, Népfürdö utca 30
Tel: 1202-203.

Széchenyi Baths
Budapest XIV, Allatkerti körút 11
Tel: 1210-310.

Ujpest Baths
Budapest IV, Arpád utca 114-120
Tel: 1690-344.

OUTDOOR POOLS
(OPEN FROM 1 MAY TO 30 SEPT.)

Arpád Pool Csillahegy
Budapest III, Pusztakúti út 3
Tel: 1804-533.

Cinkotai Pool
Budapest XVI, Alomás tér
Tel: 1833-173.

Kispest Pool
Budapest XIX, Ady Endre utca 99
Tel: 1271-701.

Palatinus Pool
Budapest XIII, Margitsziget
Tel: 1123-069.

Pünkösd Pool
Budapest II, Vörös Hadsereg útja 272
Tel: 1886-665.

Római fürdö (Roman Baths)
Budapest III, Rozgonyi Piroska utca 2.

Tungsram Baths
Budapest IV, Outer Váci út 104
Tel: 1691-175, 1694-668.

HOTELS WITH INDOOR POOLS

Nearly all equipped with sauna, sunbeds and gym.

Atrium-Hyatt
Budapest V, Roosevelt tér 2
Tel: 1383-000.

Buda-Penta
Budapest I, Krisztina körút 41-43
Tel: 1566-333.

Flamenco
Budapest XI, Tass vezér utca 7
Tel: 1252-250.

Fórum
Budapest V, Apáczai Csere János utca 12-14
Tel: 1178-088.

Grand Hotel Ramada
Budapest XIII, Margitsziget
Tel: 1111-000.

Novotel
Budapest XI, Alkotás utca 63-67
Tel: 1869-588.

Olimpia
Budapest XII, Eötvös út 40
Tel: 1568-011.

Rege
Budapest II, Pálos út 2
Tel: 1767-311.

Stadion
Budapest XIV, Ifjúság útja 1-3.

Vörös Csillag
Budapest XII, Rege út 21
Tel: 1750-522.

WATER SPORTS

Along the "Roman Bank" (Római rakpart) in Obuda you will find one boathouse after another. Here you can hire canoes and rowing boats as well as surfboards.

TENNIS

Tennis fans will find only limited opportunities to play in Budapest.

Tennis Stadium
Budapest XIII, Margitsziget
Tel: 1317-532.

Tennis Courts
Budapest XI, Bartók Béla út 63-65.

Club BXE
Budapest XII, Szamos utca 2c
Tel: 1350-127
Open daily 8 a.m.-2 p.m. Tennis racquets for hire. Minumum fee per hour's play is 400 Ft.

HOTELS WITH TENNIS COURTS

Európa
Budapest II, Hárshegyi út 5-7
Tel: 1767-122.

Expo
Budapest X, Dobi István út 10
Tel: 1842-130.

Stadion
Budapest XIV, Ifjúság útja 1-3
Tel: 1631-830.

Flamenco
Budapest XI, Tass vezér utca 7
Tel: 1252-250.

Novotel
Budapest XII, Alokotás utca 63-67
Tel: 1869-588.

Olimpia
Budapest XII, Eötvös út 40
Tel: 1568-011.

GOLF

There is a 9-hole course at the northern end of the long, narrow Szentendre Island opposite Visegrád, some 22 miles (35 km) from Budapest. Driving there (part of the way you have to use second-grade roads) is rather complicated.
Kisoroszi Golf Course
9 holes, 36 par, 3,575 square yards (2,989 sq m). Open 1 April-31 October.

HORSE-RIDING

Those who enjoy riding can take part in an organised riding excursion from Budapest.
Hungarian Riding Association
National Riding School
Budapest VIII, Kerepesi út 7
Tel: 1130-415.

Peneházi Riding School
Budapest II, Feketefej utca 5
Tel: 1164-267.

Riding tours (day trips or longer excursions – 9, 10, 15 days) are organised by the following travel agents:
Pegazus Tours
Budapest V, Károlyi Mihály utca 5
Tel: 1171-644.

IBUSZ
Budapest V, Felszabadulás tér 5
Tel: 1189-109, 1186-236.

HIKING

The Buda Hills are well provided with paths and roads. The landscape has largely been left in its natural state and there are some beautiful footpaths. For more information, contact:
Hungarian Nature Lovers' Association
Budapest VI, Bajcsy-Zsilinsky út 31
Tel: 1531-930;
Information Service
Budapest V, Váci utca 62-64
Tel: 1183-933.

ICE SKATING

Cycling Track and Artificial Ice Rink
Budapest XIV, Szabó Jószef utca 3.

Outdoor Ice Skating
Budapest XIV, Népstadion út
Tel: 1228-211.
5 November-8 March, open daily 10 a.m.-2 p.m., 4 p.m.-8 p.m.

SPORTING CALENDAR

Major sporting events of national importance mainly take place in the **Népstadion**, Budapest XIV, Istvánmezei út 3-5.
The second great centre of public interest is the **Hungaroring**, scene of Formula 1 racing every year in August and of other motorised spectaculars, such as the European Truck Driving Championships. The Hungaroring lies some 12 miles (18 km) east of Budapest in the town of Mogyoród, directly beside the M3 motorway. The total length is just under 2½ miles (4,013 m), with 15 bends, a height difference of 143 ft (34.5 m) and a maximum gradient of 7 percent. It can hold up to 200,000 spectators.

MAJOR SPORTING EVENTS

April: city marathon.
September: international tennis tournament; Budapest athletics grand prix (Népstadion).
November: international table tennis tournament (National Sports Hall).

PHOTOGRAPHY

In general, amateur photographers are not subject to restrictions. Photographing of military parades is permitted. However, it is forbidden to take pictures of industrial and railway sites, as well as military installations, barracks and convoys, with the exception of station halls and passenger trains. It is also forbidden to take photos with flash in some museums and exhibitions. There are photo machines at the railway stations and at the Ferihegy airport.

LANGUAGE

Even for foreign visitors who are skilled at languages, Hungarian remains a sealed book. Learning Hungarian is different from learning most other European languages. There are no similarities, no opportunities for comparison, no short cuts to understanding this language. The reason is that Hungarian has nothing whatsoever to do with the great Indo-European family of languages: it belongs to the Finno-Ugric group. Its only relatives within Europe are Finnish and Estonian, and its only other relatives are certain languages and dialects in Siberia and Central Asia.

Hungarian is an agglutinative language, i.e. grammatical forms are made by adding suffixes to the root syllable.

PRONUNCIATION

Stress is always on the first syllable of any word. The accent (´) does not mark the stress but indicates a long vowel (and occasionally changes its pronunciation). In all syllables the vowels are sounded clearly and fully. In the Hungarian language the difference between "stressed" and "unstressed" syllables is slight. Diphthongs (ai, ei, eu, etc.) are always pronounced as two separate vowels.

	Pronounced	As in
a	short, deep o	on
á	long a	larder
b	short, voiced	boy
c	short, unvoiced ts	Ritz
cs	short, unvoiced ch	change
d	short, voiced	down
dz	voiced ds	godson
dzs	voiced j	jungle
e	open e, higher than	pet
é	long, drawn-out	crayon
f	short, unvoiced	coffee
g	short, voiced	go
gy	voiced fricative	adieu
h	as in English	
i	long	feel
j	as English y	yes
k	unaspirated	cat
l	as in English	
ly	short voiced fricative	Goya
m	short, voiced	am
n	short, voiced	an
ng,	sounded separately,	man-kind,
nk	not run together	not: tanker
ny	short, voiced fricative	vineyard
o	short, open	top
ó	long, closed	corner
p	unaspirated	stop
r	rolled r, as in Scottish	
s	short unvoiced sh	fresh
sz	short unvoiced s	sun
t	unaspirated	batter
u	short, as in Northern English	
ú	long	coop
ü	short	German münden
ű	long	German Brüder
v	short, voiced	veto
z	short, voiced	doze
zs	short, voiced j	French journal

USEFUL WORDS & PHRASES

English-speaking visitors should have few difficulties being understood in Budapest, especially if they can switch to German in an emergency (these days, English is becoming more widely spoken, particularly among younger people, than German). It might, however, be a good idea to learn a few phrases, if only in order to be polite to your host nation.

GREETINGS

good morning	jó reggelt
hello, good day	jó napot
good evening	jó estét
good night	jó éjszakát
goodbye	viszontlátásra
enjoy your meal	jó étvágyát
pardon me	bocsánat
how are you?	hogy van?
good, well	jó

ENQUIRIES

what time is it?	hany óra van?
where is...	hol van...
when?	mikor?
where to?	hová?
how much/many	hány?/mennyi?
here	itt
there	ott
I don't understand	nem értem
how do I get to...?	merre kell menni...?
yes	igen
no	nem
please	kérem, tessék
thank you	köszönöm

NUMBERS

one	egy
two	kettö
three	haróm
four	négy
five	öt
six	hat
seven	hét
eight	nyolc
nine	kilenc
ten	tíz
eleven	tizenegy
twenty	húsz
twenty-one	huszonegy
thirty	harminc
forty	negyven
fifty	ótven
sixty	hatvan
seventy	hetven
eighty	nyolcvan
ninety	kilencven
one hundred	száz
two hundred	kétszáz
five hundred	ötszáz
one thousand	ezer

TIME/DAYS OF THE WEEK

today	ma
now	most
yesterday	tegnap
tomorrow	holnap
later	késöbb
Monday	hétfö
Tuesday	kedd
Wednesday	szerda
Thursday	csütörtök
Friday	péntek
Saturday	szombat
Sunday	vasárnap

OUT SHOPPING

open	nyitva
closed	zárva
entrance	bejárat
exit	kijárat
how much is that?	mennyibe kerül?
please show me...	kerém, mutassa meg...
expensive	drága

IN THE RESTAURANT

menu	étlap
wine list	itallap
waiter!	pincér!
restaurant	étterem
cellar	pincc
food	étel
drink	ital
coffee	kávé
wine	bor
beer	sör
red	piros/vörös
white	fehér
water	víz
large	nagy
small	kis

GETTING AROUND

baths	fürdö
house	ház
hill	hegy
bridge	híd
gate	kapu
boulevard	körút
park: small wood	liget
monument	müemlék
station	pályaudvar (pu.)
embankment: quay	rakpart
island	sziget
theatre	színház
church	templom
square	tér
street/avenue	út
street (genitive form)	útja
street/lane	utca (u.)
castle	vár
town	város
inn	vendéglö
tram	villamos

SPECIAL INFORMATION

FOR BUSINESSPEOPLE

The central organisation for business people to contact in Hungary is the Hungarian Chamber of Commerce:
Budapest V, Kossuth Lajos tér 6-8
Tel: 1533-333.
Open 8 a.m.-5 p.m.

The first preparatory contact can be made by the trade department of the appropriate Hungarian embassy in the visitor's home country. Here you will be issued with the handbook published by the Hungarian Chamber of Commerce, *Business Guide to Hungary*, which contains a wealth of useful information. Foreign business people can obtain further support from the trade department of the embassy of their own country in Hungary.

FOR CHILDREN

In general the Hungarians are definitely fond of children. There is plenty for younger guests to see and also to do, which often relieves pressure on their parents. Various organisations have their own (often free) programmes specially for children. For general information, contact:
Toptour
Budapest V, Münnich Ferenc utca 26
Tel: 1316-194.
Toptour specialises in the care of families and children. Here you can book family-friendly private accommodation or pensions with cots. There is a babysitting agency available.
Children aged 4 to 12 years can be cared for by the hour or even by the day by trained staff. Accommodation comes with full board, use of garden, play opportunities, special programmes and trips.

SUNDAY ACTIVITIES

Magyar Nemzeti Múzeum
Budapest VIII, Múzeum körút 14-16.
Tel: 1134-400.
In the **National Museum** on Sundays children, supervised by teachers, can work with plasticine, draw and paint.

Szakasits House of Culture
Budapest XII, Csörsz utca 18
Tel: 1566-649
In the Szakasits House of Culture there is a programme of events for children on Sundays from 10 a.m.-2 p.m.

Youth Centre
Budapest II, Marcibányi tér 5A
Tel: 1756-564
In the Youth Centre in Marcibányi Square there is a children's fair every Sunday from 8 a.m. to 1 p.m. Young visitors take an active part. 10 Ft (children), 20 Ft (adults).

PLAYGROUNDS

All over the city there are plenty of playgrounds for children, equipped with sand boxes, swings, and climbing frames. Some especially attractive playgrounds are in the City Park (Városliget), in the Jubilee Park on Gellért Hill and on Margaret Island.
Children's Zoo
Budapest XIV, Allatkerti körút 6-12
Tel: 1426-303.
A special attraction of the zoo in City Park is the Children's Zoo

Margaret Island Zoo
Margitsziget.
This is a little wildlife park where children can see native animals (deer, pheasants, peacocks) living freely.

ADVENTURE & AMUSEMENT PARKS

Children will be especially delighted by a trip on the **Pioneer Railway** through the Buda Hills, but even more by the fact that the train crew is entirely children!
A further attraction of the Buda Hills for children is the **Wildlife Park of Budakeszi**, a compound containing native animals. Open daily from 9 a.m. to dusk. Entrance fee 5 Ft, children and students free.

Lunapark

In the amusement park in the City Park, there is a separate mini-Lunapark for children.

Vidám Park

Budapest XIV, Allatkerti körút 14-16
Tel: 1221-025.
Open daily 10 a.m.-8 p.m., entrance fee 5 Ft.

Puppet Theatre

Main House
Budapest VI, Népköztársaság útja 69.

Puppet Theatre (Chamber performances)

Budapest VI , Jókai tér 10
Tel: 1120-622.

Circus

Fövárosi Nagycirkusz
Budapest XIV, Allatkerti körút 7
Tel: 1428-300.
Local and international stars appear in the Capital Circus in City Park, which will shortly be celebrating its 100th anniversary.

FOR STUDENTS

Students seem to live cheaply in Hungary because the cost of living is low compared to the West, and also because they are entitled to all sorts of discounts and reductions.

It is important to own an International Student Card (IUS) or an international tourist card for students (ISTC). If you also happen to be a member of the Youth Hostel Association (IYHF), all the better.

In Hungary there is a travel agency which deals exclusively with the requirements of young people and students, ranging from cheap accommodation to cultural activities. Here, too, you can learn all there is to know about student discounts – from rail tickets (if you don't already have an Inter-rail ticket) to reduced entrance fees for museums, cheap theatre tickets etc.

Express Youth and Student Travel Agency

Central Office
Budapest VI, Szabadsag tér 16
Tel: 317-777.

MEETING PLACES

A popular meeting place, particularly for young foreigners, is the space in front of the Matthias Church and the Fishermen's Bastion on Castle Hill in Buda.

Contact with Hungarian young people and students is most easily made in the youth centres and Houses of Culture and especially in the dance halls (*táncházak* – pronounced Tahnts-haasokk), where you will immediatley be invited to join in. You can also of course "join in" in the various discos where young people meet, but these places are bound to be too noisy for an exchange of ideas. You can exchange all sorts of things there, but ideas will rarely be among them.

DANCE HALLS

Petöfi Csarnok (Petöfi Hall)
Budapest XIV, Városliget
Zichy Mihály út.
Budapest's biggest youth leisure centre in City Park. Wed, Fri: folk dancing (with instruction) and folk music; Sat: disco; Fri, Sat: foreign languages club

Inner City House of Youth and Culture
Budapest V, Molnár utca 9.
Sat 6.30 p.m. dance hall.

Capital House of Culture
Budapest XI, Fehérvári út 47.
Tue 7 p.m. dance hall.

Youth and Culture Centre
Budapest II, Marczibányi tér 5A.
Sat 6 p.m. dance hall.

CHEAP ACCOMMODATION

During the vacation in July and August it is possible for foreign students to stay in Hungarian student hostels.

CHEAP FOOD

It has been our experience that it is easier to find an inexpensive place to stay than a restaurant where good food can be had for not much money. However, here are a few suggestions:

City Grill
Budapest V, Váci utca 20.
Self-service cafeteria in the Taverna Hotel.
Mon-Sat 3 p.m.-midnight (Sun till 11 p.m.)

Halló
Budapest VII, Majakovszkij utca 65.
Self-service cafeteria, open daily 6.30 p.m.-
11.30 p.m.

Stop Bistro
Budapest V, Váci utca 86.
Student's menu and light snacks, open daily
9 a.m.-7 p.m.

Mensa (student refectory)
Budapest V, Károlyi Mihály utca 4-8 / II.
Open lunchtimes only 11.30 a.m.- 2.30 p.m.

Trojka
Budapest VI, Népköztársaság útja 28
Tel: 1124-688.
A popular meeting place for young people.
There is a grill room on the ground floor, a
Russian tea room on the first floor.

Torkos Snack Bar
Budapest IX, Mester utca 12
Tel: 1138-283.
Mon-Fri 11 a.m.-8 p.m.

Zenit
Budapest XI, Ferenc körút 2-4
Tel: 1170-023.
Self-service cafeteria, open daily 5.30 a.m.-
9 p.m.

Fortuna
Budapest I, Hess András tér
Tel: 1756-857.
Self-service cafeteria, open daily 11.30
a.m.-2 p.m.

CREDITS

INDEX

F–H

V–Z

B
C
D
E
F
G
H
I
J
a
b
c
d
e
f
g

i
j
k
l